Theo Cogswell.

From Photograph. Copyright, 1898.
Published by A. W. Elson, Boston.

STRATFORD ON AVON.

Engraved by Robert Varley.

CYR'S

FIFTH READER

BY

ELLEN M. CYR

AUTHOR OF CYR'S READERS

———•❂•———

BOSTON, U.S.A.

GINN & COMPANY, PUBLISHERS

The Athenæum Press

1902

TO

MY DEAR LITTLE DAUGHTERS

Eleanore and Edith

PREFACE.

THE importance of learning to love what is best to read is hardly second to the art of reading. During childhood the imagination is most active, and this is the period when the mind should become familiar with the choicest gems of thought and expression.

The seeds sown in early life must bear fruit in later years. Long before the child can define an author's meaning the spirit of the thought has reached his heart.

It is with this firm conviction, based upon schoolroom experience, that the author of this series has gradually led her readers up the steeps of literature.

We have now reached the lofty heights and must search among the grand peaks and crags of the works of the world's greatest writers for what will appeal to children and lead them to love the grandeur which they cannot yet fully comprehend.

The majority of pupils in our public schools cannot take advantage of our high school privileges; but with libraries at their disposal, and an introduction to the world's best literature, they may continue their education after their school life is ended.

It has been the author's aim to collect the best material from the best authors. There are certain selections which can never grow old, and a reading book of this grade would be incomplete without them.

I would extend my thanks to Houghton, Mifflin & Co., for permission to use selections from the works of Thoreau and Ralph Waldo Emerson; to Harper & Bros., for extract from "Prue and I," by George William Curtis; to The Cassell Publishing Company, for poem by John Boyle O'Reilly; to R. F. Fenno & Co., for extract from "With Dewey at Manila"; to Little, Brown & Co., for extract from "The Man without a Country"; to Mr. William H. Hayne, for poem by Paul Hamilton Hayne; and to the following authors: Mrs. Julia Ward Howe, Mr. Thomas J. Vivian, and Dr. Edward Everett Hale.

The selection by James Lane Allen is published by business arrangement with Harper & Bros.

Acknowledgments are due to Messrs. Elliot and Frye, London, for use of copyright photographs of Ruskin and Carlyle, and to Messrs. Walker and Boutall, London, for permission to reproduce portraits of Mrs. Browning and Robert Burns.

I take pleasure in acknowledging my indebtedness to Mr. Austin H. Kenerson, for his hearty coöperation and valuable suggestions in the preparation of this book, as well as in the lower books of the series.

ELLEN M. CYR.

CONTENTS

————o•:•o•:•o•————

CYR'S FIFTH READER

CYR'S FIFTH READER

—o°o°o°o—

ARBACES AND THE LION.

EDWARD BULWER LYTTON.

The following selection is taken from "The Last Days of Pompeii," a famous novel written by Edward Bulwer Lytton, the author of a large number of works of fiction.

Arbaces, an Egyptian, murdered Apæcides, a priest, and accused Glaucus, a young Greek, of having committed the crime. 5
Calenus witnessed the deed, and Arbaces, after promising him a large sum for his silence, imprisoned him in a dungeon, leaving him there to die.

Glaucus was condemned, and, according to the ancient custom, was to be devoured by the lions; but Calenus escaped and 10
accused Arbaces of the crime.

The terrible eruption of Mt. Vesuvius burst forth just as the crowd rushed upon Arbaces, and the city of Pompeii was buried beneath its fury. Glaucus and some of his friends escaped, but Arbaces perished. 15

The keeper, who was behind the den, cautiously removed the grating; the lion leaped forth with a mighty and a glad roar of release. Glaucus had bent his limbs so as to give himself the firmest posture at the expected rush of the lion, with his small and shining weapon 20 raised on high, in the faint hope that one well-directed thrust might penetrate through the eye to the brain of his grim foe. But, to the unutterable astonishment of all, the beast halted abruptly in the arena; then suddenly it sprang forward, but not on the Athenian. At half speed it circled round and round the space, turning its vast head from side to side with an anxious and perturbed gaze, as if seeking only some avenue of escape. Once or twice it endeavored to leap up the parapet that divided it from the audience, and, on failing, uttered rather a baffled howl than its deep-toned and kingly roar. The first surprise of the assembly at the apathy of the lion was soon converted into resentment at its cowardice; and the populace already merged their pity for the fate of Glaucus into angry compassion for their own disappointment.

Then there was a confusion, a bustle — voices of remonstrance suddenly breaking forth, and suddenly silenced at the reply. All eyes turned, in wonder at the interruption, towards the quarter of the disturbance. The crowd gave way, and suddenly Sallust appeared on the senatorial benches, his hair disheveled — breathless — heated — half exhausted. He cast his eyes hastily around the ring. "Remove the Athenian!" he cried; "haste — he is innocent! Arrest Arbaces, the Egyptian; he is the murderer of Apæcides!"

"Art thou mad, O Sallust?" said the prætor, rising from his seat. "What means this raving?"

"Remove the Athenian! Quick! or his blood be on your head. Prætor, delay and you answer with your own life to the emperor! I bring with me the eye-witness to the death of the priest Apæcides. Room there! stand back! give way! People of Pompeii, fix every eye upon Arbaces—there he sits! Room there for the priest Calenus!" "The priest Calenus! Calenus!" cried the mob. "Is it he? No—it is a dead man." "It is the priest Calenus," said the prætor. "What hast thou to say?" "Arbaces of Egypt is the murderer of Apæcides, the priest of Isis; these eyes saw him deal the blow. Release the Athenian; he is innocent!"

"It is for this, then, that the lion spared him. A miracle! a miracle!" cried Pansa.

"A miracle! a miracle!" shouted the people. "Remove the Athenian! Arbaces to the lion!"

And that shout echoed from hill to vale, from coast to sea: "Arbaces to the lion!"

"Hear me," answered Arbaces, rising calmly, but with agitation visible in his face. "This man came to threaten that he would make against me the charge he has now made, unless I would purchase his silence with half my fortune. Were I guilty, why was the witness of this priest silent at the trial? Then I had not detained or concealed him. Why did he not proclaim my guilt when I proclaimed that of Glaucus?"

"What!" cried Calenus, turning around to the people, "shall Isis be thus contemned? Shall the blood

of Apæcides yet cry for vengeance? Shall the lion be
cheated of his lawful prey? A god! a god! I feel the
god rush to my lips! To the lion — to the lion with
Arbaces!" Sinking on the ground in strong convul-
5 sions — the foam gathered to his mouth — he was as a
man, indeed, whom a supernatural power had entered!
The people saw and shuddered. "It is a god that inspires the holy man! To the lion with the Egyptian!"

With that cry up sprang — on moved — thousands
10 upon thousands! They rushed from the heights —
they poured down in the direction of the Egyptian.
The power of the prætor was as a reed beneath the
whirlwind. The guards made but a feeble barrier —
the waves of the human sea halted for a moment, to
15 enable Arbaces to count the exact moment of his
doom! In despair, and in a terror which beat down
even pride, he glanced his eyes over the rolling and
rushing crowd — when, right above them, he beheld a
strange and awful apparition — he beheld — and his
20 craft restored his courage!

"Behold!" he shouted with a voice of thunder, which
stilled the roar of the crowd; "behold how the gods
protect the guiltless! The fires of the avenging Orcus
burst forth against the false witness of my accus-
25 ers!" The eyes of the crowd followed the gesture
of the Egyptian and beheld with ineffable dismay
a vast vapor shooting from the summit of Vesuvius
in the form of a gigantic pine tree — the trunk, blackness; the branches, fire.

At that moment they felt the earth shake beneath their feet; the walls of the theater trembled; and beyond, in the distance, they heard the crash of falling roofs. An instant more and the mountain cloud seemed to roll towards them, dark and rapid, like a torrent. 5

"BEHOLD!" SHOUTED ARBACES.

At the same time it cast forth from its bosom a shower of ashes mixed with vast fragments of burning stone! Over the crushing vines, over the desolate streets, over the amphitheater itself, far and wide, with many a mighty splash in the agitated sea, fell that awful 10 shower! No longer thought the crowd of justice

or of Arbaces; safety for themselves was their sole thought. Each turned to fly — each dashing, pressing, crushing against the other. Trampling recklessly over the fallen, — amidst groans and oaths and prayers
5 and sudden shrieks, — the enormous crowd vomited itself forth through the numerous passages. Whither should they fly for protection from the terrors of the open air?

And then darker and larger and mightier spread the
10 cloud above them. It was a sudden and more ghastly night rushing upon the realm of noon!

From " The Last Days of Pompeii."

SPRING IN KENTUCKY.

JAMES LANE ALLEN.

JAMES LANE ALLEN was born on a farm near Lexington, Ky., in 1850. The early years of his life were spent in careful study. He became interested in literature, and wrote sketches and poems for several magazines and papers.

In 1885 he went to New York City to continue this work. He wrote a number of interesting articles on the "Blue Grass Region" in Kentucky. These were published in "Harper's Magazine." His first stories appeared shortly after in "The Century."

Mr. Allen knows and loves Kentucky, and it is there that he locates his scenes. He has written a number of delightful novels which have been widely read. He resides in New York City and is popular as a writer.

IT is the middle of February. So bleak a season ₂₀ touches my concern for birds, which never seem quite at home in this world; and the winter has been most lean and hungry for them. Many snows have fallen — snows that are as raw cotton spread over their breakfast table, and cutting off connection between them and ₂₅ its bounties.

Next summer I must let the weeds grow up in my garden, so that they may have a better chance for seeds above the stingy level of the universal white.

Of late I have opened a pawnbroker's shop for my hard-pressed brethren in feathers, lending at a fearful rate of interest, for every borrower will have to pay me back in due time by monthly instalments of sing-
5 ing. But were a man never so usurious, would he not lend a winter seed for a summer song? Would he refuse to invest his stale crumbs in an orchestra of divine instruments and a choir of heavenly voices?

And to-day, also, I ordered from a nurseryman more
10 trees of holly, juniper, and fir, since the forest is naked, and every shrub and hedgerow is bare. What would become of our birds if there were no evergreens — Nature's hostelries for the homeless ones? Living in the depths of these, they can keep snow, ice, and wind
15 at bay; prying eyes cannot watch them, nor enemies so well draw near; cones, or seed, or berries are their store; and in those untrodden chambers each can have the sacred company of his mate.

But wintering here has terrible risks which few can
20 run. Scarcely in autumn have the leaves begun to drop from their high perches silently downward when the birds begin to drop away from the bare boughs silently southward. Lo! some morning the leaves are on the ground and the birds have vanished.

25 The species that remain, or that come to us then, wear the hues of the season and melt into the tone of Nature's background — blues, grays, browns, with touches of white on tail and breast and wing for coming flakes of snow.

March has gone like its winds. The other night, as I lay awake, there fell from the upper air the notes of the wild-gander as he wedged his way onward by faith, not by sight, toward his distant bourn. I rose and, throwing open the shutters, strained eyes toward the unseen explorer, startled, as a half-asleep soldier might be startled by the faint bugle-call of his commander blown to him from the clouds. What far-off lands, streaked with mortal dawn, does he believe in?

March is a month when the needle of my nature dips toward the country. I am away, greeting everything as it wakes out of a winter sleep, stretches arms upward and legs downward, and drinks goblet after goblet of young sunshine. I must find the dark-green snowdrop, and sometimes help to remove from her head, as she lifts it slowly from her couch, the frosted nightcap which the old nurse would insist that she should wear.

The pale-green tips of daffodils are a thing of beauty. There is the sunstruck brook of the field, underneath the thin ice of which drops form and fall, form and fall like big, round, silvery eyes that grow bigger and brighter with astonishment that you should laugh at them as they vanish.

But most I love to see Nature do her spring house-cleaning in Kentucky, with the rain-clouds for her water-buckets, and the wind for her brooms. What an amount of drenching and sweeping she can do in a day! How she dashes pailfuls into every dirty corner, till the whole earth is as clean as a new floor !

Another day she attacks the piles of dead leaves, where they have lain since last October, and scatters them in a trice, so that every cranny may be sunned and aired. Or, grasping her long brooms by the handles, she will go into the woods and beat the icicles off the big trees as a housewife would brush down cobwebs.

This done, she begins to hang up soft, new curtains at the forest windows, and to spread over her floor a new carpet of an emerald loveliness such as no mortal looms could ever have woven.

And then, at last, she sends out invitations through the south for the birds to come and spend the summer in Kentucky. The invitations are sent out in March, and accepted in April and May, and by June her house is full of visitors.

Not the eyes alone love Nature in March. Every other sense hies abroad. My tongue hunts for the last morsel of snow on the northern root of some aged oak. As one goes early to a concert-hall with a passion even for the preliminary tuning of the musicians, so my ear sits alone in the vast amphitheater of Nature and waits for the earliest warble of the bluebird, which seems to start up somewhere behind the heavenly curtains. And the scent of spring, is it not the first lyric of the nose — that despised poet of the senses ?

From "A Kentucky Cardinal."
Copyright, HARPER AND BROTHERS.

WILLIAM WORDSWORTH.

WILLIAM WORDSWORTH, one of the Lake poets, was born in England, on the 7th of April, 1770. His father was a lawyer who belonged to a fine old English family. His mother was descended from a family of rank.

William had three brothers, and one sister, Dorothy, who was his constant companion.

His mother died when he was but eight years old, and he remembered but little about her; but he once overheard her tell one of her friends that William was the only one of her children for whom she was anxious — he would be remarkable for good or evil.

Wordsworth spent a very free boyhood; he was strong and vigorous, and loved to be in the open air. This out-of-door life did much to make him a poet. He afterwards wrote : —

> "I had a world about me — 't was my own;
> I made it, for it only lived to me,
> And to the God who sees into the heart."

The Derwent river offered many a sport to the four brothers : —

> " the bright river passed
> Along the margin of our terrace walk ;
> A tempting playmate whom we dearly loved."

How the boy exulted in his freedom, finding delight in every season ! The winter sports were filled with happy hours. He was an excellent skater and could cut his name on the ice even after he became an old man.

All four boys attended the same school, and when they came home, their father listened with interest to the poems from Milton, Shakespeare, and Spenser which they had learned.

The father died when William was thirteen years old, and the children were left almost penniless.

His mother's family assisted in sending the future poet to Cambridge University.

The change from his country home to college life was great, and the lad was much interested in the scenes about him. He felt as though some fairy wand had touched him, for he had a fine suit of clothes, his hair was powdered according to the fashion of the times, he had money in his pocket, and a " lordly dressing gown " hung in his closet.

When he was nineteen years old William spent several weeks with his sister, and as they wandered about Dovedale together, planning and dreaming of the future, he decided to be a poet. During this year

he composed his first long poem, "An Evening Walk,
Addressed to a Young Lady" [his sister Dorothy].

In the autumn of 1790 Wordsworth and a friend
made a journey, mostly on foot, to Calais, visiting
Switzerland. They wandered across a mountainous 5
country, and were greatly disappointed when a peasant told them that they had crossed the Alps without
knowing it. Many a mile did the young men travel
together, feasting their eyes upon the wondrous
scenery: — 10

> "the ever-living universe,
> Turn where I might, was opening out its glories."

Wordsworth's uncle had already urged him to take
orders and become a clergyman, but he could not give
up his cherished dream of becoming a poet. 15

When he was twenty-one, he received his degree
and left Cambridge, spending some time with Dorothy.
The faithful sister encouraged her brother to carry out
his purpose, and they took long walks at morning and
nightfall, talking and planning together. The young 20
poet then went to London, where he spent several
months and then took another tour, this time visiting Wales. The next winter was spent in France,
where he became deeply interested in the political
affairs of that nation. 25

Although Wordsworth had begun writing verses
when he was a schoolboy, his first book of poems,
containing "An Evening Walk" and "Descriptive
Sketches," was not published until he was twenty-

three. These poems attracted very little attention, and did not have a rapid sale, but they were appreciated by a few, who recognized the true spirit of poetry in them.

5　His relatives were disappointed in him and thought him a hopeless and idle dreamer. Dorothy wrote one of her friends: "This favorite brother of mine happens to be no favorite with any of his near relatives except his brothers, by whom he is adored."
10 His sister understood him and encouraged him continually. She was devoted to him, and they planned to have a home together as soon as he had sufficient means.

　About this time Wordsworth began to write for a
15 London paper. In 1795 a friend whom he had nursed during his last illness left him a legacy of nine hundred pounds. With this sum the brother and sister began house-keeping in a modest little cottage. Here, far from the world, but surrounded with beautiful
20 scenery, they read, walked, talked, and wrote verses. In this quiet home the poet listened to his own thoughts and to the messages that the tiniest dewdrop held for him. He wrote: "To me, the meanest flower that blows can give thoughts that lie too deep for tears."
25　At this time he made the acquaintance of Samuel T. Coleridge, and the two poets became lifelong friends. Coleridge visited Wordsworth at his home, and was charmed with him and his sister. In 1797 Wordsworth moved to Alfoxden, where Coleridge and his

wife were staying, so that he might enjoy their society. This close friendship brought him into touch with other literary men, and he became acquainted with Robert Southey and Charles Lamb.

Meanwhile his pen was active and some of his most 5 beautiful poems were written. "It was," says Wordsworth, "a very pleasant and profitable time of my life." The next summer, during a tour with his sister along the river Wye, he wrote "Tintern Abbey," an exquisite poem which was published early in September of that 10 year in his volume of "Lyrical Ballads."

Shortly afterwards the Wordsworths left their home at Alfoxden, and spent the winter at the foot of the Hartz mountains. It was bitterly cold and nothing could have been more dreary than this season at 15 Goslar; but the poet's heart turned with longing to old scenes, and some of the poems written among these bleak and wintry surroundings are filled with the breath of springtide and nature's most smiling moods. 20

The next December, the brother and sister went to live at Dove Cottage, Grasmere. They had been traveling for four days, much of the way on foot, but such was their delight in nature that Wordsworth wrote Coleridge an enthusiastic account of their journey:— 25

> "The frosty wind, as if to make amends
> For its keen breath, was aiding to our steps,
> And drove us onward like two ships at sea
> Or like two birds, companions in mid-air."

Dove Cottage is still standing by the roadside close to the lake, with a garden where some of the plants which Wordsworth set out may still be found. It was here that he wrote "To a Butterfly," "To the Small Celan-
5 dine," and "Daffodils."

On the 4th of October, 1802, Wordsworth was married to Mary Hutchinson, and for nearly fifty years she made his life happy by her loving devotion. His poems contain many references to her, as in "She was a Phantom of Delight" and others.

WORDSWORTH'S HOME AT RYDAL MOUNT.

During the next ten years Wordsworth wrote his finest poems, among them his wonderful ode, "Intimations of Immortality from Recollections of Early Childhood," "The Prelude," and the greater part of "The Excursion." These poems will always
25 be associated with the valley of Easedale, surrounded by mountains. Along the green pathways many lines were murmured by the poet, and often was he accompanied by his wife and sister, who were ready to write the verses as they fell from the poet's lips.

In 1803 Wordsworth and his sister Dorothy went to Scotland, and there met Sir Walter Scott. They were impressed by the love and respect with which Scott was everywhere received. Two years later Scott and his wife returned this visit and were delighted with 5 their reception at the humble cottage at Grasmere.

In 1813 Rydal Mount being vacant, the family moved there, where they remained the rest of Wordsworth's life. The home at Rydal was a gray cottage, almost hidden by ivy and roses, with a picturesque, old- 10 fashioned garden.

"The Excursion" and "The White Doe of Rylstone" appeared during the year 1815.

When he was from sixty to seventy years of age, Wordsworth reached the height of his popularity and 15 was looked upon as the distinguished poet of the period. He still retained his simplicity and rustic ways, and enjoyed a ramble with a little child as well as a philosophical talk with some great man. He was made poet laureate when he was seventy-three. 20

His life closed gently and quietly upon the 23d of April, 1850, and he was laid in the quiet churchyard at Grasmere.

TO THE SMALL CELANDINE.

WILLIAM WORDSWORTH.

PANSIES, lilies, kingcups, daisies,
Let them live upon their praises;
Long as there's a sun that sets,
Primroses will have their glory;
Long as there are violets,
They will have a place in story:
There's a flower that shall be mine,
'T is the little celandine.

Eyes of some men travel far
For the finding of a star;
Up and down the heavens they go,
Men that keep a mighty rout!
I'm as great as they, I trow,
Since the day I found thee out,
Little flower!—I'll make a stir,
Like a sage astronomer.

Ere a leaf is on a bush,
In the time before the thrush
Has a thought about her nest,
Thou wilt come with half a call,
Spreading out thy glossy breast
Like a careless prodigal;
Telling tales about the sun,
When we've little warmth, or none.

Comfort have thou of thy merit,
Kindly, unassuming spirit!
Careless of thy neighborhood,
Thou dost show thy pleasant face
On the moor, and in the wood,
In the lane; — there's not a place,
Howsoever mean it be,
But 't is good enough for thee.

Ill befall the yellow flowers,
Children of the flaring hours!
Buttercups, that will be seen,
Whether we will see or no;
Others, too, of lofty mien,
They have done as worldlings do,
Taken praise that should be thine,
Little, humble celandine!

DAFFODILS.

WILLIAM WORDSWORTH.

I WANDERED lonely as a cloud
    That floats on high o'er vales and hills,
When all at once I saw a crowd,
    A host, of golden daffodils;
Beside the lake, beneath the trees,
Fluttering and dancing in the breeze.

Continuous as the stars that shine
    And twinkle on the milky way,
They stretched in never-ending line
    Along the margin of a bay:
Ten thousand saw I at a glance,
Tossing their heads in sprightly dance.

The waves beside them danced; but they
    Out-did the sparkling waves in glee:
A poet could not but be gay,
    In such a jocund company:
I gazed — and gazed — but little thought
What wealth the show to me had brought:

For oft, when on my couch I lie
    In vacant or in pensive mood,
They flash upon that inward eye
    Which is the bliss of solitude;
And then my heart with pleasure fills,
And dances with the daffodils.

WALDEN POND.

HENRY DAVID THOREAU.

HENRY DAVID THOREAU was born in Concord, Mass., on the 12th of July, 1817. His father was of French descent, and his mother was the daughter of a New England clergyman.

Henry's life as a country boy, driving the cow to pasture and roaming about the woods, made him familiar with Nature; new 5 discoveries of her beauties and the constant changes of the seasons soon became his greatest delight.

The meadows and stream sides were stored with treasures, and when only twelve years of age he had already made a number of collections for Professor Agassiz, the great naturalist. Ralph 10 Waldo Emerson says of him : —

> " It seemed as if the breezes brought him,
> It seemed as if the sparrow taught him,
> As if by secret signs he knew
> Where in far fields the orchis grew." 15

Thoreau attended Harvard College, and was graduated in 1837. He then joined his brother in teaching a private school; but soon turned aside from this profession and decided to devote himself to the study of nature.

He was never idle, but preferred to earn what money he re- 20 quired by building a fence or a boat, or by laboring on some farm, rather than to be confined to any regular occupation. He, how-ever, became a land surveyor, as this employment led him con-stantly to new ground for observation.

A Robinson Crusoe's life, with only his own efforts and na- 25 ture to depend upon, would have suited this child of nature. Still, although so hermit like, he was really fond of sympathy, delighted to entertain his friends with stories of field and river, and was always ready to lead a party in search for nuts or berries. 30

In 1845 he made an experiment to prove that man could live
as independent of his kind as the birds and squirrels. Upon a
pine slope on the shores of Walden Pond he built and furnished
a small house. During two years he lived here studying, writ-
5 ing, and learning to know the fishes, birds, and other woodland
creatures.

Birds came at his call, and even the fishes swam fearlessly
through his hands. He would sit immovable, until the bird,
reptile, or fish which had been startled by his presence would
10 return, sometimes out of curiosity to observe him, or to resume
its habits.

While a young man, he became acquainted with Ralph Waldo
Emerson, who was his lifelong friend. Thoreau so loved nature
that his books are filled with descriptions of beautiful scenery,
15 ever-changing wild flowers, and the habits of animals. He was
so happy in solitude that it made him heavy-hearted to see houses
springing up among the woods and meadows where he had wandered as a boy. The axe was always destroying his forest.
" Thank God," he said, " they cannot cut down the clouds ! "

20 Thoreau died on the 6th of May, 1862. His grave is in the
beautiful cemetery of Sleepy Hollow, Concord, beside those of
Hawthorne and Emerson.

In such a day, in September or October, Walden is a
perfect forest mirror, set round with stones as precious
25 to my eye as if fewer or rarer. Nothing so fair, so
pure, and at the same time so large as a lake, perchance, lies on the surface of the earth. It needs no
fence. Nations come and go without defiling it.

It is a mirror which no stone can crack, whose
30 quicksilver will never wear off, whose gilding Nature
continually repairs; no storms, no dust, can dim its
surface ever fresh; a mirror in which all impurity presented to it sinks, swept and dusted by the sun's hazy

brush, — this the light dust-cloth, — which retains no breath that is breathed on it, but sends its own to float as clouds high above its surface, and be reflected in its bosom still.

A field of water betrays the spirit that is in the air. It is continually receiving new life and motion from above. It is intermediate in its nature between land and sky. On land only the grass and trees wave, but the water itself is rippled by the wind. I see where the breeze dashes across it by the streaks or flakes of light. It is remarkable that we can look down on its surface. We shall, perhaps, look down thus on the surface of air at length, and mark where a subtler spirit sweeps over it. . . .

One November afternoon, in the calm at the end of a rainstorm of several days' duration, when the sky was completely overcast and the air was full of mist, I observed that the pond was remarkably smooth, so that it was difficult to distinguish its surface; though it no longer reflected the bright tints of October, but the sad, somber November colors of the surrounding hills.

Though I passed over it as gently as possible, the slight undulations produced by my boat extended almost as far as I could see, and gave a ribbed appearance to the reflections. But, as I looked over the surface, I saw here and there at a distance, a faint glimmer, as if some skater insects which had escaped the frosts might be collected there, or, perchance, the surface, being so smooth, betrayed where a spring welled up from the bottom.

Paddling gently to one of these places, I was surprised to find myself surrounded by myriads of small
5 perch, about five inches long, of a rich bronze color in the green water, sporting there and constantly rising to the surface and dimpling it, sometimes leaving bubbles on it. In such transparent and seemingly bottomless water, reflecting the clouds, I seemed to be floating
10 through the air as in a balloon, and their swimming impressed me as a kind of flight or hovering, as if they were a compact flock of birds passing just beneath my level on the right or left, their fins, like sails, set all around them.

15 There were many such schools in the pond, apparently improving the short season before winter would draw an icy shutter over their broad skylight, sometimes giving to the surface an appearance as if a slight breeze struck it, or a few raindrops fell there. When
20 I approached carelessly and alarmed them, they made a sudden splash and rippling with their tails, as if one had struck the water with a brushy bough, and instantly took refuge in the depths.

Even as late as the 5th of December, one year, I
25 saw some dimples on the surface, and thinking it was going to rain hard immediately, the air being full of mist, I made haste to take my place at the oars and row homeward; already the rain seemed rapidly increasing, though I felt none on my cheek, and I antici-

pated a thorough soaking. But suddenly the dimples ceased, for they were produced by the perch, which the noise of my oars had scared into the depths, and I saw their schools rapidly disappearing; so I spent a dry afternoon after all.

An old man who used to frequent this pond nearly sixty years ago, when it was dark with surrounding forests, tells me that in those days he sometimes saw it all alive with ducks and other waterfowl, and that there were many eagles about it. He came here a-fishing and used an old log canoe which he found on the shore. It was made of two white-pine logs dug out and pinned together, and was cut off square at the ends.

It was very clumsy, but lasted a great many years before it became water-logged and sank to the bottom. He did not know whose it was; it belonged to the pond.

He used to make a cable for his anchor, of strips of hickory bark tied together. An old man, a potter, who lived by the pond before the Revolution, told him once that there was an iron chest at the bottom, and that he had seen it. Sometimes it would come floating up to the shore; but when you went toward it, it would go back into deep water and disappear.

I was pleased to hear of the old log canoe, which took the place of an Indian one of the same material but more graceful construction, which perchance had first been a tree on the bank, and then, as it were, fell into the water, to float there for a generation, the most proper vessel for the lake.

THE PUPPET SHOW.

JOHANN WOLFGANG VON GOETHE.

JOHANN WOLFGANG VON GOETHE, one of the greatest writers that Germany has ever produced, was born at Frankfort on the Main, August 28, 1749.

Goethe attended no school during his early years, but his
5 surroundings were an education, and his father and mother encouraged him in reading and studying the books with which their home was filled.

During the Seven Years' War there were many French soldiers at Frankfort, and they greatly influenced the boy. From them

he learned passages from plays, and soon became well versed in the French language.

When he was sixteen, Goethe entered the university at Leipsic. His father sent him there to study law, but he had already decided to devote himself to literature. He also became interested in art and studied drawing, for which he had considerable talent. He remained there three years and then went to Strasburg, entering the university.

At this time he made the acquaintance of a noted German scholar and thinker, who taught him the
25 true value of nature in art, and revealed to him the beauty of classic and English literature.

Goethe returned to Frankfort on his twenty-second birthday. His sister Cornelia sympathized with him in all his hopes and aspirations, but he had outgrown many of the friends of his boy-
30 hood. He spent his time in writing, and produced a number of poems and several essays; but one of his greatest works was a

drama founded on the history of Gottfried, the imperial knight of the Middle Ages, and was called "Götz von Berlichingen." This work was received with enthusiasm throughout Germany. It was like a trumpet call, appealing to the courage and chivalry of the German spirit. 5

The following spring Goethe left Frankfort for Wetzlar, and while there wrote "Werther." "Götz" and "Werther" were read from one end of Germany to the other. "Werther" was translated into every language in Europe.

Beside these two works, Goethe translated Goldsmith's "De- 10 serted Village," and wrote a number of poems. His literary success brought the young author a large number of friends, among them the Grand Duke of Saxe-Weimar. Goethe accepted the duke's invitation to visit his little capital. He was treated as an honored guest and won the affection of all. The duke gave 15 him a little home near his palace, where he lived during the next eight years.

After a time Goethe returned to Weimar and devoted his time to writing history. He also began to write "Wilhelm Meister's Apprenticeship," which is filled with scenes from his own life. 20 In 1821 "Wilhelm Meister's Travels" appeared. These books are filled with truth, beauty, and life, and stand in the first ranks of the author's works.

For many years he had had the story of "Faust" in his mind. The first part was published when he was sixty years old, in 25 company with a thirteen-volume edition of his works. This was the crowning effort of Goethe's life and the greatest of his works. The second part of "Faust" was written after the poet had passed his seventieth birthday, and when it was completed Goethe felt that his life work was over. 30

His death occurred on the 15th of March, 1832.

I NEVER can forget that happy Christmas day. I see it still before me. I remember how surprised we were when, after we had received our customary presents, mother seated us before the door that leads to the other 35

room. The door opened, but not, as formerly, to let
us pass; the entrance was occupied by an unexpected
show.

Within it rose a porch concealed by a mysterious
5 curtain. All of us were standing at a distance; our
eagerness to see what glittering or jingling article
lay hid behind the half-transparent veil was mounting higher and higher, when we were told to sit down
and wait with patience.

10 At length we were all seated and silent; a whistle
gave the signal; the curtain rolled aloft and showed
us the interior of the temple, painted in deep red colors.
The high-priest Samuel appeared with Jonathan, and
their strange voices seemed to me the most striking
15 thing on earth.

Shortly after, Saul entered, overwhelmed with confusion at the impertinence of that giant warrior who
had defied him and all his people. How glad I was
when the valiant young son of Jesse, with his shep-
20 herd's pouch and sling, came forth and said: "Dread
king and sovereign lord! let no one's heart sink down
because of this. If your Majesty will give me leave, I
will go out to battle with this blustering giant."

Here ended the first act; leaving the spectators more
25 curious than ever to see what further would happen,
and wishing that the music might soon be done. At
last the curtain rose again. David devoted the flesh of
the monster to the fowls of the air and the beasts of the
field; the Philistine scorned and bullied him, stamped

mightily with his feet, and at length fell like a mass of clay, affording a splendid ending for the piece. And then the maidens sang "Saul has slain his thousands, but David his ten thousands!" The giant's head was borne before his little victor.   5

Next morning, alas! the magic apparatus had vanished; the mysterious veil was carried away. My brothers and sisters were running up and down with their playthings; I alone kept gliding to and fro; it seemed to me impossible that two bare doorposts could 10 be all that now remained, where the night before so much enchantment had displayed itself.

"I can easily imagine," said the mother, "how these things should lodge so firmly in your mind; I well remember what an interest you took in them; how you 15 found the book and learned the whole piece by heart. I then felt such a motherly contentment at your fine recitation and good memory that I resolved to give the whole wooden troop to your own disposal."

By good fortune this happened at a time when the 20 lieutenant — a young officer who had made this little theater himself and presented it to us children — had himself been expressing a desire to initiate me into the mysteries of the art. He now contrived to persuade my parents to offer him the use of two chambers in the 25 top story of the house, that he might accommodate the spectators in one, while the other held his actors.

At last the wished-for day arrived. At five in the evening, my instructor came and took me upstairs with him.   Trembling with joy, I entered and beheld on both sides of the framework the puppets all hanging in order, as they were to advance to view.

I considered them carefully, mounted the steps which raised them above the scene, and hovered aloft above that little world.   Not without reverence did I look down between the pieces of board and recollect what a glorious effect the whole would produce, and feel into what mighty secrets I was now admitted.   We made a trial which succeeded well.

A party of children were invited on the next day. We performed rarely, except that once, in the fire of action, I let poor Jonathan fall, and was obliged to reach down with my hand and pick him up again; an accident which sadly marred the illusion, produced a peal of laughter, and vexed me greatly.   My father, however, seemed to relish this misfortune not a little. Prudently hiding his contentment at the expertness of his little boy, after the piece was finished he dwelt on the mistakes we had committed, saying it would all have been very pretty had not this or that gone wrong with us.

I was vexed to the heart at these things and sad for all the evening.   By next morning, however, I had quite slept off my sorrow and was blest in the persuasion that, but for this one fault, I had played delightfully. The spectators also flattered me with their unanimous approval; they all maintained that though the lieutenant, in regard to the coarse and the fine voices, had done great things, yet his declamation was in general

too stiff and affected; whereas the new aspirant spoke
his Jonathan and David with exquisite grace. My
mother in particular commended the gallant tone in
which I had challenged Goliath and acted the modest
victor before the king.   5

From this time, to my extreme delight, the theater
continued open; and as the spring advanced, so that
fires could be dispensed with, I passed all my hours of
recreation lying in the garret and making the puppets
caper and play together.   10

Often I invited my comrades, or my brothers and
sisters; but when they would not come, I stayed by
myself. My imagination brooded over that tiny world.
My greatest pleasure lay in the inventive part and the
employment of my fancy. But it happened with me   15
as it often happens with children; they embrace wide
plans, make mighty preparations, then a few trials, and
the whole undertaking is abandoned.

This or that piece inspired me with interest for a few
scenes of it, and immediately I set about providing new   20
costumes suitable for the occasion. I surrendered myself to my imagination; I rehearsed and prepared forever ; built a thousand castles in the air, and saw not
that I was at the same time undermining the founda-
tions of these little edifices.   25

From " Wilhelm Meister's Apprenticeship."

THE DESCENT INTO THE MAELSTROM.

[ABRIDGED.]

EDGAR ALLAN POE.

EDGAR ALLAN POE was born in Boston on the 19th of January, 1809. His father and mother were actors and died in Richmond, Va., when Edgar was but two years old.

The beauty and attractive manners of the boy won the atten-
5 tion of Mr. John Allan, a wealthy gentleman living at Richmond, and he adopted the little fellow.

Edgar was an interesting child, bright, loving, and generous. He was dressed like a little prince and had his own pony and dogs and a groom, with whom he rode every day. He soon showed
10 a love of poetry and repeated long passages to visitors with such appreciation of their meaning as to delight his hearers. At the age of eleven Edgar attended a school at Richmond. He was a very apt pupil, progressing rapidly in Latin and Greek, and showing a deep love of poetry. He began to write poems to his
15 girl playmates before he was ten years old.

His schoolmates found him a brave, unselfish boy, championing those who were weak, and taking many a hard blow in defending his friends.

After leaving this school, Poe entered the University of Vir-
20 ginia, and was a successful student during his year there. While at college he had engaged in gambling, and when Mr. Allan learned of debts of this kind he refused to pay them. Edgar then left him in anger, going to the home of his father's sister, Mrs. Clemm.

25 Upon the death of his adopted mother, he hastened to his childhood's home. Mr. Allan became reconciled to him and obtained for him a West Point scholarship. He entered the military school when he was twenty-one, and for a time was a diligent student; but he became restless and determined to leave. Mr. Allan would
30 not consent to this, but Poe neglected his duties and conducted himself in so disorderly a manner that he was expelled.

He returned to Richmond for a while and then enlisted in the army, but was taken ill, and his friends procured his discharge.

About the year 1832 a Baltimore paper called "The Saturday Visitor" offered two prizes — one for the best tale and the other for the best poem.

Poe sent a poem and a number of tales which so fascinated the judges that it was with difficulty that they decided upon one. "The Descent into the Maelstrom" was at first chosen, but "A MS. Found in a Bottle" was finally preferred, and received the hundred-dollar prize.

Poe spent several years in Baltimore, writing for periodicals, but after a time went to New York and accepted the invitation of some literary men to join them in editing a paper. After a year in New York, Poe removed to Philadelphia and became editor of a magazine. Some of his best prose tales were written at this time, among them "Ligeia," which was inspired by a dream.

He was married in Baltimore to his cousin, Virginia Clemm. Their home was a happy one, and the poet was devoted to his wife, who was an invalid. In his poem "Annabel Lee" he touchingly describes her loving character. He returned to New York, and it was there that "The Raven," his greatest poem, was written. The fame gained by its publication assisted him in bringing out a new edition of his poetry and two volumes of tales.

In 1846 Poe removed to Fordham, N. Y., where he lived in a picturesque little cottage at the top of a hill. He was greatly saddened by the illness of his wife and his poverty.

The last year of Poe's life was filled with dark scenes, and he died at Baltimore on the 7th of October, 1849.

WE had now reached the summit of the loftiest crag. For some minutes the old man seemed too much exhausted to speak.

"Not long ago," said he at length, "I could have
5 guided you on this route as well as the youngest of my sons; but, about three years past, there happened to me an event such as never happened before to mortal man, — or at least such as no man ever survived to tell of, — and the six hours of deadly terror which I then
10 endured have broken me up body and soul. Do you know I can scarcely look over this little cliff without getting giddy?

"We are now," he continued, "upon the Norwegian coast. The mountain upon whose top we sit is Hel-
15 seggen, the Cloudy. Now raise yourself up a little higher — hold on to the grass if you feel giddy — so — and look out, beyond the belt of vapor beneath us, into the sea."

I looked dizzily, and beheld a wide expanse of ocean.
20 To the right and left, as far as the eye could reach, there lay outstretched, lines of black and beetling cliff.

"Do you hear anything? Do you see any change in the water?" exclaimed the old man.

As he spoke I became aware of a loud and gradually
25 increasing sound, like the moaning of a vast herd of buffaloes upon an American prairie. In five minutes the whole sea was lashed into ungovernable fury; but it was between Moskoe and the coast that the main uproar held its sway. Here the vast bed of the waters

burst suddenly into frenzied convulsion,—heaving, boil-
ing, hissing,—and all whirling and plunging on to
the eastward.

The edge of the whirl, which was more than a mile
in diameter, was represented by a broad belt of gleaming spray; but no particle of this slipped into the
mouth of the terrific funnel, whose interior, as far as
the eye could fathom it, was a smooth, shining, and
jet-black wall of water, speeding dizzily round and
round, and sending forth to the winds an appalling
voice, half shriek, half roar, such as not even the
mighty cataract of Niagara ever lifts up in its agony
to Heaven.

The mountain trembled to its very base.

"This," I cried, "this can be nothing else than the
great whirlpool of the Maelstrom!"

"So it is sometimes termed," said he. "We Nor-
wegians call it the Moskoe-ström, from the island of
Moskoe in the midway.

"Myself and my two brothers once owned a schooner-
rigged smack of about seventy tons burden, with which
we were in the habit of fishing among the islands beyond Moskoe.

"It is now within a few days of three years since
what I am going to tell you occurred. It was on the
10th of July, 18—. The three of us — my two brothers
and myself — had crossed over to the islands about two
o'clock P.M., and soon nearly loaded the smack with
fine fish. It was just seven, *by my watch*, when we

weighed and started for home, so as to make the worst
of the Ström at slackwater, which we knew would be
at eight.

⟨ "We set out with a fresh wind at our starboard
5 quarter, and for some time sped along at a great rate,
never dreaming of danger. All at once we were taken
aback by a breeze from over Helseggen. We put the
boat on the wind, but could make no headway at all
for the eddies, and I was upon the point of proposing
10 to return to the anchorage, when, looking astern, we
saw the whole horizon covered with a singular copper-
colored cloud that rose with the most amazing velocity.

"In less than a minute the storm was upon us; in
less than two the sky was entirely overcast; and what
15 with this and the driving spray, it became suddenly so
dark that we could not see each other in the smack.

"Such a hurricane as then blew it is folly to attempt
describing. At the first puff, both our masts went by
the board as if they had been sawed off — the main-
20 mast taking with it my youngest brother, who had
lashed himself to it for safety.

"For some moments we were completely deluged, but
presently our little boat gave herself a shake, just as a
dog does in coming out of the water, and thus rid her-
25 self, in some measure, of the seas. I was now trying
to get the better of the stupor that had come over me,
and to collect my senses so as to see what was to be
done, when I felt somebody grasp my arm. It was my
elder brother, and my heart leaped for joy, for I had

felt sure that he was overboard; but the next moment all this joy was turned into horror, for he put
his mouth close to my ear and screamed out the word
' Moskoe-ström!'

"I knew what he meant by that one word well 5
enough — I knew what he wished to make me understand. With the wind that now drove us on, we were
bound for the whirl of the Ström and nothing could
save us!

"A singular change had come over the heavens. 10
Around in every direction it was still as black as pitch,
but nearly overhead there burst out, all at once, a circular rift of clear sky — as clear as I ever saw — and
of a deep, bright blue — and through it there blazed
forth the full moon with a luster that I never before 15
knew her to wear. She lit up everything about us
with the greatest distinctness — but, oh, what a scene
it was to light up!

"A hideous thought flashed upon me. I dragged my
watch from its fob. It was not going. I glanced at 20
its face by the moonlight, and then burst into tears as
I flung it far away into the ocean. It had run down at
seven o'clock! We were behind the time of the slack,
and the whirl of the Ström was in full fury!

"So far we had ridden the swells very cleverly; but 25
presently a gigantic sea happened to take us right
under the counter, and bore us with it as it rose — up
— up — as if into the sky. I would not have believed
that any wave could rise so high. And then down we

came with a sweep, a slide, and a plunge that made
me feel sick and dizzy, as if I were falling from some
lofty mountain-top in a dream. But while we were up
I had thrown a quick glance around; and that one
5 glance was all-sufficient. I saw our exact position in
an instant. The Moskoe-ström whirlpool was about a
quarter of a mile dead ahead — but no more like the
everyday Moskoe-ström than the whirl as you now
see it is like a mill-race.

10 ⌐ " It could not have been more than two minutes afterward when we suddenly felt the waves subside and were
enveloped in foam. We were now in the belt of surf that
always surrounds the whirl; and I thought, of course,
that another moment would plunge us into the abyss.

15 " It may appear strange, but now, when we were in
the very jaws of the gulf, I felt more composed than
when we were only approaching it. I began to reflect
how magnificent a thing it was to die in such a
manner, and how foolish it was in me to think of so
20 paltry a consideration as my own individual life, in
view of so wonderful a manifestation of God's power.
After a little while I became possessed with the keenest curiosity about the whirl itself. I positively felt a
wish to explore its depths, even at the sacrifice I was
25 going to make.

" We careered round and round for perhaps an hour,
flying rather than floating, going gradually more and
more into the middle of the surge, and then nearer and
nearer to its horrible inner edge. Suddenly we gave

a wild lurch to starboard and rushed headlong into the abyss.

"Never shall I forget the sensations of awe, horror, and admiration with which I gazed about me. The boat appeared to be hanging, as if by magic, midway down, upon the interior surface of a funnel vast and deep, whose perfectly smooth sides might have been mistaken for ebony, but for the bewildering rapidity with which they spun around, and for the gleaming and ghastly radiance they shot forth, as the rays of the full moon from that circular rift amid the clouds which I have already described streamed in a flood of golden glory along the black walls, and far away down into the inmost recesses of the abyss.

"The rays of the moon seemed to search the very bottom of the profound gulf, over which there hung a magnificent rainbow.

"Both above and below us were visible fragments of vessels, large masses of building timber, and trunks of trees, with many smaller articles. I called to mind the great variety of buoyant matter that strewed the coast of Lofoden, having been absorbed and then thrown forth by the Moskoe-ström. By far the greater number of the articles were shattered in the most extraordinary way; but then I distinctly recollected that there were some of them which were not disfigured at all.

"I resolved to lash myself securely to a water cask, to cut it loose, and to throw myself with it into the water. I tried to induce my brother to do likewise, but he shook his head despairingly and refused to move. The emergency admitted of no delay; and so with a bitter struggle I resigned him to his fate, fastened myself to the cask, and precipitated myself with it into the sea, without another moment's hesitation.

"The result was precisely what I had hoped it might be. It might have been an hour, or thereabout, after my quitting the smack, when, having descended to a vast distance beneath me, it made three or four wild gyrations in rapid succession, and, bearing my loved brother with it, plunged headlong, at once and forever, into the chaos of foam below. The barrel to which I was attached sank very little farther than half the distance between the bottom of the gulf and the spot at which I leaped overboard, before a great change took place in the character of the whirlpool. The slope of the sides of the vast funnel became less and less steep. The gyrations of the whirl grew gradually less and less violent. By degrees the froth and the rainbow disappeared, and the bottom of the gulf seemed slowly to uprise. The sky was clear, the winds had gone down, and the full moon was setting radiantly in the west, when I found myself on the surface of the ocean, in full view of the shores of Lofoden, and above the spot where the pool of the Moskoe-ström had been. I was borne violently into the channel of the Ström, and in a few minutes was hurried down the coast into the grounds of the fishermen, where a boat picked me up."

THE ALBATROSS.

SAMUEL TAYLOR COLERIDGE.

SAMUEL TAYLOR COLERIDGE was born in England on the 21st of October, 1772. His father was both vicar and school-master of the parish.

Samuel was the youngest of thirteen children. He was a sensitive, delicate child, with a vivid imagination, and loved to 5 be by himself.

He began his education at the free grammar school, and was found to have a remarkable mind. His father died before he was nine years old, and the boy felt his loss deeply. The mother was poor, and Samuel was sent to London to live with an uncle, never returning to his native town except on occasional visits. The scenes of his early home were, however, so impressed upon his memory that he afterwards said that whenever he closed his eyes in the sunlight he saw afresh the waters of the Otter, its willowy

banks, the plank that crossed it, and the sand of varied tints that lay in its bed.

After spending three months in London, Coleridge was ad-mitted to the charity school at Christ's Hospital. There was little in his life to make him happy, but he was obliged to remain 25 there from eight to nine years. He made some warm friends, among them a timid, sensitive boy named Charles Lamb, who in after years became famous, under the pen-name of "Elia," as the author of a number of quaint and charming essays.

Coleridge was a born poet, and in spite of his hardship began 30 writing poems during these school days. He used to act out what he had read, and imagine himself the hero of legend or history. Lamb wrote of him : " The walls of the old Grey Friars reëchoed to the accents of the inspired charity boy ! "

Coleridge entered Cambridge University when he was nineteen. He enjoyed the social life there, and his rooms at college became 5 a center of attraction. In spite of this, his life was not happy and he fled from college, enlisting under an assumed name in a regiment of dragoons. He was a poor horseman, but a favorite in camp because of his gift at telling stories and his readiness to nurse the sick and write letters for his comrades.

10 One day he wrote a Latin quotation on a stall, and an officer, seeing that he was a scholar, made him his orderly. It was part of Coleridge's duty to walk behind his officer in the streets, where he was recognized one day by a student, and his friends procured his discharge.

15 He returned to Cambridge, and was soon busily engaged in his studies.

During the vacation of his last year at Cambridge, Coleridge visited one of his old school-fellows at Bristol. While there he made the acquaintance of Sara Fricker, who became his wife 20 in October of 1795. He, in company with other friends, had decided to go to America and there establish a colony, but their plan was given up.

Coleridge had sold some poems for thirty guineas, and with this sum he started in life. He found a pretty little cottage 25 at Clevedon, near Bristol. It was one story high, with a rose tree peeping in at the window. Here the youthful pair began their married life.

Literature now became his chosen profession. His first volume of poems was published when he was twenty-four years old. 30 This was followed by a volume of sonnets ; and still later he published his " Ode to the Departing Year."

Hartley Coleridge, the poet's first son, was born during the next fall ; and soon after the family went to Nether Stowey. Coleridge had made the acquaintance of Wordsworth. The latter moved to 35 Alfoxden and the two poets became lifelong friends. At this time Coleridge wrote " The Rime of the Ancient Mariner," " The

Dark Ladie," and the first part of "Christabel," and was also engaged in writing for several newspapers.

"The Rime of the Ancient Mariner" was planned during a walk, and the story of the albatross was suggested by Wordsworth. For two years Coleridge led a happy life. He then became discouraged and burdened by debt. Some friends furnished him with the necessary funds and he sailed for Germany, remaining there about a year.

In the summer of 1800 Coleridge took his family to Greta Hall, near Keswick. A painful disease led him to take drugs, and he became a slave to the use of opium.

Coleridge soon left Keswick and went to London, where he lived in poverty. A friend had left him a pension, and the poet set it aside for the support of his family.

His poems had at this time become well known, and he might have spent his last years in comfort had it not been for his terrible bondage; but the last twenty years of his life were spent in wretchedness and failure.

Coleridge died on the 25th of July, 1834. Life had lost hope for him, and his success as a poet failed to cheer him. His works are exquisite in thought and expression, and command the admiration of all true lovers of poetry.

PART I.

THE ship was cheered, the harbor cleared,
Merrily did we drop
Below the kirk, below the hill,
Below the lighthouse top.

The Sun came up upon the left,
Out of the sea came he!
And he shone bright, and on the right
Went down into the sea.

. . . . . .

And now the Storm-blast came, and he
Was tyrannous and strong:
He struck with his o'ertaking wings,
And chased us south along.

With sloping masts and dipping prow,
As who pursued with yell and blow
Still treads the shadow of his foe,
And forward bends his head,
The ship drove fast, loud roared the blast,
And southward aye we fled.

And now there came both mist and snow,
And it grew wondrous cold;
And ice, mast-high, came floating by,
As green as emerald.

And through the drifts the snowy clifts
Did send a dismal sheen:
Nor shapes of men nor beasts we ken —
The ice was all between.

The ice was here, the ice was there,
The ice was all around:
It cracked and growled, and roared and howled,
Like noises in a swound!

At length did cross an Albatross:
Thorough the fog it came;
As if it had been a Christian soul,
We hailed it in God's name.

It ate the food it ne'er had eat,
And round and round it flew.
The ice did split with a thunder-fit;
The helmsman steered us through!

And a good south wind sprung up behind;
The Albatross did follow,
And every day, for food or play,
Came to the mariner's hollo!

In mist or cloud, on mast or shroud,
It perched for vespers nine;
Whiles all the night, through fog-smoke white,
Glimmered the white moon-shine.

"God save thee, ancient Mariner!
From the fiends, that plague thee thus!—
Why look'st thou so?"—With my cross-bow
I shot the Albatross.

PART II.

The Sun now rose upon the right:
Out of the sea came he,
Still hid in mist, and on the left
Went down into the sea.

And the good south wind still blew behind,
But no sweet bird did follow,
Nor any day for food or play
Came to the mariner's hollo!

.   .   .   .   .

"FOR ALL AVERRED I HAD KILLED THE BIRD."

For all averred I had killed the bird
That made the breeze to blow.
Ah wretch! said they, the bird to slay,
That made the breeze to blow!

 . . . . .

The fair breeze blew, the white foam flew,
The furrow followed free;
We were the first that ever burst
Into that silent sea.

Down dropt the breeze, the sails dropt down,
'T was sad as sad could be;
And we did speak only to break
The silence of the sea!

All in a hot and copper sky,
The bloody Sun, at noon,
Right up above the mast did stand,
No bigger than the Moon.

Day after day, day after day,
We stuck, nor breath nor motion;
As idle as a painted ship
Upon a painted ocean.

Water, water, everywhere,
And all the boards did shrink;
Water, water, everywhere,
Nor any drop to drink.

   .   .   .   .   .   .

About, about, in reel and rout
The death-fires danced at night;
The water, like a witch's oils,
Burnt green, and blue, and white.

   .   .   .   .   .   .

And every tongue, through utter drought,
Was withered at the root;
We could not speak, no more than if
We had been choked with soot.

Ah! well-a-day! what evil looks
Had I from old and young!
Instead of the cross, the Albatross
About my neck was hung.

From " The Ancient Mariner."

PICCIOLA.

X. B. SAINTINE.

X. B. SAINTINE, the pen name of a well-known French writer, was born at Paris in 1798. His earliest works were so full of good cheer and sympathy that they won many readers.

5 Saintine received a prize for his writings from the French Academy when he was but twenty-one, and two years later a second prize was awarded him by the same Academy.

In 1823 he published a book of poems; but his most famous work is "Picciola." The story is beautifully told, and its charm seems everlasting.

10 The Academy awarded it a prize of three thousand francs, and decorated the author with the cross of the Legion of Honor.

Saintine laid aside his writing during his later years and enjoyed a peaceful and happy old age, surrounded by his many friends and all the comforts of life. His death occurred in 15 1865.

ONE day Charney was breathing the fresh air in the little court of the fortress, his head declining, his eyes downcast, his arms crossed behind him, pacing with slow and measured steps.

20 Spring was breaking. A milder air breathing around tantalized him with a vain inclination to enjoy the season at liberty. He was proceeding to number, one by one, the stones paving the courtyard, when he perceived a small mound of earth rising between two 25 stones of the pavement, cleft slightly at the summit.

The Count stopped short, his heart beat hurriedly. Who could decide that this trifling irregularity on the surface might not indicate important operations underground? Perhaps his former friends had been mining to procure access to his dungeon and restore him to light and liberty. He listened! He fancied he could detect a low murmur. He raised his head, and 5 the loud and rapid clang of the tocsin saluted his ear. The ramparts were echoing with the prolonged roll of drums, like the call to arms in time of war. Is his liberation at hand? Has France a new ruler?

Again he lends a listening ear, and the same noises 10 recur; but they mislead him no longer. The supposed tocsin is only the church-bell which he has been accustomed to hear daily at the same hour; and the drums, the usual evening signal for retreat to quarters. With a bitter smile Charney begins to pity his own folly 15 which could mistake the insignificant labors of some wandering mole or field-mouse for the result of human fidelity.

Resolved, however, to bring the matter to the test, Charney, bending over the little hillock, gently removed 20 the earth from its summit; when he had the mortification to perceive that the wild though momentary emotion by which he had been overcome was not produced by so much as the labors of an animal armed with teeth and claws, but by the efforts of a feeble 25 plant to pierce the soil — a pale and sickly scatterling of vegetation.

Deeply vexed, he was about to crush with his heel the miserable weed, when a refreshing breeze, laden

with the sweets of some bower of honeysuckles or
syringas swept past, as if to intercede for mercy toward
the poor plant, which might perhaps hereafter reward
him with its flowers and fragrance.

5   A new thought led him to suspend his act of vengeance. How had this tender plant, so soft and fragile
as to be crushed with a touch, contrived to pierce and
cleave asunder the soil, daily trodden by his own footsteps, and all but cemented to the flags of granite be-
10 tween which it was enclosed? On stooping again to
examine the matter with more attention, he observed
at the extremity of the plant a sort of fleshy lobe,
affording protection to its first and tenderest leaves
from the injurious contact of any hard bodies that they
15 might have to encounter in penetrating the earthy
crust in search of light and air.

   "This then is the secret!" cried he, already interested in the discovery. "Nature has imparted strength
to the vegetable germ, even as the unfledged bird which
20 is able to break asunder with its beak the eggshell in
which it is imprisoned; happier than myself — in possession of instruments to secure its liberation!" And
after gazing another minute on the inoffensive plant,
he lost all inclination for its destruction.

25   On resuming his walk the next day, with wide and
careless steps, Charney was on the point of setting his
foot on it, but drew back in time. Amused to find
himself interested in the preservation of a weed, he
paused to take note of its progress. The plant was

strangely grown, and the free light of day had already effaced the pale and sickly complexion of the preceding day. Charney was struck by the power in plants to absorb rays of light, and, strengthened by the nourishment, to borrow, as it were, from the prism, the very 5 colors destined to distinguish its various parts.

"The leaves," thought he, "will probably imbibe a hue different from that of the stem. And the flowers? what color, I wonder, will be the flowers? Nourished by the same sap as the green leaves and stem, how do 10 they manage to acquire from the influence of the sun their tints of azure, pink, or scarlet? For already their hue is appointed. But lo, the fleshy lobes which served to facilitate the plant's progress through the soil, though now useless, are feeding themselves at its 15 expense, and weighing upon its slender stalk."

Even as he spoke, daylight became obscured. A chilly spring evening, threatening a frosty night, was setting in; and the two lobes, gradually rising, seemed to reproach him by enclosing the still tender foliage, 20 which they secured from the attacks of insects or the inclemency of the weather by the screen of their protecting wings. In the weariness of captivity Charney was soon satisfied to occupy his idle hours in observing the changes in the plant. But when he attempted to 25 argue with it, the answers of the simple herb were too much for him.

"To what purpose these stiff bristles, disfiguring a slender stem?" demanded the Count. And the following morning he found them covered with frost; thanks to their defence, the delicate bark had been secured from all contact with the rime.

"To what purpose, for the summer season, this win-
5 ter garment of wool and down?" he again inquired. And when the summer season really breathed upon the plant, he found the new shoots array themselves in their light spring clothing, the downy vestments being laid aside.

10 "Storms may be impending!" cried Charney with a bitter smile; "and how will these slender and flex-ible shoots resist the cutting hail, the driving wind?" But when the stormy rain arose and the winds blew, the slender plant, yielding to their force, replied to the
15 sneers of the Count by prudent prostration. Against the hail it fortified itself in a different way; the leaves, rapidly uprising, clung to the stalks for protection, presenting to the attacks of the enemy the strength of their under surface; and union, as usual, produced
20 strength. Firmly closed together they defied the pelt-ing shower, and the plant remained the master of the field.

Count Charney delighted in watching day by day the constant changes of the plant. Even after his
25 return to his cell he often watched the little solitary through his prison bars. One morning, as he stood at the window, he saw the jailer, who was rapidly cross-ing the courtyard, pass so close to it that the stem seemed on the point of being crushed under his feet.

The Count actually shuddered! When Ludovico, the jailer, arrived with his breakfast, Charney inquired after his little boy, and, taking from his box a small gilt goblet, charged him to present it to the child.

Ludovico refused the gift; but Charney resolved to persevere. "I am aware that a toy, a rattle, a flower would be a present better suited to Antonio's age; but you can sell the goblet and buy those trifles with the money. And lo! speaking of flowers," — the Count made his plea.

"Sir Count," replied the jailer, "keep your goblet. Were this pretty bauble missing from your case its companions might fret after it; and with respect to your gillyflower" —

"Is it a gillyflower?" interrupted Charney with eagerness.

"How should I know? All flowers are more or less gillyflowers. But as to sparing the life of yours, me-thinks the request comes late in the day. My boot would have been better acquainted with it long ago, had I not perceived your affection for the weed."

"Oh, as to my partiality," interrupted Charney, "I beg to assure you" —

"Tut, tut! What need of assurance?" cried Ludo-vico. "Men must have something to love; and state prisoners have little choice. Some amuse themselves with rearing linnets and goldfinches; others have a fancy for white mice. For my part, poor souls! I have this much respect for their pets — that I had a fine

Angora cat of my own, with long silken hair — you'd
have sworn it was a muff when it was asleep! — a cat
that my wife doted on, to say nothing of myself.
Well, I gave it away, lest the creature should take a
5 fancy to some of their favorites. All the cats in creation ought not to weigh against so much as a mouse
belonging to a captive!"

   .   .   .   .

Charney became daily more attached to the object
of his care, and had the satisfaction of seeing the plant
10 expand and acquire new beauties every hour. "If it
would but flower!" he frequently exclaimed. "What
a delight to hail the opening of its first blossom! a blossom whose beauty, whose fragrance will be developed
for the sole enjoyment of my eager senses. What will
15 be its color, I wonder? what the form of its petals?
Time will show. How I long for the moment! Bloom,
Picciola! bloom, and reveal yourself in all your beauty
to him to whom you are indebted for the preservation
of your life!"

20 Picciola [poor little thing] was the name, borrowed
from the lips of Ludovico, which Charney had bestowed
upon his favorite.

Returning one morning to the accustomed spot, the
Count's eyes were suddenly attracted toward a shoot of
25 unusual form gracing the principal stem of the plant.
He felt the beating of his heart accelerated, and,
ashamed of his weakness, the color rose to his cheek
as he stooped to examine it. The spherical shape,

covered with glossy scales, announced a bud! Eureka!
—a flower must be at hand!

One evening, after his customary visit to Picciola, an
attack of faintness overpowered him; he threw himself
on the bed, with aching brows and shivering limbs.
He fancied sleep would restore him. But instead of
sleep came pain and fever; and on the morrow, when
he tried to rise, an influence stronger than his will
held him to his pallet, and there he remained for many
days.

As the convalescence of the Count proceeded, he was
seated one morning in his chamber, when the door was
suddenly burst open, and Ludovico, with a radiant
countenance, rushed into the room.

"Victory!" cried he. "The creature is in bloom!
Picciola! Picciola!"

"In bloom!" cried Charney, starting up. "Let me
see her— I must see the blossom."

In vain did the jailer implore the Count to delay the
undertaking for a day or two. Charney was deaf to
all remonstrance. He consented only to wait an hour,
in order that the sun might become one of the party.

At the appointed moment Ludovico reappeared, to
offer the Count de Charney the support of his arm
down the steep steps of the stone staircase.

The enchantress had, indeed, attired herself in all
her charms! Her brilliantly streaked corolla, in which
crimson, pink, and white were blended, her large transparent petals, bordered by a little, silvery fringe, ex-

ceeded the utmost anticipations of the Count as he
gazed with delight upon it. He was filled with love
and admiration for the delicate thing, whose fragrance
and beauty breathed enchantment. But he was soon
5 startled from his revery. The Count noticed for the
first time traces of mutilation — branches half cut
away, and faded leaves wounded by some sharp instrument. Tears started to his eyes.

"Come, come, compose yourself!" said Ludovico.
10 "Picciola, the stout-hearted little weed, brought you
out of your illness. Did not the three humbugs pronounce you to be dying? I snipped off enough of
these leaves for a strong infusion, and a single cup
of it acted like a charm. 'T is a recipe that I mean
15 to keep as the apple of my eye; and if ever poor little
Antonio should fall ill, he shall drink broths of this
herb. Though her foliage is a little thinner, I've a
notion the plant will not suffer from thinning. Picciola
will, perhaps, be the better for the job, as well as her
20 master."

Charney gazed once more at the object of his care ;
but instead of admiration for the delicate lines and the
perfume of those expanding blossoms, he experienced
only gratitude for the gift of life. He beheld a bene-
25 factress in Picciola.

THE BATTLE AT MANILA.

THOMAS J. VIVIAN.

PART I.

WHEN we arrived off Subig Bay on the afternoon of Saturday, April 30, 1898, the Commodore called the commanding officers of the ships over to his cabin and outlined to them his plan of attack.

He told them he had every reason to believe that the 5 Spaniards were in Manila Bay, and that his purpose was to carry out the President's instructions and destroy their fleet. We were told that the first thing was to slip into the bay, and if possible to pass the shore forts without drawing their fire. 10

Sunday morning came on still and hot, and before dawn the fleet steamed slowly into the harbor. First went the flagship "Olympia," then the "Baltimore," then the "Raleigh," next the "Petrel," following her the "Concord," and last the "Boston." After the 15 fighting fleet came the supply ships.

As we rounded out beyond the last point before reaching the entrance, we saw the lights of the great cone of Corregidor burning bright and still, but saw nothing in the shape of a searchlight. Every man was 20 called up and ordered to wash and take a cup of coffee. While this light and early refreshment was being served all the ships' lights were extinguished, except those on the taffrail, and these were hooded. So we crept along until we came into the channel, moving in single file.

In that still air it seemed absolutely impossible for us to escape the attention of the entrance forts, yet we would all have been inside — squadron, supply ships, and convoy — without the Spanish fleet receiving the faintest intimation of our approach if it had not been for an enthusiastic fireman. Throwing open the furnace doors, he ladled in a few shovelfuls of soft coal. Up from the smokestack of the cutter went a great shower of sparks.

Some minutes elapsed before out of the west there came a bugle call, then a flash, and then the rolling boom of a great gun.

Twice more the battery spoke, and with the third shot there came a crack from the "Concord," and we knew that our first shot had gone out in the shape of a four-inch shell. Then still further back of us the "Boston" sent in an eight-inch shell, and still further to the rear the "Mc Culloch" sounded a few of her four-pounders.

The batteries kept on flashing and booming a few minutes longer, and then became as silent as they were before we had steamed up.

As soon as we had passed the batteries at the harbor mouth we slowed down, until it seemed as though we were almost at a standstill. The Commodore was talking in an undertone to the rebel Filippino who was acting as pilot; I could see the figures of the

men standing silently at their posts up and down the
ship; and looking over her sides I could distinguish no
line of demarcation between the dull gray of the vessels
and the dark waters of the bay through which we were
so slowly slipping.   5

This creeping, creeping, creeping, with invisible mines
below us and an invisible fleet ahead, was a test out of
which no man came without a sigh of relief. We were
all keyed up, but it was not long before the fighting
string in every man's heart was twanging and singing 10
like that of a taut bow.

As is the fashion of nature in these parts, the dawn
turned as suddenly into day as though a curtain had
been torn down from the sunlight, and there right
ahead of us lay the Spanish fleet tucked up under the 15
forts of Cavité.

Commodore Dewey's fleet consisted of seven vessels,
exclusive of the transports. There were four cruisers,
two gunboats, one cutter, fifty-seven classified big
guns, seventy-four rapid firers and machine guns, and 20
one thousand eight hundred and eight men.

Against us were pitted seven cruisers, five gunboats,
two torpedo boats, fifty-two classified big guns, eighty-
three rapid firers and machine guns, and one thousand
nine hundred and forty-eight men.   25

It cannot be denied that we had a greater number
of heavy guns and that our ships were of modern construction, nor must it be overlooked that the Spanish
fleet was much more numerous, and that it had the

immense assistance of protecting forts manned with
strong garrisons and mounting an unknown number
of guns, of whose caliber and force we had been told
most terrifying things.

5 · As we passed on the eastward curve before actually
beginning the engagement, our lookouts reported that
Admiral Montojo's flag was flying on the cruiser "Reina
Cristina." They reported also that the Spaniards appeared to be protected by a sort of roughly con-
10 structed boom of logs.

As we steamed slowly along then, after dropping the
supply ships, there came a flash of flame and a boom
from the bastions of Cavité, followed immediately by
another flame and a sharper report from one of the
15 Spanish flagship's modern guns. Both shots dropped
somewhere in the bay, and our only answer was in
sending up a string of flags bearing the code watchword, "Remember the 'Maine'!"

On steamed the fleet, with every gun loaded and
20 every man at his post; but not a lanyard was pulled.
Even the Spaniards at Cavité ceased firing as we
moved down toward Manila. As we rounded past
the city's water-front, with about four miles of blue
water between us and it, we could with our glasses
25 make out the city walls, church towers, and other
high places, crowded with sight-seers. As we turned
from Manila, the Commodore said something about the
picturesqueness of the city, adding that the blue hills
at the back of the town reminded him of those of Ver-

mont. It was most unaffectedly said, and was no more tinged with bravado than was Captain Wildes's use of a palm-leaf fan during the engagement.

As we headed toward the Spanish fleet, their gunners and those of the forts began a right merry fusillade. With all this thundering and snapping of the Spaniards, however, there was no answer from us. Up went the signal, "Hold your fire until close in," and on went the squadron. Suddenly something happened. Close off the bow of the "Baltimore" there came a shaking of the bay and a geyser of mud and water. Then right ahead of the "Raleigh" came another ugly fountain of harbor soil and water.

We were among the mines at last.

But we did not strike any. These two upheavals marked the extent of our experience with the "terrible mines" of Manila Bay. The Commodore, his chief of staff, Commander Lamberton, the executive officer, Lieutenant Reese, and the navigator were on the forward bridge. Captain Gridley was in the conning tower. With a glance at the shore the Commodore turned to the officer next to him and said: "About five thousand yards I should say; eh, Reese?"

"Between that and six thousand, I should think, sir," Reese answered.

The Commodore then leaned over the railing and called out:—

"When you are ready you may fire, Gridley."

Instantly the floor of the bridge sprang up beneath

our feet as the port eight-inch gun of our forward turret gave its introductory roar. Our first aim was at the center of the Spanish fleet, the "Olympia's" shot being particularly directed, as a sort of interna-
5 tional mark of courtesy, to the "Reina Cristina."

As our turret gun rang out, the "Baltimore" and "Boston" took up the chorus, their forward guns pitching in two-hundred-and-fifty-pound shells. The reply of the Spaniards was simply terrific. Their ship and
10 shore guns seemed to unite in one unending snap and roar, while the scream of their shot, the bursting of shells, made up a din that was as savage as it was unceasing. It was, however, but as the scraping of fiddle strings to the blare and crash of a full orchestra
15 when compared with that which was to follow.

One wailing, shrieking shell was making straight for the "Olympia's" forward bridge when it exploded about a hundred feet in front of us, one fragment sawing the rigging just over our heads. Another fragment chis-
20 elled a long splinter from the deck just under where the Commodore stood ; a third smashed the bridge gratings, and all around and about and above us there was the sputter and shriek and roar of projectiles.

But the miracle was that none of us was hit.
25 Through this hail of miraculously impotent steel we steered until within a distance of four thousand yards of the Spanish column.

"Open with all the guns," said the Commodore ; and they were opened. That is, all on the port broadside.

By the time the last ship had passed the Spaniards, the "Olympia" had swung around on her return line of attack, and once more we were steaming past Montojo with our starboard guns flaming, roaring, spitting, and smoking as we went. As we passed, the batteries on 5 shore and the Spanish batteries afloat banged away at us, fighting gallantly and furiously. One shot went clean through the "Baltimore," but hit no one. Another cut the signal halyards from Lieutenant Brumby's hands on the after bridge. Another shell passed 10 through the "Boston's" foremast, not far from where Captain Wildes was, on the bridge.

END OF PART I.

BATTLE HYMN OF THE REPUBLIC.

JULIA WARD HOWE.

MRS. JULIA WARD HOWE was born in New York City on the 27th of May, 1819. Her father, Mr. Samuel Ward, was a well-known banker. Her mother was a cultured woman and was the author of several poems.

5 The young girl was carefully educated, and early showed a love for literature. She read a large share of the books in her father's library and wrote verses during her childhood.

She was married to Dr. Samuel Howe, who was the superintendent of the Blind Asylum, at Boston, and traveled with him 10 through Europe.

"Passion Flowers," Mrs. Howe's first volume of poems, was published in 1854, and another collection, "Words for the Hour," appeared two years later.

Her "Battle Hymn" was published with other poems in a 15 book entitled "Later Lyrics."

Mrs. Howe resides in Boston, and is actively engaged in writing and lecturing.

MINE eyes have seen the glory of the coming of the
    Lord:
He is trampling out the vintage where the grapes of
    wrath are stored;
He hath loosed the fateful lightning of his terrible
    swift sword;
      His truth is marching on.

I have seen him in the watch-fires of a hundred cir-
    cling camps;

They have builded him an altar in the evening dews
 and damps;
I can read his righteous sentence by the dim and flaring lamps.
   His day is marching on.

I have read a fiery gospel, writ in burnished rows of
 steel:
"As ye deal with my contemners, so with you my
 grace shall deal;
Let the Hero, born of woman, crush the serpent with
 his heel,
   Since God is marching on."

He has sounded forth the trumpet that shall never
 call retreat;
He is sifting out the hearts of men before his judg-
 ment-seat;
Oh, be swift, my soul, to answer him! be jubilant, my
 feet!
   Our God is marching on.

In the beauty of the lilies Christ was born, across the
 sea,
With a glory in his bosom that transfigures you and
 me;
As he died to make men holy, let us die to make men
 free,
   While God is marching on.

THE BATTLE AT MANILA.

THOMAS J. VIVIAN.

PART II.

It was on the third turn that the great naval duel between the two flagships took place.

When we sighted the Spanish fleet, I remarked that the enemy seemed to have no steam up, and that the fleet seemed to lie behind a breakwater. As we came closer to them, however, we saw more clearly the scheme of their order. Put out your right hand with the thumb extended; call the thumb the Cavité spit, and the space between the thumb and the forefinger Cavité Bay. Manila lies about where the nail of the forefinger is. The town of Cavité lies in the pocket of the thumb and forefinger, and the thumb's nail stands for the main Cavité batteries, four in number. Put a pencil halfway across from the thumb's nail to the first joint of the forefinger, and it will stand for the Cavité arsenal with its boom extension. Behind this boom lay the gunboats of the Spanish fleet, while in front of it, facing Manila Bay, were the Spanish cruisers.

They lay anchored while we made our first and second parallels of attack, but by the time we were sweeping up on the third course the smoke poured out of the "Reina Cristina's" smokestacks; there was a fleece of white gathered about the steam pipe, and

Drawn by Frank T. Merrill.

Engraved by Robert Varley.

THE BATTLE OF MANILA BAY.

the flagship moved out to the attack. She gallantly
stood for the "Olympia," and it looked as though it were
her intention to ram us. The Commodore passed the
word to concentrate all possible fire on the "Reina Cris-
5 tina," and she actually shivered under the battering of
our storm of shot and shell. Rents appeared near her
water-line where the eight-inch shells had torn their
way. One shot struck the port bridge on which Admiral Montojo stood, upon which, like the brave man
10 he was, the Admiral coolly stepped to the other end.

But no bravery could stand the driving, crushing,
rending of the tons of steel which we poured into the
"Cristina," and there was quite a little cheer from our
forward men as the Spanish flagship slowly turned and
15 made for the shore.

In the whole duel between the "Cristina" and the
"Olympia" sixty of the Spanish crew were killed, including the chaplain and the first lieutenant. It was
small wonder she retreated. It was during the fright-
20 ful hubbub of the duel between the Admiral and the
Commodore that two gunboats crept out from behind the Cavité pier and started in to do desperate
deeds. One stole out along the shore, then turned and
made for the supply ships, while the other headed for
25 the "Olympia."

The "Petrel" was sent after the first, and after a
sharp bark or two from her four-pounders, the Spaniard
evidently gave up the job and made for the shore. The
"Petrel" made after her, and while the Spanish crew

clambered over their boat's sides and on to the beach
and up into the underbrush, the "Petrel" turned her
rapid-fire guns on their craft and literally blew her to
pieces.

The other torpedo boat, which was bound to destroy 5
our flagship, made a better fight. Our secondary battery was concentrated on her, but still she kept on
until within five hundred yards, and matters were
beginning to look serious for us. Then the machine
guns in the tops began to treat her to a hailstorm, 10
and this proved too much for this representative of
Spanish naval daring. She turned, and as she did so
a shell struck her just inside the stern railing, exploded,
and the gunboat dipped suddenly in the middle; her
stern and bow rose as suddenly in the air, and she 15
disappeared.

After passing five times in front of the enemy,
the men having been at their blazing work for two
uninterrupted hours, the Commodore concluded that it
would be well to call a halt. 20

"What time is it, Reese?" asked the Commodore.

"Seven forty-five, sir."

"Breakfast time," said the Commodore with an odd
smile; "run up the signals for 'cease firing' and follow
me." 25

With that the "Olympia's" bows were set for a run
to the eastern side of the bay where the storeships lay.
As we swung out, the Spaniards gave a cheer. They
possibly imagined as they saw our line forming to with-

draw, that the fight was over. So, too, might the
Manila gunners on the Luneta fort have done, for as
we passed them they let fly with their Krupp guns.

"No reply, I suppose, sir?" said Lamberton, looking
5 meaningly over to the forward turret, while the men
at the five-inch guns were cocking their eyes inquisi-
tively up at the bridge.

"Oh, no," said the Commodore; "let them amuse
themselves if they will. We shall have plenty of op-
10 portunity to burn powder. We haven't begun fighting yet."

No sooner had we reached the anchorage ground
beside the transport ships than the Commodore called
all the commanders on board to report. Then it was
15 that the wonder of it came to pass.

Not a ship disabled!

Not a gun out of order!

Not a man killed!

Not a man injured!

20 It seemed incredible that this should have been the
result to us in that awful two hours' fight, while to the
Spaniards it had meant such destruction and desolation.
Captain after captain reported the same astounding
news to the Commodore.

25 The Commodore had decided on three hours' rest,
and this being ample time for all the preparatory work
needed, there was no hurry. First of all, all hands
were piped to breakfast, and while I am not historian
enough to have the details of every great combat at my

pen's point, it strikes me that this deliberate hauling off and sitting down to breakfast in the middle of a sea-fight, stands as a situation unique in the chronicles of maritime warfare.

The programme for the second act was that we were to finish up the enemy's fleet, taking one ship after another, and then attend to the forts. Again we sailed around to the Manila channel; and as we drew near the Spaniards we saw that the "Cristina," the "Castilla," and the transport "Mindanao," which latter had been beached about midway between Cavité and Manila, were all ablaze, and that their crews were busy as so many ants trying to put out the flames.

The condition of the Spanish flagship was most pitiable, and before we had commenced firing the second time we saw Admiral Montojo transferring his flag from the "Cristina" to the "Isla de Cuba."

The "Baltimore" headed for the "Cristina" and "Austria." As she came within range she caught all of the Spanish fire that was left on board those two ships. It seemed that in their desperation the Spaniards fired better at this time than they had in the earlier morning, for one of the foreigners' shells exploded on the "Baltimore's" deck, wounding five men with the splinters. No reply came from the "Baltimore."

A few minutes passed and another shell landed on the "Baltimore's" decks, and three other men were hit. Still the "Baltimore" did not reply. Shells plunged about her until she seemed ploughing through a park of fountains. Then, when she reached about a three-thousand-yard range, she swung and poured a broadside into the "Reina Cristina."

5 The smoke clouds hid everything for a minute or two, but when they lifted we saw the "Cristina" blow up, and the waters about her beaten with a rain of descending fragments and men. When the rain of her fragments had ceased the "Cristina" settled and sank, 10 the remainder of her crew jumping overboard and swimming for the nearest consort.

The "Baltimore" then turned her attention to the "Don Juan de Austria," the "Olympia" and "Raleigh" steaming up to complete the destruction in as mercifully 15 brief a time as possible. The three cruisers poured a continuous stream of deadly steel into the Spaniard, which rocked under the smashing.

The Spaniard replied as best she could, but in the midst of it all there came a roar that drowned all pre- 20 vious noises. A shell had struck the Spaniard's magazine and exploded it. Up shot the "Austria's" decks in the flaming volcano, and so terrific was the explosion that the flying fragments of the cruiser actually tore away all the upper works of the gunboat which lay 25 beside her.

The cruisers "Velasco" and "Castilla" were the next of the enemy's ships to be wiped out.

Every ship in the Spanish fleet, with one exception, fought most valiantly, but to the "Don Antonio de

Ulloa" and her commander Robion should be given the
palm for that sort of desperate courage and spirit which
leads a man to die fighting. Shot after shot struck the
Spaniard's hull, until it was riddled like a sieve.   Shell
after shell swept her upper decks, until under the awful 5
fire all of her upper guns were useless ; but there was
no sign of surrender. The main deck crew escaped,
but the captain and his officers clung to their wreck.
On the lower deck her gun crews stuck to their posts
like the heroes they were.   10

As shot after shot struck the shivering hulk, and
still her lower guns answered back as best they could,
it seemed as though it were impossible to kill her. At
last we noticed that sickening, unmistakable lurch of a
sinking ship.   Her commander noticed it too; still 15
there was no surrender.   He nailed the Spanish ensign
to what was left of the mast, and the "Don Antonio de
Ulloa" went down, not only with her colors flying, but
also with her lower guns still roaring defiance.   It was
a brave death, and I am sure every man in the squad- 20
ron would like to have shaken Commander Robion by
the hand.

As the firing grew faster and more furious, and the
smoke settled down again, it was again almost impossible to distinguish exact and particular acts.   Ship after 25
ship was sunk or burned, until poor old Admiral Montojo, seeing but the shattered and blackened remnants
of his fleet, hauled down his colors and, together

with the surviving Spaniards, hastily escaped from the sinking and burning hulk, Admiral and officers alike leaving behind them all their personal property and valuables.

5 One after the other of the shore batteries was settled, and then at 12.45 came the final blow. The bastions of the Cavité forts had been crumbling under the shells of the "Boston," "Baltimore," and "Concord," while the "Raleigh," "Olympia," and "Petrel" had been de-
10 voting themselves to the reduction of the arsenal.

After half an hour's fight of this sort the Cavité gunners evidently became demoralized and began to fire wildly. Those guns left in position continued firing, however, until at their back there was a thunder-
15 ous roar, followed by a heart-shaking concussion. A shell had landed in the arsenal magazine. With the upward rush of flames, fragments, and dead, the heart of the Spaniard went out of him, a white flag was run up at the Cavité citadel, and the battle of Manila was
20 over.

Again the commanders were called over to the flagship. Again came the reports: not a gun overthrown! not a vessel disabled! not a man killed!

From " With Dewey at Manila."

THE MOONLIGHT MARCH.

REGINALD HEBER.

REGINALD HEBER, an English clergyman and hymn-writer, was born in 1783. He was appointed Bishop of Calcutta in 1823.

His devotion to his work and the trying climate were too great a strain upon his health, and he died on the 3d of April, 1826.

Bishop Heber's hymns are among the finest and best known in the English language.

I SEE them on their winding way,
About their ranks the moonbeams play;
Their lofty deeds and daring high
Blend with the notes of victory;
And waving arms and banners bright
Are glowing in the mellow light.

They're lost and gone; the moon is past,
The woods' dark shade is o'er them cast;
And fainter, fainter, fainter still
The march is rising o'er the hill.
Again, again the pealing drum,
The clashing horn — they come, they come;
Through rocky pass, o'er wooded steep,
In long and glittering files they sweep;
And nearer, nearer, yet more near,
Their softened chorus meets the ear.

Forth, forth, and meet them on their way;
The trampling hoofs brook no delay;
With thrilling fife and pealing drum,
And clashing horn, they come, they come!

A PERILOUS ADVENTURE.

VICTOR HUGO.

VICTOR HUGO was born in France, on the 26th of February, 1802. His father was a general in the French army.

Hugo began to devote himself to literary work when he was nineteen. The next year his volume of "Odes and Ballads"
5 was published, and the king of France was so pleased with the verses that he conferred a pension of a thousand francs upon the young poet.

He then wrote several volumes of poems and romances, as well as a number of dramas, which created great excitement among
10 the political parties of France.

In 1837 he was made officer of the Legion of Honor and held a number of important positions during the next fourteen years. His writings and influence against Napoleon had created so strong a feeling by that time that he was obliged to leave
15 France and take refuge in the Island of Guernsey. There he remained for nearly twenty years.

During his exile he wrote a number of books, among them "Les Misérables," one of the greatest novels ever published. He continued writing throughout his life.

20 Victor Hugo died on the 22d of May, 1885. His last years were made happy by the love and admiration of his countrymen, and his death was mourned throughout the nation.

THE old man sat motionless. For the moment it seemed to him that in escaping from the sea, and in
25 touching land, all danger had vanished. No one knew his name; he was alone, lost to the enemy, without a trace left behind him. He felt a strange composure. A little more and he would have been asleep.

Suddenly he started to his feet.

He was looking at the steeple of Cormeray, directly in front of him beyond the plain. Something extraordinary was taking place in this steeple.

The belfry appeared alternately open and closed at regular intervals; its lofty windows showed all white, then all black; the sky could be seen through it, then it disappeared; a gleam of light would come, then an eclipse, and the opening and shutting followed each other a second apart, with the regularity of a hammer on an anvil.

He looked at all the steeples on the horizon. The belfries of all the steeples were alternately black and white. What did this mean?

It meant that all the bells were ringing.

They were sounding the alarm, sounding it frantically, sounding it everywhere, in all the belfries, in every parish, in every village, and not a sound reached his ears.

This was owing to the distance, which prevented the sounds from reaching so far, and because of the sea breeze blowing from the opposite direction, which carried all land noises far away from him.

All these bells madly calling from every side, and at the same time, silence; nothing could be more weird.

Certainly they were after somebody.

Whom?

This man of steel shuddered.

It could not be he. No one could have discovered his coming; he had just landed, and he finally assured himself, by repeating, "Surely, no one knows of my arrival, and no one knows my name."

For some moments there had been a slight sound above and behind him. This sound was like the rust-
5 ling of a leaf on a wind-shaken tree. At first he paid no heed to it; then, as the sound continued, he at last turned around. The wind was trying to detach a large placard pasted on the pillar above his head.

He mounted the stone on which he had been sitting,
10 and placed his hand on the corner of the placard which was flapping in the wind; a part of the placard was printed in large letters, and there was still enough day-light to read them. He read this:—

THE FRENCH REPUBLIC, ONE AND INDIVISIBLE.

15 We, Prieur de la Marne, acting representative of the people for the army of the coast of Cherbourg, order: The former Mar-quis de Lantenac, Viscount de Fontenay, the so-called Prince of Brittany, secretly landed on the coast of Granville, is declared an outlaw. A price is set on his head. The sum of sixty thou-
20 sand francs will be paid to him who will deliver him up, dead or alive. A battalion of the army of the coast of Cherbourg will be sent immediately in pursuit of the former Marquis de Lantenac. The parishes are ordered to lend every assistance. Given at the town hall of Granville, this second day of June, 1793. Signed

25   PRIEUR DE LA MARNE.

The old man pulled down his hat over his eyes, drew his cloak closely up under his chin, and went quickly down the dune. It was evidently unsafe to remain longer on this prominent summit.

The plain was deserted. It was an hour when there were no passers-by. He stopped behind a thicket, took off his cloak, turned the hairy side of his vest out, fastened his ragged cloak around his neck again by the cord, and started on his way.   5

"Where are you going?" said a voice.

He turned around.

A man was there in the thicket, tall like himself, old like himself, with white hair like his own, and with garments more ragged. Almost his double. This man   10 was leaning on a long stick. He repeated:—

"I ask where you are going."

"In the first place, where am I?" he said with an almost haughty calmness.

The man replied:—   15

"You are in the province of Tanis. I am its beggar; you are its lord."

"I?"

"Yes, you, sir, the Marquis de Lantenac."

The Marquis de Lantenac—henceforth we shall call   20 him by his name—replied gravely:—

"You are right. Deliver me up."

The man continued:—

"We are both at home here: you in the castle, I in the thicket."   25

"Make an end of it. Do your work. Betray me," said the Marquis.

The man pointed to the roof of the farmhouse, which could be seen some distance away, above the trees.

"They are searching for you. There is a half battalion there."

"Well," said the Marquis, "let us go on."

And he took a step in the direction of the farm.

5 The man seized him by the arm.

"Do not go there."

"And where would you have me go?"

"Home with me."

The Marquis looked at the beggar.

10 "Listen, Marquis, my home is not fine; but it is safe. A hut lower than a cave. For a floor, a bed of seaweed; for a ceiling, a roof of branches and grass. Come. You would be shot at the farm. With me you will go to sleep. You must be tired; and to-15 morrow morning the Blues will march away, and you can go wherever you please."

The Marquis studied the man.

"And you wish to save me?"

"Yes."

20 "Why?"

"Because I said: 'There is another poorer than I. I have the right to breathe, he has not.'"

"But do you know that a price has been put on my head?"

25 "Yes."

"How did you know?"

"I read the placard."

"Then, since you have read the placard, you know that the man who betrays me will win sixty thousand francs."

" I know it."

" Do you know that sixty thousand francs is a fortune?"

" Yes."

" And that the one who will deliver me up will make 5
his fortune?"

" That is just what I thought. When I saw you I said to myself: ' Only think of it, the one who betrays this very man will win sixty thousand francs and make his fortune!   Let us hasten to conceal him.' " 10

The Marquis followed the poor man.   They entered a thicket.   Here was the beggar's den.   It was a sort of room that a grand old oak had let this man have in its heart.   It was hollowed out under its roots and covered with its branches. 15

They stooped, crept along a little way, entered the room cut up into odd compartments by the great tree-roots, and sat down on a heap of seaweed, which served as a bed.   The space between two roots, where they entered, and which served as a doorway, let in 20
some light.   A reflection from the moon threw a dim light over the entrance.   In a corner there was a jug of water, a loaf of buckwheat bread, and some chestnuts.

They shared the chestnuts; the Marquis added his 25
piece of biscuit; they bit the same loaf of buckwheat and drank from the jug one after the other.

" You belong to this country?" asked the Marquis.

" I have never been out of it."

"Have I ever met you before?"

"Often, for I am your own beggar. I was the poor man at the foot of the road to your castle. You used to give me alms. I held out my hand, you saw the hand

5 only, and you dropped in it the alms which I needed in the morning to keep me from dying of hunger at night. Sometimes a sou saved my life. I owe you my life. I pay the debt."

His voice grew serious. "On one condition."

10 "What is that?"

"That you do not come here to work evil."

"I come here to do good," said the Marquis.

"Let us sleep," said the beggar.

They lay down side by side on the bed of seaweed.

15 The beggar fell asleep immediately. The Marquis, although very tired, remained absorbed in thought for a time, then he looked at the poor man in the darkness and lay down again. Lying on this pallet was like lying on the ground; he took advantage of it to put

20 his ear to the earth and listen. There was a dull humming underground; he heard the noise of the bells.

The tocsin was still sounding.

The Marquis fell asleep.

When he awoke it was day.

25 Tellmarch, the beggar, was outside near the entrance. He was leaning on his stick. The sun shone on his face.

"Monseigneur," said Tellmarch, "it has just struck four from the belfry of Tanis. I heard the four strokes.

So the wind has changed, it is blowing offshore; I hear no other sound, so the tocsin has ceased. Everything is quiet at the farm and in the hamlet. The worst of the danger is over; it will be wise for us to separate. It is my hour for setting out."

He indicated a point on the horizon.

" I am going that way."

He pointed in the opposite direction.

" You must go this way."

The beggar saluted the Marquis solemnly.

A moment later he had disappeared among the trees.

The Marquis rose and went in the direction Tellmarch had pointed out to him.

It was the charming morning hour, called in the old Norman peasant tongue " the song sparrow of the day." The finches and hedge sparrows were chirping. The Marquis followed the path by which they had come the night before.

At the foot of the crossroad where he was stealing along, he could see only the roofs of the farms which lay to the left. He was skirting a steep height. At the foot of the height the view was abruptly lost in the trees. The foliage seemed bathed in light. All nature was filled with the deep joy of the morning.

Suddenly the landscape became terrible. It was like the bursting forth of an ambuscade. A strange deluge of wild cries and gunshots fell over the fields and woods full of sunlight, and in the direction of the farm a great smoke pierced by bright flames arose, as if the hamlet and the farm were nothing but a bundle of burning straw. It was sudden and fearful, an abrupt change from peace to madness, a horror without warning. The Marquis stopped.

5 There is no one who, under similar circumstances, would not have felt that curiosity is stronger than danger; one must know, if he has to die in consequence. He climbed up the height, at the foot of which passed the hollow path. From there he could 10 see, but he might also be seen. He looked about him.

To be sure, there was firing and a fire. The noise could be heard, the fire could be seen. The farm was the center of some terrible calamity. What was it? 15 Was the farm attacked? And by whom? Was it a battle? The Blues, as they had been ordered, very often punished refractory farms and villages by setting them on fire; to make an example of them they burned every farm and every hamlet which had not felled the 20 trees prescribed by law, and which had not opened passages through the thickets for the republican cavalry. It was evident that none of the openings ordered by the decree had been made in the thickets and hedges of Tanis. Was this the punishment?

25 While the Marquis, hesitating to go down, hesitating to remain, was listening and watching, this din ceased. The Marquis was aware of something in the thicket like the scattering of a wild and joyous troop. There was a frightful swarming under the trees. They were

rushing from the farm into the woods. Drums were beating. No more firing was heard. They seemed to be hunting about, pursuing, tracking; it was evident that they were in search of some one; the noise was scattered and deep; it was a medley of words of anger 5 and of triumph, a clamorous uproar; suddenly, as an outline becomes visible in a cloud of smoke, something became articulate and distinct in this tumult. It was a name — a name repeated by a thousand voices, and the Marquis heard clearly this cry: — 10

"Lantenac! Lantenac! the Marquis de Lantenac!"

It was he for whom they were hunting.

✗Suddenly, all around him and on every side at once, the thicket was filled with guns, bayonets, and swords, a tricolored flag arose in the shade, the cry of "Lante- 15 nac!" burst on his ear, and at his feet through the brambles and branches passionate faces appeared.

The Marquis was alone, standing on a summit which could be seen from every point of the wood. He could scarcely see those who were crying his name, but he 20 was seen by all. If there were a thousand guns in the woods, he was a target for them. He could distinguish nothing in the thicket but eager eyes fixed upon him.

He took off his hat, turned up the rim, broke a long, 25 dry thorn from a furze bush, drew a white cockade from his pocket, fastened the brim and the cockade back to the crown of the hat with the thorn, and putting the hat on his head again, so that the raised rim showed his forehead and his cockade, he said in a loud voice, speaking to the whole forest at once: —

"I am the man you are seeking. I am the Marquis de Lantenac, Prince of Brittany, Lieutenant-General of 5 the armies of the king. Make an end of it. Aim! Fire!"

And, tearing open his goatskin vest, he bared his naked breast.

He looked down, expecting to meet loaded guns, and 10 saw himself surrounded with kneeling men.

A great shout arose: "Long live Lantenac! Long live the general!"

At the same time hats were thrown in the air, swords flourished joyfully, and throughout the whole thicket 15 sticks were seen rising, on whose points whirled brown woolen caps.

He was surrounded by a Vendean band. This troop fell on their knees when they saw him.

All these eyes, full of a terrible fire, were fixed on 20 the Marquis with a sort of savage love.

A young, noble-looking man made his way through the kneeling soldiers, and with long strides went up towards the Marquis. Like the peasants, he wore a felt hat with turned-up rim and a white cockade, and 25 was wrapped in a fur jacket, but his hands were white and his linen fine, and he wore over his vest a white silk scarf, from which hung a sword with a gold hilt.

When he reached the height he threw down his hat,

unfastened his scarf, knelt on one knee, and presented scarf and sword to the Marquis, saying : —

"We were searching for you, and we have found you. Accept the sword of command. These men are now yours. I was their commander; I am promoted to a higher rank, for I become your soldier. Accept our homage, my lord. General, give me your orders."

From " Ninety-Three."

RALPH WALDO EMERSON.

RALPH WALDO EMERSON was born in Boston on the
25th of May, 1803. His father, William Emerson, was
a minister. The parsonage was on Summer Street, where
at that time were many pretty homes with gardens.

5   Mr. Emerson took great interest in the education of
his children, and Ralph was sent to a private school

before he was three years
old. His father died dur-
ing his early boyhood, and
his mother worked hard
to support and educate
her five sons.

The boys were very
fond of their books and
were manly and helpful,
doing all they could for
their mother. Their aunt,
Mary Emerson, lived with
them, and she guided their
20 choice of reading and led them to think. "Lift your
aims"; "Always do what you are afraid to do";
"Scorn trifles" were the maxims which she gave to
her nephews.

Ralph entered the Latin School when he was ten
25 years old, remaining there until he entered college. His
books were his chief source of happiness, and the scenes
in them were so real to him and his brothers that when

they visited their grandmother at Concord, they imagined in their play that the barns, garret, or woods were battlefields or mountain-tops.

Many were the poems which they could repeat, and a clerk in one of the Concord stores used to stand little Ralph on a barrel so that he might entertain the customers with his recitations.

Each of the boys was fitted for college, and helped pay his own expenses by teaching and acting as usher or waiter. Ralph entered Harvard College when he was but fourteen. He occupied a room at the President's house, and paid for it by carrying official messages. He won five dollars at the prize declamations and sent the money home, hoping that it would enable his mother to purchase a new shawl, but it was needed to pay a debt.

Ralph was graduated when he was eighteen, and was chosen class poet. He and his brother William, two years his senior, opened a school for young ladies in Mrs. Emerson's house. It was fairly successful, but as soon as they were well established, William went to Germany and left Ralph in charge. He taught during more than a year, and then entered the Divinity School at Harvard College.

Within a month his health failed, and he was obliged to give up his studies. He went to visit an uncle at Newton, spending much of his time out of doors. The next fall he went to Chelmsford to teach in the Academy. He remained there three months, and then left on account of ill-health. In the spring he took a school at Cambridge, in order to be where he might gain some benefit from the Divinity School, and in October of this year, 1826, he was " approbated to preach."

5 His health, however, had so failed that his physician ordered him to go south. He traveled as far as St. Augustine, and the next summer returned home, improved in health, but not fully recovered.

He was married, soon after his return, to Ellen 10 Tucker, a very beautiful young lady, but of delicate health. She died a year and a half after her marriage.

Mr. Emerson was for a time the pastor of a church in Boston. He then sailed for Europe, desiring to see the ancient cities and to make the acquaintance of 15 some of the men whose works had influenced him, among them being Wordsworth, Coleridge, and Carlyle. He found the latter among the lonely hills of Nithsdale, and the two philosophers formed a friendship which lasted throughout their lives.

20 On Emerson's return to this country he engaged in lecturing, and preached at Plymouth during that winter. There he met Lydia Jackson, to whom he was married the following September. Mr. Emerson took his bride to their new home in Concord, where he lived the rest 25 of his life, and which is still occupied by the family. He spent much of his time out of doors; and the grove near by, rather than his library, was used by him as a study. He believed that his thoughts were clearer and truer in this solitude, with only the winds and the voices

of birds to distract him. He found inspiration in the
stars at night and even braved the wind storms, revel-
ing in their grandeur.

Friends gathered in Concord, among them Hawthorne,
Thoreau, Alcott, and the Curtis boys, while near by were 5
Longfellow, Holmes, and Lowell. Their society afforded
him much pleas-
ure. Emerson was
also a favorite
among the village
farmers, and the
little children
loved him dearly.

Much of his time
was spent in lectur-
ing. He received
but little from his

EMERSON'S HOME AT CONCORD, MASS.

books of "Essays," "Poems," "Representative Men,"
and other works until the latter years of his life. In
his seventieth year he went abroad for the third time, 20
revisiting his old friend Carlyle. On his return to
Concord the whole village welcomed him, and his
friends and neighbors accompanied him to his home,
under a triumphal arch.

His last few years were quiet and peaceful. He 25
died on the 27th of April, 1882, and was buried under
a great pine tree in Sleepy Hollow cemetery.

EACH AND ALL.

RALPH WALDO EMERSON.

LITTLE thinks, in the field, yon red-cloaked clown,
Of thee, from the hilltop looking down;
The heifer that lows in the upland farm,
Far-heard, lows not thine ear to charm;
The sexton, tolling his bell at noon
Deems not that great Napoleon
Stops his horse, and lists with delight
Whilst his files sweep round yon Alpine height;
Nor knowest thou what argument
Thy life to thy neighbor's creed has lent.
All are needed by each one —
Nothing is fair or good alone.

I thought the sparrow's note from heaven,
Singing at dawn on the alder-bough;
I brought him home, in his nest, at even;
He sings the song, but it pleases not now;
For I did not bring home the river and sky;
He sang to my ear — they sang to my eye.

The delicate shells lay on the shore;
The bubbles of the latest wave
Fresh pearls to their enamel gave,
And the bellowing of the savage sea
Greeted their safe escape to me.

I wiped away the weeds and foam —
I fetched my sea-born treasures home;
But the poor, unsightly, noisome things
Had left their beauty on the shore,
With the sun, and the sand, and the wild uproar.

Then I said : " I covet truth;
Beauty is unripe childhood's cheat;
I leave it behind with the games of youth." —
As I spoke, beneath my feet
The ground-pine curled its pretty wreath,
Running over the club-moss burrs;
I inhaled the violet's breath;
Around me stood the oaks and firs;
Pine-cones and acorns lay on the ground;
Over me soared the eternal sky,
Full of light and of deity;
Again I saw, again I heard
The rolling river, the morning bird; —
Beauty through my senses stole —
I yielded myself to the perfect whole.

EYES.

RALPH WALDO EMERSON.

MAN cannot fix his eye on the sun, and so far seems imperfect. In Siberia a late traveler found men who could see the satellites of Jupiter with their unaided eye. In some respects the animals excel us. The birds have
5 a longer sight, besides the advantage by their wings of a higher observatory. A cow can bid her calf, by secret signal, probably of the eye, to run away, or to lie down and hide itself. The jockeys say of certain horses, that "they look over the whole ground." The outdoor life
10 and hunting and labor give equal vigor to the human eye. A farmer looks out at you as strong as the horse; his eye-beam is like the stroke of a staff. An eye can threaten like a loaded and leveled gun, or can insult like hissing or kicking; or, in its altered mood, by beams
15 of kindness, it can make the heart dance with joy.

The eye obeys exactly the action of the mind. When a thought strikes us, the eyes fix, and remain gazing at a distance; in enumerating the names of persons or of countries, as France, Germany, Spain,
20 Turkey, the eyes wink at each new name. There is no nicety of learning sought by the mind, which the eyes do not vie in acquiring. "An artist," says Michael Angelo, "must have his measuring tools, not in the hand, but in the eye"; and there is no end to
25 the catalogue of its performances.

Eyes are bold as lions — roving, running, leaping, here and there, far and near. They speak all languages. They wait for no introduction; . . . ask no leave of age or rank ; they respect neither poverty nor riches, neither learning nor power, . . . but intrude, and come again, and go through and through you, in a moment of time. . . . The glance is natural magic. The mysterious communication established across a house between two entire strangers moves all the springs of wonder. The communication by the glance is in the greatest part not subject to the control of the will. It is the bodily symbol of identity of nature. We look into the eyes to know if this other form is another self, and the eyes will not lie, but make a faithful confession what inhabitant is there. . . .

The eyes of men converse as much as their tongues, with the advantage that the ocular dialect needs no dictionary, but is understood all the world over. When the eyes say one thing, and the tongue another, a practised man relies on the language of the first. If the man is off his centre, the eyes show it. You can read in the eyes of your companion whether your argument hits him, though his tongue will not confess it. There is a look by which a man shows he is going to say a good thing, and a look when he has said it. Vain and forgotten are all the fine offers and offices of hospitality if there is no holiday in the eye. How many furtive inclinations avowed by the eye, though dissembled by the lips ! One comes away from a com-

pany in which it may easily happen he has said nothing, and no important remark has been addressed to him, and yet, if in sympathy with the society, he shall not have a sense of this fact, such a stream of life
5 has been flowing into him, and out from him, through the eyes. There are eyes, to be sure, that give no more admission into the man than blueberries. Others are liquid and deep — wells that a man may fall into; others are aggressive and devouring, seem to call out
10 the police, take all too much notice, and require crowded Broadways, and the security of millions, to protect individuals against them. . . . There are asking eyes, asserting eyes, prowling eyes; and eyes full of fate — some of good and some of sinister omen. The
15 alleged power to charm down insanity, or ferocity in beasts, is a power behind the eye. It must be a victory achieved in the will, before it can be signified in the eye.

From the Essay on " Behavior."

THE PERCEPTION OF BEAUTY.

WILLIAM ELLERY CHANNING.

BEAUTY is an all-pervading presence. It unfolds in the numberless flowers of the spring. It waves in the branches of the trees and the green blades of grass. It haunts the depths of the earth and sea, and gleams out in the hues of the shell and the precious stone. And not only these minute objects, but the ocean, the mountains, the clouds, the heavens, the stars, the rising and setting sun, all overflow with beauty. The universe is its temple, and those men who are alive to it cannot lift their eyes without feeling themselves encompassed with it on every side.

Now this beauty is so precious, the enjoyments it gives are so refined and pure, so congenial with our tenderest feelings, and so akin to worship, that it is painful to think of the multitude of men as living in the midst of it, and living almost as blind to it as if they were tenants of a dungeon. An infinite joy is lost to the world by the want of culture of this spiritual endowment. The greatest truths are wronged if not linked with beauty, and they win their way most surely and deeply into the soul when arrayed in this their natural and fit attire. Now no man receives the true culture of a man, in whom the sensibility to the beautiful is not cherished; and I know of no condition of life from which it should be excluded.

LOST ON THE MOUNTAIN.

BERNARDIN DE ST. PIERRE.

BERNARDIN DE ST. PIERRE was born at Havre, France, in 1737.

He was very fond of nature, books, and animals, but cared little for other companionship. At twelve years of age he became
5 absorbed in the adventures of "Robinson Crusoe." To please the boy his parents allowed him to take a sea voyage with his uncle.

On his return he studied at Caen, where he made great progress. He completed his studies at Rome, and soon after was
10 granted a commission as an engineer. He was then sent to Dusseldorf, and might have attained honor and a fortune, but he had a faulty temper and was unwilling to obey orders, so that in spite of his bravery and talents he was sent back to France.

After years of changes and trouble he went to Paris and
15 devoted himself to literature.

His "Paul and Virginia" is one of the most beautiful stories ever written, and has been translated into many languages. It is said that Napoleon slept with a copy of this book beneath his pillow during his Italian campaign, and Joseph Bonaparte
20 awarded a pension of six thousand francs to the author.

St. Pierre was elected a member of the French Academy as a mark of honor, and his last years were happier than his youth had ever been. He died at the age of seventy-seven.

ONE Sunday, at daybreak, the children perceived a
25 negro woman beneath the plantains which surrounded their habitation. She threw herself at the feet of Virginia and said: "My good young lady, have pity on a poor runaway slave. For a whole month I have wandered among these mountains, half dead with hun-

ger and often pursued by the hunters and their dogs. I fled from my master, a rich planter of the Black River, who has used me as you see"; and she showed her body marked with scars from the lashes she had received. She added: "I was going to drown myself, 5 but hearing you lived here, I said to myself: Since there are still some good white people in this country, I need not die yet."

Virginia answered with emotion: "Take courage, unfortunate creature! here is something to eat"; and 10 she gave her the breakfast she had been preparing, which the slave in a few minutes devoured. When her hunger was appeased, Virginia said to her: "Poor woman! I should like to go and ask forgiveness for you of your master. Surely the sight of you will 15 touch him with pity. Will you show me the way?"

"Angel of heaven!" answered the poor negro woman, "I will follow you where you please!" Virginia called her brother and begged him to accompany her. The slave led the way, by winding and difficult paths, until, 20 about the middle of the day, they reached the borders of the Black River. There they perceived a well-built house, surrounded by extensive plantations, and a number of slaves employed in their various labors. Their master was walking among them with a pipe in his 25 mouth and a switch in his hand. Virginia, holding Paul by the hand, drew near, and with much emotion begged him, for the love of God, to pardon his poor slave, who stood trembling a few paces behind.

The planter at first paid little attention to the children, but when he observed the elegance of Virginia's form and the profusion of her beautiful light tresses which had escaped from beneath her blue cap; when
5 he heard the soft tone of her voice which trembled, as well as her whole frame, while she implored his compassion, — he took his pipe from his mouth, and, lifting up his stick, said that he pardoned his slave, for the love of her who asked his forgiveness. Vir-
10 ginia made a sign to the slave to approach her master, and instantly sprang away, followed by Paul.

They climbed up the steep they had descended, and, having gained the summit, seated themselves at the foot of a tree, overcome with fatigue, hunger, and thirst.
15 Paul said to Virginia : " My dear sister, it is past noon, and I am sure you are thirsty and hungry; we shall find no dinner here; let us go down the mountain again and ask the master of the poor slave for some food." — " Oh, no," answered Virginia, " he frightens
20 me too much. Remember what mamma sometimes says, ' The bread of the wicked is like stones in the mouth.' God will take care of us; he listens to the cry even of the little birds when they ask him for food."

25 Scarcely had she pronounced these words when they heard the noise of water falling from a neighboring rock. They ran thither, and having quenched their thirst at this crystal spring, they gathered and ate a few cresses which grew on the border of the stream.

Soon afterwards, while they were wandering backwards
and forwards in search of more solid nourishment, Virginia perceived in the thickest part of the forest a
young palm tree. The kind of cabbage which is found
at the top of the palm, enfolded within its leaves, is 5
well adapted for food; but although the stock of the
tree is not thicker than a man's leg, it grows to above
sixty feet in height. The wood of the tree, indeed, is
composed only of very fine filaments; but the bark is
so hard that it turns the edge of the hatchet, and Paul 10
was not furnished even with a knife.

At length he thought of setting fire to the palm tree,
but a new difficulty occurred; he had no steel with
which to strike fire; and although the whole island is
covered with rocks, I do not believe it is possible to 15
find a single flint. Paul determined to kindle a fire
after the manner of the negroes. With the sharp end
of a stone he made a small hole in the branch of a tree
that was quite dry, and which he held between his
feet; he then, with the edge of the same stone, brought 20
to a point another dry branch of a different sort of
wood, placing the piece of pointed wood in the small
hole of the branch which he held with his feet and
turning it rapidly between his hands. In a few minutes
smoke and sparks of fire issued from the point of 25
contact. Paul then heaped together dried grass and
branches, and set fire to the foot of the palm tree,
which soon fell to the ground with a tremendous
crash. Having thus succeeded in obtaining this

fruit, they ate part of it raw, and part dressed upon the ashes.

After dinner they were much embarrassed by the recollection that they had now no guide, and that they 5 were ignorant of the way. Paul, whose spirit was not subdued by difficulties, said to Virginia: "The sun shines full upon our huts at noon; we must pass, as we did this morning, over that mountain, with its three points, which you see yonder. Come, let us be mov-10 ing." They then descended the steep bank of the Black River on the northern side, and arrived, after an hour's walk, on the banks of a large river, which stopped their further progress.

The stream, on the banks of which Paul and Virginia 15 were now standing, rolled foaming over a bed of rocks. The noise of the water frightened Virginia, and she was afraid to wade through the current. Paul there-fore took her up in his arms and went thus loaded over the slippery rocks, which formed the bed of the river, 20 careless of the tumultuous noise of its waters. "Do not be afraid," cried he to Virginia; "I feel very strong with you. If that planter at the Black River had refused you the pardon of his slave, I would have fought with him." — "What!" answered Virginia, 25 "with that great wicked man? To what have I exposed you! Dear me! how difficult it is to do good! and yet it is so easy to do wrong."

When Paul had crossed the river he wished to con-tinue the journey carrying his sister, but his strength

soon failed, and he was obliged to set down his burden
and to rest himself by her side. Virginia then said to
him: "My dear brother, the sun is going down; you
have still some strength left, but mine has quite failed;
do leave me here and return home alone to ease the 5
fears of our mothers." — "Oh, no," said Paul, "I will
not leave you; if night overtakes us in this wood, I
will light a fire and bring down another palm tree;
you shall eat the cabbage, and I will form a covering
of the leaves to shelter you." 10

In the mean time Virginia being a little rested, she
gathered from the trunk of an old tree, which overhung
the bank of the river, some long leaves of the plant
called hart's-tongue, which grew near its root. Of
these leaves she made a sort of buskin, with which she 15
covered her feet which were bleeding from the sharp-
ness of the stony paths; for in her eager desire to do
good she had forgotten to put on her shoes. Feeling
her feet cooled by the freshness of the leaves, she
broke off a branch of bamboo and continued her walk, 20
leaning with one hand on the staff, and with the other
on Paul.

They walked slowly through the woods; but from
the height of the trees, and the thickness of their
foliage, they soon lost sight of the mountain by which 25
they had hitherto directed their course, and also of the
sun, which was now setting. At length they wandered from the beaten path in which they had hitherto
walked, and found themselves in a labyrinth of trees,

underwood, and rocks, whence there appeared to be no
outlet.

Paul made Virginia sit down, while he ran backwards and forwards, half frantic, in search of a path
5 which might lead them out of this thick wood; but
he fatigued himself to no purpose. He then climbed
to the top of a lofty tree, whence he hoped at least to
perceive the mountain; but he could discern nothing
around him but the tops of trees, some of which were
10 gilded with the last beams of the setting sun. The
most profound silence reigned in those awful solitudes,
which was only interrupted by the cry of the deer
which came to their lairs in that unfrequented spot.
Paul, in the hope that some hunter would hear his voice,
15 called out as loud as he was able: "Come, come to
the help of Virginia!" But the echoes of the forest
alone answered his call, and repeated again and again,
" Virginia — Virginia!"

Paul at length descended from the tree, overcome by
20 fatigue and vexation. He looked around in order to
make some arrangement for passing the night in that
desert; but he could find neither fountain, nor palm
tree, nor even a branch of dry wood fit for kindling a
fire. He was then impressed, by experience, with the
25 sense of his own weakness and began to weep. Virginia said to him: "Do not weep, my dear brother,
or I shall be overwhelmed with grief. I am the cause
of all your sorrow and of all that our mothers are suffering at this moment. I find we ought to do nothing,

not even good, without consulting our parents. Oh, I have been very imprudent!"—and she began to shed tears. "Let us pray to God, my dear brother," she again said, "and he will hear us." They had scarcely finished their prayer when they heard the barking of 5 a dog. "It must be the dog of some hunter," said Paul, "who comes here at night, to lie in wait for the deer." Soon after, the dog began barking again with increased violence.

"Surely," said Virginia, "it is Fidele, our own dog. 10 Yes; now I know his bark." A moment after Fidele was at their feet, barking, howling, moaning, and devouring them with caresses. Before they could recover from their surprise, they saw Domingo running towards them. At the sight of the good old negro 15 who wept for joy, they began to weep too.

When Domingo had recovered himself a little, "Oh, my dear children," said he, "how miserable have you made your mothers! How astonished they were when they returned, on not finding you at home! I ran back- 20 wards and forwards in the plantation, not knowing where to look for you. At last I took some of your old clothes, and showing them to Fidele, the poor animal, as if he understood me, immediately began to scent your path, and conducted me, wagging his tail all the while, to 25 the Black River.

"I there saw a planter who told me you had brought back a Maroon negro woman, his slave, and that he had pardoned her at your request. After that, Fidele,

l on the scent, led me up the steep bank of the Black
er, where he again stopped and barked with all his
might. At last he led me to this very spot. We
are now at the foot of the mountain and still four
5 good leagues from home. Come, eat and recover your
strength."

Domingo then presented them with a cake, some
fruit, and a large gourd full of beverage. But when
they prepared to continue their journey a new difficulty
10 occurred; Paul and Virginia could no longer walk,
their feet being swollen and inflamed. Domingo knew
not what to do; whether to leave them and go in search
of help, or remain and pass the night with them on
that spot. "There was a time," said he, "when I
15 could carry you both together in my arms! But now
you are grown big, and I am old."

While he was in this perplexity, a troop of Maroon
negroes appeared at a short distance from them. The
chief of the band, approaching Paul and Virginia, said
20 to them: "Good little white people, do not be afraid.
We saw you pass this morning with a negro woman of
the Black River. You went to ask pardon for her of
her wicked master; and we, in return for this, will
carry you home upon our shoulders." He then made
25 a sign, and four of the strongest negroes immediately
formed a sort of litter with the branches of trees and
lianas, and having seated Paul and Virginia on it, carried them upon their shoulders. Domingo marched in
front with his lighted torch, and they proceeded amidst

the rejoicings of the whole troop, who overwhelmed
them with their benedictions.

It was midnight when they arrived at the foot of
their mountain, on the ridges of which several fires
were lighted. As soon as they began to ascend, they 5
heard voices exclaiming: "Is it you, my children?"
They answered immediately, and the negroes also:
"Yes, yes, it is." A moment after they could distinguish their mothers coming towards them with lighted
torches in their hands. "Unhappy children!" cried 10
Madame de la Tour, "where have you been? what
agonies you have made us suffer!"—"We have been,"
said Virginia, "to the Black River, where we went to
ask pardon for a poor Maroon slave, to whom I gave
our breakfast this morning, because she seemed dying 15
of hunger; and these Maroon negroes have brought us
home." Madame de la Tour embraced her daughter,
without being able to speak; and Virginia, who felt
her face wet with her mother's tears, exclaimed: "Now
I am repaid for all the hardships I have suffered." Mar- 20
garet, in a transport of delight, pressed Paul in her arms,
exclaiming: "And you also, my dear child, you have done
a good action." When they reached the cottages with
their children, they entertained all the negroes with a
plentiful repast, after which the latter returned to the 25
woods praying Heaven to shower down every description
of blessing on those good white people.

From " Paul and Virginia."

OLIVER GOLDSMITH.

OLIVER GOLDSMITH was born in 1728, in a little Irish hamlet called Pallas.   His father was a clergyman, who found it hard to provide for his large family of eight children.   When Oliver was two years old, his father  was offered a place as curate at Lissoy, and the family moved to a large house near that village.

A servant, named Elizabeth Delop, taught the alphabet to little Oliver, and he was afterwards sent to the village school. His teacher was an old quartermaster named Thomas Byrne, who used to shoulder a crutch and show the boys "how fields were won."   He told the children Irish folk-stories and wild legends and sang them many a song.

While at this school, Oliver was taken ill with 25 smallpox, and was sent, on recovering, to the Griffin school at Roscommon.   The pale-faced little fellow learned very slowly and was looked upon as a dunce.

The boys laughed at him and imposed upon him, although they all regarded him as kind-hearted and affectionate.

Oliver was no dunce, though he seemed so stupid and awkward. After he became famous, these very 5 playmates remembered bright answers he had given when they had roused him beyond endurance. While attending school at Roscommon, Oliver stayed with his Uncle John. A country dance was once given at the house. The gay music led Oliver to forget his shyness, 10 and he began to dance the hornpipe. The fiddler laughed and called him " Ugly Æsop." Oliver quickly turned to him and said : —

> " Heralds, proclaim aloud! all saying,
>   See Æsop dancing and his monkey playing."   15

In spite of these flashes of wit, his playmates continued to laugh at him and cheat him into buying their worthless toys, and he was thought to be the dullest boy in the village.

At the age of eleven he was sent to a school at Athlone, 20 about five miles away, and two years later attended a school at Edgeworthstown. The master, Rev. Patrick Hughes, took an interest in the lad, and was the only teacher who recognized his good qualities.

The story is told that Oliver was returning to school 25 after a holiday, riding a horse and carrying a guinea in his pocket. He loitered along the way, enjoying the scenes, and at nightfall found himself several miles from school.

The guinea gave him such a sense of wealth that he inquired the way to the best house in the village, meaning the best inn. The man of whom he inquired was amused at the boy's importance, and directed him to the home of Squire Featherstone. Oliver rang at the gate, gave his orders to the servant, and called for a supper and the best room in the house. The squire, seeing his mistake, carried on the joke, and it was not until Oliver produced the guinea to settle his account that he learned the truth.

He afterwards wrote a play, which has such an incident for its foundation.

In his seventeenth year Oliver went to Trinity College, Dublin, entering as a "sizar," a name given to those students who were educated at little expense but were obliged to act as servants. He swept the courts and waited on the table. He had a room in a garret, and after he became famous it was found that he had scrawled his name upon one of the windows.

The unhappy sizar little thought that some day this pane of glass would be given a place of honor in the College Library.

Poor Oliver led an unhappy life. He cared little for study and had a brutal tutor. A year and a half after he entered college his father died and he was in want.

Music afforded him his only delight, and he loved to play upon his flute and sing. He wrote street ballads to keep himself from starving and sold them for five shillings apiece. The happiest hours he spent were those when he crept out after dark to listen to the singing of these ballads by the street beggars.

He was so kind-hearted that he seldom reached home with the whole of his five shillings. Each beggar's cry would touch his tender heart, and he often robbed him- 5 self of his clothing that he might cover some shivering form.

When he was twenty-one, Goldsmith received the degree of Bachelor of Arts and returned to his home. There he spent a happy period of two years, helping 10 his brother, who taught the village school, and assisting his widowed mother.

After trying a number of professions without success, Goldsmith decided to emigrate to America. He started with thirty pounds and mounted on a good horse. In 15 six weeks he returned, riding a forlorn-looking beast. He said that he had reached a seaport and paid his passage to America, but that the winds were unfavorable, and while waiting he had taken a little trip into the country. During his absence a fair wind had arisen 20 and the ship had sailed without him.

Goldsmith then decided to study law. Mr. Contarine, an uncle, lent him fifty pounds, and he set out for London. Stopping at Dublin, he met an old schoolmate who persuaded him to try his luck at doubling his 25 money at a card table, and he lost it all.

Mr. Contarine did not entirely lose faith in his wayward nephew, and, learning that he had some taste for chemistry, gave him the means to start the study of medicine. Goldsmith went to Edinburgh and spent eighteen months there. He then continued his medical studies at Leyden. He left Leyden in his twenty-seventh year. The day before his departure he had seen some rare plants in a florist's window. Remembering that his uncle had expressed a desire for these varieties, he purchased them with the little money he had and sent them to Ireland.

The next year was spent in journeying on foot through Flanders, France, and Switzerland. He had little or no money, and slept in barns and even under hedges. When he came to a convent or a monastery, he found shelter for the night; and his flute often earned him a supper and a lodging, for the peasants, as well as the little children, enjoyed and rewarded him for the merry strains which set them to dancing.

The wanderer landed at Dover, friendless and penniless. He turned strolling player, but his face and figure were not received with favor. He reached London, but led a hard life there. Unable to find suitable employment, he pounded drugs and ran errands for a chemist, served as usher in a school, and was even reduced to a life among the beggars.

His medical education was of little use to him. He tried to open a practice in London, but had few patients, and while at their bedsides was obliged to hold his hat over his coat to hide the worn places.

Goldsmith now began to toil with his pen, lodging in a garret at the top of a flight of stairs called "Break-

neck Steps." In this wretched abode, he wrote many
articles for magazines and newspapers, essays, and poems,
as were called for by the bookseller who employed him.
His style was pure and graceful, and his humor happy.
There was beauty in all that he wrote, and he gradually 5

DR. JOHNSON READING "THE VICAR OF WAKEFIELD."

grew in favor. He made the acquaintance of Dr. Johnson, one of the greatest English writers; Reynolds, a
famous English painter; and Edmund Burke, a distinguished orator.

Goldsmith left the garret at the top of "Breakneck 10
Steps" and took rooms in a better locality; but he
was constantly in debt. At one time he was arrested
for not paying his rent, and he appealed to Johnson

for help. The good doctor sent him a guinea and soon followed the messenger. He found that Goldsmith had changed the guinea, bought a bottle of wine, and was upbraiding the landlady. Dr. Johnson put the cork
5 into the bottle, and told Goldsmith to think of some way out of his difficulty.

Goldsmith told him that he had a novel all ready for the press. Johnson read it, saw that it was good, and carrying it to a bookseller, sold it for sixty pounds.
10 The debt was paid and the sheriff's officer withdrew. The novel that acted as rescuer was "The Vicar of Wakefield." Before it was published, however, "The Traveler" appeared. This poem, which was the first work to which Goldsmith had signed his name, received
15 highest praise from the critics.

"The Vicar of Wakefield" was published when Goldsmith was thirty-eight years of age. Few books have been more popular. The story sparkles with wit, and the fresh home life appeals to every one.
20 "The Deserted Village," a picture of simple, village life, was published four years later. Even Goldsmith's enemies had nothing to say to the praise which greeted this poem.

He wrote a play called "She Stoops to Conquer,"
25 and after some difficulty found a manager who was willing to put it upon the stage. It was received with enthusiasm, and is still popular.

The last years of his life were attended with success, but his extravagant way of living, and readiness to respond to the call of every needy person, kept him always in debt.

Goldsmith died in 1774, in his forty-sixth year. His grave has been forgotten, but he has been honored with a monument in Westminster Abbey, bearing an inscription written by his friend, Dr. Johnson.

MOSES AT THE FAIR.

[ABRIDGED.]

OLIVER GOLDSMITH.

As we were now to hold up our heads a little higher in the world, it would be proper to sell the colt, which was grown old, at a neighboring fair, and buy us a horse that would carry single or double upon an occasion and make a pretty appearance at church or upon a visit.

As the fair happened on the following day, I had intentions of going myself; but my wife persuaded me that I had a cold, and nothing could prevail upon her to permit me from home. " No, my dear," said she, " our son Moses is a discreet boy and can buy and sell to very good advantage; you know all our great bargains are of his purchasing. He always stands out and higgles, and actually tires them till he gets a bargain."

As I had some opinion of my son's prudence, I was willing enough to intrust him with this commission; and the next morning I perceived his sisters busy in fitting out Moses for the fair, trimming his hair, brush-
5 ing his buckles, and cocking his hat with pins. The business of the toilet being over, we had at last the satisfaction of seeing him mounted upon the colt, with a deal box before him to bring home groceries in. He had on a coat made of that cloth they call thunder and
10 lightning, which, though grown too short, was much too good to be thrown away. His waistcoat was of gosling green, and his sisters had tied his hair with a broad, black ribbon. We all followed him several paces from the door, bawling after him, "Good luck!
15 good luck!" till we could see him no longer.

He was scarce gone when Mr. Thornhill's butler came to congratulate us upon our good fortune, saying that he overheard his young master mention our names with great commendation.
20 Good fortune seemed resolved not to come alone. Another footman from the same family followed, with a card for my daughters, importing that the two ladies had received such pleasing accounts from Mr. Thornhill of us all, that after a few previous inquiries
25 they hoped to be perfectly satisfied. "Ay," cried my wife, "I now see it is no easy matter to get into the families of the great; but when one once gets in, then, as Moses says, one may go to sleep." To this piece of humor, for she intended it for wit, my daughters

assented with a loud laugh of pleasure. In short, such
was her satisfaction at this message that she actually
put her hand in her pocket and gave the messenger
sevenpence halfpenny.

This was to be our visiting day. The next that
came was Mr. Burchell, who had been at the fair. He
brought my little ones a pennyworth of gingerbread
each, which my wife undertook to keep for them and
give them by little at a time. He brought my daughters
also a couple of boxes, in which they might keep wafers,
snuff, patches, or even money, when they got it. My
wife was unusually fond of a weasel-skin purse, as being
the most lucky; but this by the by.

I wondered what could keep our son so long at the
fair, as it was now almost nightfall. "Never mind
our son," cried my wife; "depend upon it he knows
what he is about. I'll warrant we'll never see him
sell his hen on a rainy day. I have seen him buy
such bargains as would amaze one. But, as I live,
yonder comes Moses, without a horse, and the box at
his back."

As she spoke, Moses came slowly on foot, and sweat-
ing under the deal box, which he had strapped round
his shoulders like a peddler. "Welcome, welcome,
Moses; well, my boy, what have you brought us from
the fair?"—"I have brought you myself," cried Moses
with a sly look and resting the box on the dresser.—
"Ah, Moses," cried my wife, "that we know, but
where is the horse?"—"I have sold him," cried

Moses, "for three pounds five shillings and twopence." — "Well done, my good boy," returned she; "I knew you would touch them off. Between ourselves, three pounds five shillings and twopence is no bad day's
5 work. Come, let us have it, then." — "I have brought back no money," cried Moses again. "I have laid it all out in a bargain, and here it is," pulling out a bundle from his breast; "here they are, a gross of green spectacles with silver rims and shagreen cases." —
10 "A gross of green spectacles!" repeated my wife in a faint voice. "And you have parted with the colt and brought us back nothing but a gross of paltry, green spectacles!" — "Dear mother," cried the boy, "why won't you listen to reason? I had them a dead bar-
15 gain or I should not have bought them. The silver rims alone will sell for double the money." — "A fig for the silver rims!" cried my wife. "I dare say they won't sell for above half the money at the rate of broken silver, five shillings an ounce." — "You need
20 be under no uneasiness," cried I, "about selling the rims. They are not worth sixpence, for I perceive they are only copper varnished over." — "What!" cried my wife, "not silver! the rims not silver!" — "No," cried I, "no more silver than your saucepan."
25 — "And so," returned she, "we have parted with the colt, and have only a gross of green spectacles with copper rims and shagreen cases! The blockhead has been imposed upon, and should have known his company better." — "There, my dear," cried I, "you are

wrong; he should not have known them at all." —
"The idiot!" returned she, "to bring me such stuff!
If I had them I would throw them into the fire." —
"There again you are wrong, my dear," said I, "for
though they be copper we will keep them by us, as 5
copper spectacles, you know, are better than nothing."

By this time the unfortunate Moses was undeceived.
He now saw that he had indeed been imposed upon
by a prowling sharper, who had marked him for an
easy prey. I, therefore, asked the circumstances of 10
his deception. He sold the horse, it seems, and walked
the fair in search of another. A reverend looking man
brought him to a tent under pretense of having one to
sell. "Here," continued Moses, "we met another man,
very well dressed, who desired to borrow twenty pounds 15
upon these, saying that he wanted money, and would
dispose of them for a third of the value. The first
gentleman, who pretended to be my friend, whispered
to me to buy them, and cautioned me not to let so good
an offer pass. I sent for Mr. Flamborough, and they 20
talked him up as finely as they did me, and so at last
we were persuaded to buy the two gross between us."

From " The Vicar of Wakefield."

THE VILLAGE PREACHER.

OLIVER GOLDSMITH.

SWEET was the sound, when oft, at evening's close,
Up yonder hill the village murmur rose;
There, as I pass'd with careless steps and slow,
The mingling notes came soften'd from below;
The swain responsive as the milkmaid sung,
The sober herd that low'd to meet their young;
The noisy geese that gabbled o'er the pool,
The playful children just let loose from school;
The watch-dog's voice that bay'd the whispering wind,
And the loud laugh that spoke the vacant mind;
These all in sweet confusion sought the shade,
And fill'd each pause the nightingale had made.

But now the sounds of population fail,
No cheerful murmurs fluctuate in the gale,
No busy steps the grass-grown foot-way tread,
But all the bloomy flush of life is fled, —
All but yon widow'd, solitary thing,
That feebly bends beside the plashy spring:
She, wretched matron, forced in age, for bread,
To strip the brook with mantling cresses spread,
To pick her wintry fagot from the thorn,
To seek her nightly shed, and weep till morn;
She only left of all the harmless train,
The sad historian of the pensive plain.

Near yonder copse, where once the garden smiled,
And still where many a garden-flower grows wild;
There, where a few torn shrubs the place disclose,
The village preacher's modest mansion rose.
A man he was to all the country dear,
And passing rich with forty pounds a year;
Remote from towns he ran his godly race,
Nor e'er had changed, nor wish'd to change his place;
Unskilful he to fawn, or seek for power
By doctrines fashion'd to the varying hour;
Far other aims his heart had learn'd to prize,
More bent to raise the wretched than to rise.

His house was known to all the vagrant train,
He chid their wanderings, but relieved their pain;
The long remember'd beggar was his guest,
Whose beard descending swept his aged breast.
The ruin'd spendthrift, now no longer proud,
Claim'd kindred there, and had his claims allow'd;
The broken soldier, kindly bade to stay,
Sat by his fire, and talk'd the night away;
Wept o'er his wounds, or tales of sorrow done,
Shoulder'd his crutch, and show'd how fields were won.

Pleased with his guests, the good man learn'd to
        glow,
And quite forgot their vices in their woe;
Careless their merits or their faults to scan,
His pity gave ere charity began.

Thus to relieve the wretched was his pride,
And e'en his failings lean'd to Virtue's side:
But in his duty prompt at every call,
He watch'd and wept, he pray'd and felt for all;
And, as a bird each fond endearment tries,
To tempt its new-fledged offspring to the skies,
He tried each art, reproved each dull delay,
Allured to brighter worlds, and led the way.

At church, with meek and unaffected grace,
His looks adorn'd the venerable place;
Truth from his lips prevail'd with double sway,
And fools, who came to scoff, remain'd to pray.
The service past, around the pious man,
With steady zeal, each honest rustic ran;
E'en children follow'd with endearing wile,
And pluck'd his gown, to share the good man's smile.

His ready smile a parent's warmth express'd,
Their welfare pleased him, and their cares distress'd;
To them his heart, his love, his griefs were given,
But all his serious thoughts had rest in heaven.
As some tall cliff that lifts its awful form,
Swells from the vale, and midway leaves the storm,
Though round its breast the rolling clouds are spread,
Eternal sunshine settles on its head.

From " The Deserted Village."

CASTLES IN SPAIN.

GEORGE WILLIAM CURTIS.

GEORGE WILLIAM CURTIS was born at Providence, R. I., on the 24th of February, 1824.   He received his early education at Jamaica Plain, Mass.

The Curtis family went to New York City when George was fifteen years old, and he spent a year in the counting office of a   5 merchant.

Three years later George and his brother went to Brook Farm, in West Roxbury, Mass., where some literary men had formed a community.   They spent two years there, studying, and enjoying the outdoor life.

After a winter at home they went to Concord, working on a farm half the day, and spending the remaining hours in study.   Mr. Curtis recalled that season in these words: —

"The soft, sunny spring in the silent Concord meadows, where I sat in the great, cool barn through the long, still, golden afternoons and read the history of Rome."

He had already become acquainted with Mr. Emerson, and became a member of a club where he met Hawthorne, Thoreau, and Alcott.   It was at this time that Thoreau built his hut, and the Curtis brothers helped to raise it.   25

Mr. Curtis sailed for Europe in 1846, and spent four years in traveling about Italy, France, Germany, and Palestine.   On his return his first book, "Nile Notes of a Howadji," was published, and he began to deliver lectures.   He became connected with the publishing house of Harper & Brothers, and also wrote for   30 the "New York Tribune" and "Putnam's Monthly."   In this last-named magazine appeared his "Potiphar Papers" and "Prue and I." They were afterward published in book form and met with success. The charm of the latter book is as fresh to-day as when it was first written.

5 For many years, Curtis held the position of editor of "Harper's Weekly," and was engaged in writing and lecturing until his death in August, 1892.

I AM the owner of great estates. Many of them lie in the west, but the greater part are in Spain. You 10 may see my western possessions any evening at sunset, when their spires and battlements flash against the horizon.

It gives me a feeling of pardonable importance, as a proprietor, that they are visible, to my eyes at least, 15 from any part of the world in which I chance to be. In my long voyage around the Cape of Good Hope to India (the only voyage I ever made, when I was a boy and a supercargo), if I fell homesick, or sank into a revery of all the pleasant homes I had left behind, I had 20 but to wait until sunset, and then looking toward the west, I beheld my clustering pinnacles and towers, brightly burnished, as if to salute and welcome me.

So, in the city, if I get vexed and wearied, and cannot find my wonted solace in sallying forth at dinner-25 time to contemplate the gay world of youth and beauty, I go quietly up to the house-top, toward evening, and refresh myself with a distant prospect of my estates. And if I sometimes wonder at such moments whether I shall find those realms as fair as they appear, I am 30 suddenly reminded that the night air may be noxious,

and, descending, I enter the little parlor where my
wife, Prue, sits stitching, and surprise that precious
woman by exclaiming with the poet's enthusiasm:

> "Thought would destroy their Paradise
> No more; — where ignorance is bliss
> 'T is folly to be wise."

Columbus also had possessions in the west; and as I
read aloud the romantic story of his life, my voice
quivers when I come to the point in which it is related
that sweet odors of the land mingled with the sea air,
as the admiral's fleet approached the shores; that tropical birds flew out and fluttered around the ships, glittering in the sun, the gorgeous promises of the new
country; that boughs, perhaps with blossoms not all
decayed, floated out to welcome the strange wood from
which the craft was hollowed. Then I cannot restrain
myself. I think of the gorgeous visions I have seen
before I have even undertaken the journey to the west,
and I cry aloud to Prue: —

"What sun-bright birds and gorgeous blossoms and
celestial odors will float out to us, my Prue, as we
approach our western possessions!"

The placid Prue raises her eyes to mine with a
reproof so delicate that it could not be trusted to
words; and after a moment she resumes her knitting
and I proceed.

These are my western estates, but my finest castles
are in Spain. It is a country famously romantic, and

my castles are all of perfect proportions and appro-
priately set in the most picturesque situations. I have
never been to Spain myself, but I have naturally con-
versed much with travelers to that country. The wisest
5 of them told me that there were more holders of real
estate in Spain than in any other region he had ever
heard of, and they are all great proprietors. Every
one of them possesses a multitude of the stateliest
castles. From conversation with them you easily gather
10 that each one considers his own castles much the largest
and in the loveliest positions. And after I heard this
said, I verified it by discovering that all my immediate
neighbors in the city were great Spanish proprietors.

One day, as I raised my head from entering some
15 long and tedious accounts in my books, and began to
reflect that the quarter was expiring, and that I must
begin to prepare the balance sheet, I observed my subordinate in office, but not in years (for the poor old
clerk will never see sixty again!) leaning on his hand,
20 and much abstracted.

"Are you not well?" asked I.

"Perfectly, but I was just building a castle in Spain,"
said he.

I looked at his rusty coat, his faded hands, his sad
25 eye, and white hair for a moment in great surprise, and
then inquired: —

"Is it possible that you own property there too?"

He shook his head silently; and still leaning on his
hand, and with an expression in his eye as if he were

looking upon the most fertile estate of Andalusia, he
went on making his plans: laying out his gardens, I
suppose, building terraces for the vines, determining a
library with a southern exposure, and resolving which
should be the tapestried chamber.   5

"What a singular whim!" thought I as I watched
him and filled up a check for four hundred dollars, my
quarterly salary, "that a man who owns castles in Spain
should be a bookkeeper at nine hundred dollars a year!"   10

.   .   .   .

It is not easy for me to say how I know so much,
as I certainly do, about my castles in Spain.   The sun
always shines upon them.   They stand lofty and fair
in a luminous, golden atmosphere, — a little hazy and
dreamy, perhaps, like the Indian summer, but in which   15
no gales blow and there are no tempests.   All the sublime mountains and beautiful valleys and soft landscape
that I have not yet seen are to be found in the grounds.
They command a noble view of the Alps; so fine,
indeed, that I should be quite content with the pros-   20
pect of them from the highest tower of my castle, and
not care to go to Switzerland.

The neighboring ruins, too, are as picturesque as those
of Italy.   The rich gloom of my orange groves is gilded
by fruit as brilliant of complexion and exquisite of   25
flavor as any that ever dark-eyed Sorrento girls, looking over the high plastered walls of southern Italy, hand
to the youthful travelers, climbing on donkeys up the
narrow lane beneath.

The Nile flows through my grounds. The desert lies
upon their edge, and Damascus stands in my garden.
From the windows of those castles look the beautiful
women whom I have never seen, whose portraits the
5 poets have painted. They wait for me there, and chiefly
the fair-haired child, lost to my eyes so long ago, now
bloomed into an impossible beauty. In the long, summer mornings the children that I never had, play in the
gardens that I never planted. I hear their sweet voices
10 sounding low and far away, calling, "Father! father!"
I see the lost, fair-haired girl, grown now into a woman,
descending the stately stairs of my castle in Spain,
stepping out upon the lawn, and playing with those
children. They bound away together down the garden;
15 but those voices linger, this time airily calling, "Mother!
mother!"

But there is a stranger magic than this in my Spanish
estates. The lawny slopes on which, when a child, I
played in my father's old country place, which was sold
20 when he failed, are all there, and not a flower faded,
nor a blade of grass sere. The green leaves have not
fallen from the spring woods of half a century ago, and
a gorgeous autumn has blazed undimmed for fifty years
among the trees I remember.

25 Chestnuts are not especially sweet to my palate now,
but those with which I used to prick my fingers when
gathering them in New Hampshire woods are exquisite
as ever to my taste when I think of eating them in
Spain. I never ride horseback now at home; but in

Spain, when I think of it, I bound over all the fences in the country, bareback upon the wildest horses.

Yes; and in those castles in Spain, Prue is not the placid helpmate with whom you are acquainted, but her face has a bloom which we both remember, and her movement a grace which my Spanish swans emulate, and her voice a music sweeter than orchestras discourse. She is always there what she seemed to me when I fell in love with her many and many years ago.

So, when I meditate my Spanish castles, I see Prue in them as my heart saw her standing by her father's door. "Age cannot wither her." There is a magic in the Spanish air that paralyzes Time. He glides by unnoticed and unnoticing. I greatly admire the Alps, which I see so distinctly from my Spanish windows; I delight in the taste of the southern fruit that ripens upon my terraces; I enjoy the pensive shade of the Italian ruins in my gardens; I like to shoot crocodiles, and talk with the Sphinx upon the shores of the Nile flowing through my domain; but I would resign all these forever rather than part with that Spanish portrait of Prue for a day.

From "*Prue and I.*"
By permission of HARPER AND BROTHERS.

THREE HEROINES.

AGNES REPPLIER.

To Spain belongs Augustina, the Maid of Saragossa; to England, brave Mary Ambree; and to America, Molly Pitcher, the stout-hearted heroine of Monmouth; and these three women won for themselves honor and
5 renown by the same valorous exploits.

Augustina is the most to be envied, for her praises have been sung by a great poet; Mary Ambree has a noble ballad to perpetuate her fame; Molly Pitcher is still without the tribute of a verse to remind her
10 countrymen occasionally of her splendid courage in the field.

The Spanish girl was of humble birth, young, poor, and very handsome. When Saragossa was besieged by the French, during the Peninsular War, she carried
15 food every afternoon to the soldiers who were defending the batteries. One day the attack was so fierce, and the fire so deadly, that by the gate of Portillo not a single man was left alive to repulse the terrible enemy.

20 When Augustina reached the spot with her basket of coarse and scanty provisions, she saw the last gunner fall bleeding on the walls. Not for an instant did she hesitate; but springing over a pile of dead bodies, she snatched the match from his stiffening fingers and
25 fired the gun herself.

Then calling on her countrymen to rally their broken ranks, she led them back so unflinchingly to the charge that the French were driven from the gate they had so nearly captured, and the honor of Spain was saved.

For the story of Mary Ambree we must leave the chroniclers, who to their own loss and shame never mention her at all, and take refuge with the poets. From them we learn all we need to know; and it is quickly told.

Her lover was slain treacherously in the war between Spain and Holland, the English being then allies of the Dutch; and, vowing to avenge his death, she put on his armor and marched to the siege of Ghent, where she fought with reckless courage on its walls.

Fortune favors the brave, and wherever the maiden turned her arms the enemy was repulsed, until at last the Spanish soldiers vied with the English in admiration of this valorous foe. . . .

And now for Molly Pitcher, who, unsung and almost unremembered, should nevertheless share in the honors heaped so liberally upon the English and Spanish heroines. "A red-haired, freckle-faced young Irish woman," without beauty and without distinction, she was the newly wedded wife of an artilleryman in Washington's little army. On June 28, 1778, was fought the battle of Monmouth, famous for the admirable tactics by which Washington regained the advantages lost through the negligence of General Charles Lee.

It was a Sunday morning, close and sultry. As the day advanced, the soldiers on both sides suffered terribly from that fierce, unrelenting heat in which America rivals India. The thermometer stood at 96° in the
5 shade. Men fell dead in their ranks without a wound, smitten by sunstroke; and the sight of them filled their comrades with dismay.

Molly Pitcher, regardless of everything save the anguish of the sweltering, thirsty troops, carried buckets
10 of water from a neighboring spring and passed them along the line. Backward and forward she trudged, this strong, brave, patient young woman, while the sweat poured down her freckled face, and her bare arms blistered in the sun.

15 She was a long time in reaching her husband, — so many soldiers begged for drink as she toiled by, — but at last she saw him, parched, grimy, and spent with heat, and she quickened her lagging steps. Then suddenly a ball whizzed past, and he fell dead by the side
20 of his gun before ever the coveted water had touched his blackened lips.

Molly dropped her bucket and for one dazed moment stood staring at the bleeding corpse. Only for a moment, for, amid the turmoil of battle, she heard the
25 order given to drag her husband's cannon from the field.

The words roused her to life and purpose. She seized the rammer from the grass and hurried to the gunner's post. There was nothing strange in the work to her. She was too well versed in the ways of war for either ignorance or alarm.

Strong, skilful, and fearless, she stood by the weapon and directed its deadly fire until the fall of Monckton turned the tide of victory. The British troops under Clinton were beaten back after a desperate struggle, the Americans took possession of the field, and the battle of Monmouth was won.

On the following day poor Molly, no longer a furious Amazon, but sad-faced, with swollen eyes and a scanty bit of crape pinned on her bosom, was presented to Washington, and received a sergeant's commission with half pay for life.

It is said that the French officers, then fighting for the freedom of the colonies, that is, against the English, were so delighted with her courage that they added to this reward a cocked hat full of gold pieces, and christened her " La Capitaine."

What befell her in after years has never been told. She lived and died obscurely, and her name has well-nigh been forgotten in the land she served. But the memory of brave deeds can never wholly perish, and Molly Pitcher has won for herself a niche in the Temple of Fame, where her companions are fair Mary Ambree and the dauntless Maid of Saragossa.

ENSIGN EPPS, THE COLOR-BEARER.

JOHN BOYLE O'REILLY.

JOHN BOYLE O'REILLY was born in Ireland, June 28, 1844. He began life as a type-setter, and later went to England and became a reporter for various newspapers. Returning to Ireland, he joined the 10th Hussars, with the secret intention of spread-
5 ing the Irish cause among the soldiers. His purpose was dis-covered, and he was sentenced to be shot. This sentence was commuted, and he was sent to the English prison colony in Aus-tralia. From there he escaped in an open boat and was picked up at sea by Captain Gifford of the American ship, "Gazelle,"
10 and brought to America. He wrote and lectured in this country, and became the editor of the "Boston Pilot."

Among his works are "Songs of the Southern Seas," "Songs, Legends, and Ballads," and "In Bohemia." He died in Hull, Mass., Aug. 10, 1890.

ENSIGN EPPS, at the battle of Flanders,
Sowed a seed of glory and duty,
That flowers and flames in height and beauty
Like a crimson lily with heart of gold,
To-day, when the wars of Ghent are old,
And buried as deep as their dead commanders.

Ensign Epps was the color-bearer —
No matter on which side, Philip or Earl;
Their cause was the shell — his deed was the pearl.
Scarce more than a lad, he had been a sharer
That day in the wildest work of the field.
He was wounded and spent, and the fight was lost;
His comrades were slain, or a scattered host.

But stainless and scathless out of the strife
He had carried his colors, safer than life.
By the river's brink, without weapon or shield,
He faced the victors.   The thick heart-mist
He dashed from his eyes, and the silk he kissed
Ere he held it aloft in the setting sun,
As proudly as if the fight had been won,
And he smiled when they ordered him to yield.

Ensign Epps, with his broken blade,
Cut the silk from the gilded staff,
Which he poised like a spear till the charge was made,
And hurled at the leader with a laugh.
Then round his breast, like the scarf of his love,
He tied the colors his heart above,
And plunged in his armor into the tide,
And there, in his dress of honor, died.

.   .   .   .   .   .

Where are the lessons ye kinglings teach?
And what is the text of your proud commanders?
Out of the centuries, heroes reach
With the scroll of a deed, with the word of a story,
Of one man's truth and of all men's glory,
Like Ensign Epps at the battle of Flanders.

THE BATTLE OF LANDEN.

[ABRIDGED.]

THOMAS BABINGTON MACAULAY.

THOMAS BABINGTON MACAULAY was born in England on the 25th of October, 1800.

He gave proof of a decided taste for literature when a little child. From the time he was three years old he spent the
5 greater part of his time in reading, and liked to lie on a rug

before the fire with his book before him. He was a quaint little fellow and talked in the language of the books which he read.

Before he was eight years old he had written a history and a romance. His early education was received in private schools, and he entered Trinity College, Cambridge, when he was eighteen years old. He enjoyed his college life, and succeeded in gaining a fellowship of three hundred pounds and a prize for an essay.

20 After his graduation he began to practice law in London, but had little business, and spent more time at the House of Commons than in the court.

When he was twenty-four he made a speech which surprised the audience by its eloquence and was praised in the " Edinburgh
25 Review." The next year this magazine published an essay on Milton written by Macaulay, which made the young man famous.

He was invited to dinners and honored by the most distinguished persons in London. His gift as a brilliant and entertaining talker increased his popularity.

In 1830 he became a member of the House of Commons and distinguished himself by his eloquent speeches. He continued to contribute to the "Edinburgh Review," and took an active part in the question of slavery in India.

A few years later he was sent by the Government to India, 5 where his services proved of great value. One of his sisters accompanied him, and he remained there four years.

On his return he became a member of Parliament, and for two years was Secretary of War. His duties were light, and he engaged in literary work. He became deeply interested in writing 10 a history of England, and retired to private life in order to devote his time to this work. He worked slowly and carefully, sparing no pains in searching for material.

The first two volumes, published in 1849, had an enormous sale, both in England and America. Three more volumes were 15 completed seven years later. This history has been published in a dozen different languages, and Macaulay received many flattering marks of admiration and respect.

After resigning his seat in Parliament he went to Holly Lodge, Kensington. It was a delightful house, with a large library and 20 a garden. Macaulay was very happy there. On his return to Holly Lodge, after a trip through Germany and Italy, he writes: "My garden is really charming. The flowers are less brilliant than when I went away, but the turf is perfect emerald. All the countries through which I have been traveling could not show 25 such a carpet of soft, rich, green herbage as mine." He died on the 28th of December, 1859, and was buried in the Poets' Corner at Westminster Abbey.

THOUGH the French army in the Netherlands had been weakened by the departure of forces, and though 30 the allied army was daily strengthened by the arrival of fresh troops, Luxembourg still had a superiority of force; and that superiority he increased by an adroit stratagem.

He marched towards Liege, and made as if he were
about to form the siege of that city. William was
uneasy, and the more uneasy because he knew there
was a French party among the inhabitants. He quitted
5 his position near Louvain, advanced to Nether Hespen,
and encamped there, with the river Gette in his rear.

This was exactly what General Luxembourg had expected and desired. He turned his back on the fortress, which had hitherto seemed to be his object, and
10 hastened toward the Gette.

William, Prince of Orange, who had but fifty thousand left in his camp, was alarmed by learning from
his scouts that the French general, with near eighty
thousand, was close at hand.

15 It was still in the king's power, by a hasty retreat,
to put the narrow but deep waters of the Gette between his army and the enemy. But the site which
he occupied was strong; and it could easily be made
still stronger. He set all his troops to work. Ditches
20 were dug, mounds thrown up, palisades fixed in the
earth, and the king trusted that he should be able to
repel the attack even of a force greatly outnumbering
his own.

Luxembourg, however, was determined to try
25 whether even this position could be maintained against
the superior numbers and the impetuous valor of his
soldiers. Soon after sunrise the roar of the cannon
began to be heard. William's batteries did much execution before the French artillery could be so placed

as to return fire. It was eight o'clock before the close fighting began. The village of Neerwinden was regarded by both commanders as the point on which everything depended.

There an attack was made by the French left wing, 5 commanded by Montchevreuil, a veteran officer of high reputation, and by Berwick, who, though young, was fast rising to a high place among the captains of his time.

Berwick led the onset and forced his way into the village, but was soon driven out again with a terrible 10 carnage. His followers fled or perished; he, while trying to rally them, was surrounded by foes. He concealed his white cockade and hoped to be able, by the help of his native tongue, to pass himself off as an officer of the English army. But his face was recog- 15 nized by one of his mother's brothers, who held on that day the command of a brigade. A hurried embrace was exchanged between the kinsmen, and the uncle conducted the nephew to William.

By this time, the French, who had been driven in 20 confusion out of Neerwinden, had been reinforced by a division and came gallantly back to the attack. This second conflict was long and bloody. The assailants again forced entrance into the village. They were driven out with tremendous slaughter, and showed 25 little inclination to return to the charge.

Meanwhile the battle had been raging all along the intrenchments of the allied army. Again and again Luxembourg brought up his troops within pistol-shot of the breastwork, but he could bring them no nearer. At length Luxembourg formed his decision. A last attempt must be made to carry Neerwinden; and the invincible household troops, the conquerors of Stein-kirk, must lead the way.

The household troops came on in a manner worthy of their long and terrible renown. A third time Neerwinden was taken. A third time William tried to retake it. At the head of some English regiments he charged the guards of Louis, the French king, with such fury that, for the first time in the memory of the oldest warrior, that far-famed band gave way. It was only by strenuous exertions that the broken ranks were rallied.

A little after four in the afternoon the whole line gave way. All was havoc and confusion. The Duke of Ormond was struck down in the press; and in another moment he would have been a corpse, had not a rich diamond on his finger caught the eye of one of the French guards, who justly thought that the owner of such a jewel would be a valuable prisoner. The duke's life was saved; and he was speedily exchanged for Berwick.

It was only on such occasions as this that the whole greatness of William's character appeared. Amidst the rout and uproar, while arms and standards were flung away, while multitudes of fugitives were choking up the bridges and fords of the Gette, or perishing in its waters, the king put himself at the head of a few brave regiments and by desperate efforts arrested the progress of the enemy.

His risk was greater than that which others ran, for he could not be persuaded to encumber his feeble frame with a cuirass, or to hide the ensigns of the garter. He thought his star a good rallying point for his own troops, and only smiled when he was told that it was a good mark for the enemy.

Many fell at his right hand and at his left. Two led horses, which in the field always followed his person, were struck dead by cannon shots. One musket ball passed through the curls of his wig, another through his coat, a third bruised his side and tore his blue riband to tatters.

Many years later, gray-headed old pensioners, who crept about the arcades and alleys of Chelsea Hospital, used to relate how he charged at the head of Galway's horse, how he dismounted four times to put heart into the infantry, how he rallied one corps which seemed to be shrinking: "That is not the way to fight, gentlemen. You must stand close up to them. Thus, gentlemen, thus." "You might have seen him," an eyewitness wrote only four days after the battle, "with his sword in his hand, throwing himself upon the enemy. It is certain that one time, among the rest, he was seen at the head of two English regiments, and that he fought seven with these two in sight of the whole army, driving them before him above a quarter of an hour. Thanks be to God who preserved him!"

The enemy pressed on him so close that it was with difficulty that he at length made his way over the Gette. A small body of brave men who shared his peril to the last, could hardly keep off the pursuers as
5 he crossed the bridge. Never, perhaps, was the change which the progress of civilization has produced in the art of war more strikingly illustrated than on that day. Ajax beating down the Trojan leader with a rock which two ordinary men could scarcely lift, Horatius defend-
10 ing the bridge against an army, Richard the Lionhearted spurring along the whole Saracen line without finding an enemy to stand his assault, Robert Bruce crushing with one blow the helmet and head of Sir Henry Bonun in sight of the whole array of England
15 and Scotland, — such are the heroes of dark ages.

At Landen two poor sickly beings, who in a rude state of society would have been regarded as too puny to bear any part in combats, were the souls of the two great armies. But their lot had fallen on a time when
20 men had discovered that the strength of the muscles is far inferior in value to the strength of the mind.

From " The History of England."

THE PLANTING OF THE APPLE TREE.

WILLIAM CULLEN BRYANT.

For an account of the life of Bryant, see "Cyr's Third Reader."

COME, let us plant the apple tree.
Cleave the tough greensward with the spade;
Wide let its hollow bed be made;
There gently lay the roots, and there
Sift the dark mould with kindly care,
    And press it o'er them tenderly,
As round the sleeping infant's feet,
We softly fold the cradle-sheet;
    So plant we the apple tree.

What plant we in this apple tree?
Buds, which the breath of summer days
Shall lengthen into leafy sprays;
Boughs where the thrush with crimson breast,
Shall haunt, and sing, and hide her nest;
    We plant upon the sunny lea,
A shadow for the noontide hour,
A shelter from the summer shower,
    When we plant the apple tree.

What plant we in this apple tree?
Sweets for a hundred flowery springs
To load the May-wind's restless wings,
When, from the orchard-row, he pours
Its fragrance through our open doors;

A world of blossoms for the bee,
Flowers for the sick girl's silent room,
For the glad infant sprigs of bloom,
  We plant with the apple tree.

What plant we in this apple tree?
Fruits that shall swell in sunny June,
And redden in the August noon,
And drop when gentle airs come by,
That fan the blue September sky,
  While children come, with cries of glee.
And seek them where the fragrant grass
Betrays their bed to those who pass,
  At the foot of the apple tree.

And when, above this apple tree,
The winter stars are quivering bright,
And winds go howling through the night,
Girls, whose young eyes o'erflow with mirth,
Shall peel its fruit by the cottage hearth,
  And guests in prouder homes shall see,
Heaped with the grape of Cintra's vine
And golden orange of the line
  The fruit of the apple tree.

The fruitage of this apple tree
Winds and our flag of stripe and star
Shall bear to coasts that lie afar,
Where men shall wonder at the view
And ask in what fair groves they grew;

And sojourners beyond the sea
Shall think of childhood's careless day
And long, long hours of summer play,
 In the shade of the apple tree.

Each year shall give this apple tree
A broader flush of roseate bloom,
A deeper maze of verdurous gloom,
And loosen, when the frost-clouds lower,
The crisp brown leaves in thicker shower.

And time shall waste this apple tree.
Oh, when its aged branches throw
Thin shadows on the ground below,
Shall fraud and force and iron will
Oppress the weak and helpless still?
 What shall the tasks of mercy be,
Amid the toils, the strifes, the tears
Of those who live when length of years
 Is wasting this apple tree?

"Who planted this old apple tree?"
The children of that distant day
Thus to some aged man shall say;
And, gazing on its mossy stem,
The gray-haired man shall answer them:
 "A poet of the land was he,
Born in the rude but good old times;
'T is said he made some quaint old rhymes
 On planting the apple tree."

A HIGHLAND SNOWSTORM.

[ABRIDGED.]

JOHN WILSON.

JOHN WILSON, better known as "Christopher North," was born at Paisley, Scotland, in 1785, and died in Edinburgh in 1854.

He entered the University at Glasgow when he was twelve years old and completed his education at Oxford.

5 After leaving college he went to live on his estate, which was delightfully situated on Lake Windermere, near the homes of Wordsworth and Coleridge. He spent four years there in boating, fishing, and hunting. He was married when he was twenty-six, and soon afterwards published a volume of poems. He continued 10 to live an idle, out-of-door life until the loss of a large share of his fortune, when he went to Edinburgh and began to study law.

He decided, however, to devote himself to literature, and wrote many articles for "Blackwood's Magazine," signing himself "Christopher North."

15 When he was thirty-five years old, Mr. Wilson was elected professor in the University at Edinburgh, and held this position for thirty years.

ONE family lived in Glencreran, and another in Glencoe — the families of two brothers. Each had an 20 only child — a son and a daughter — born on the same day. Thus had these cousins grown up before their parent's eyes — Flora Macdonald, a name hallowed of yore, the fairest, and Ronald Cameron, the boldest of all the living flowers in Glencoe and Glencreran.

25 It was now their seventeenth birthday, and Flora was to pass the day in Glencreran. Ronald was to meet her in the mountains, that he might bring her

down the precipitous passes to his father's hut; and soon they met at the trysting place, a bank of birch trees beneath a cliff that takes its name from the eagles.

On their meeting, seemed not to them the whole of 5 nature suddenly inspired with joy and beauty? From tree roots, where the snow was thin, little flowers, or herbs flower-like, now for the first time, were seen looking out as if alive; the trees seemed budding, as if it were already spring; and rare as in that rocky region 10 are the birds of song, a faint trill for a moment touched their ears, and the flutter of a wing. Deep down beneath the snow they listened to the tinkle of rills unreached by the frost, and merry, thought they, was the music of these contented prisoners. 15

The boy starts to his feet, and his keen eye looks along the ready rifle; for his sires had all been famous deer-stalkers, and the passion of the chase was in his blood. Lo! a deer from Dalness, hound-driven, or sullenly astray, slowly bearing his antlers up the glen, 20 then stopping for a moment to snuff the air, then away — away! The rifle-shot rings dully from the scarce echoing snow cliffs, and the animal leaps aloft, struck by a certain death wound. Laboring and lumbering heavily along, the huge animal at last disappears 25 around some rocks at the head of the glen.

"Follow me, Flora!" the boy-hunter cries; and flinging down their plaids they turn their bright faces to the mountain, and away up the glen after the stricken deer. Redder and redder grew the snow, and more heavily trampled, as they winded around the rocks.

Yonder is the deer, staggering up the mountain, not half a mile off — now standing at bay, as if before his swimming eyes came Fingal, the terror of the forest, whose howl was known to all the echoes, and quailed the herd while their antlers were yet afar off. "Rest, Flora, rest! while I fly to him with my rifle and shoot him."

The boy, maddened by the chase, pressed forward, now alone, and thus he was hurried on for miles, till at last he struck the noble quarry, and down sank the antlers in the snow, while the air was spurned by the convulsive beatings of feet. Then leaped Ronald upon the red deer and lifted a look of triumph to the mountain-tops.

Where is Flora? Ronald has forgotten her, and he is alone — he and the deer — an enormous animal, fast stiffening in the frost of death.

Some large flakes of snow are in the air, and they seem to waver and whirl, though an hour ago there was not a breath. Faster they fall and faster; the flakes are as large as leaves; and overhead whence so suddenly has come that huge, yellow cloud? "Flora, where are you? where are you, Flora?" and from the huge animal the boy leaps up and sees that no Flora is at hand.

But yonder is a moving speck, far off upon the snow.

'T is she! 'tis she! Shrill as the eagle's cry he sends a shout down the glen, and Flora is at last by his side. Panting and speechless she stands, and then dizzily sinks upon his breast. Her hair is ruffled by the wind, and her face moistened by the snowflakes, now 5 not falling but driven. Her shivering frame misses the warmth of the plaid which almost no cold can penetrate.

What would the miserable boy give now for the coverings lying far away, which in his foolish passion 10 he had flung down to chase that fatal deer? "Oh, Flora, if you would not fear to stay here by yourself, under the protection of God, soon would I go and come from the place where our plaids are lying; and under the shelter of the deer we may be able to outlive the 15 hurricane."

"I will go with you down the glen, Ronald"; but, weak as a day-old lamb, she tottered and fell down in the snow. The cold had chilled her very heart, after the heat of that long race; and it was manifest that 20 here she must be for the night, to live or to die.

"I will go and leave you with God," said Ronald; and he went and came as if he had been endowed with eagles' wings.

All at once Ronald lifted Flora in his arms, and 25 walked up the glen. Some walls of what had once been a house, he had suddenly remembered, were but a short way off. There it was — a snowdrift at the opening that had been once a door; the wood of the roof had been carried off for fuel, and the snowflakes were falling in, as if they would soon fill the inside of the ruin. The snow in front was all trampled, as if by sheep; and carrying in his burden, Ronald saw 5 the place was filled with a flock that, all huddled together, looked on him as on a shepherd come to see how they were faring in the storm.

And a young shepherd he was, with a lamb apparently dying in his arms. All color, all motion, all 10 breath seemed to be gone; and yet something convinced his heart that she was yet alive. The ruined hut was roofless, but across an angle of the walls some pine branches had been flung, as a sort of shelter for the sheep or cattle that might repair thither in stormy 15 weather.

Into that corner the snowdrift had not yet forced its way, and he sat down there with Flora. The chill air was somewhat softened by the breath of the huddled flock, and the edge of the cutting wind blunted 20 by the stones.

Bright was the peat fire in the hut of Flora's parents in Glencoe, and they were among the happiest of the humble happy, blessing this the birthday of their blameless child. They thought of her singing her 25 sweet songs by the fireside of the hut in Glencreran, and tender thoughts of her cousin Ronald were with them in their prayers.

So was it now with the dwellers in the hut at the head of Glencreran. Their Ronald had left them in the morning; night had come, and he and Flora were not there; but they never doubted that the happy creatures had changed their minds, and that Ronald had returned with Flora to Glencoe.

But the inland storm had been seen brewing among 5 the mountains, and down through the long cliff-pass went a band of shepherds, trampling their way across a hundred frozen streams. Away over the drift-bridged chasms toiled that gathering, with their sheep-dogs scouring the loose snows in the van, Fingal, the Red 10 Beaver, with his head aloft on the lookout for deer. Following the dogs, who know their duties, the band are now close to the ruined hut.

Why bark the sheep-dogs so? and why howls Fingal, as if some spirit passed athwart the night? He 15 scents the body of the boy who so often had shouted him on in the forest when the antlers went by. Not dead — nor dead she who is on his bosom. Yet will the red blood in their veins ever again be thawed?

Almost pitch dark is the roofless ruin; and the 20 frightened sheep know not what is that terrible shape that is howling there. But a man enters and lifts up one of the bodies, giving it into the arms of those at the doorway, and then lifts the other; and by the flash of a rifle they see it is Ronald Cameron and Flora 25 Macdonald, seemingly both frozen to death. But the noble dog knows that death is not there, and licks the face of Ronald, as if he would restore life to his eyes.

The storm was with them all the way down the

glen; nor could they have heard each other's voices; but mutely they shifted the burden from strong hand to hand, thinking of the hut at Glencoe, and of what would be felt there on their arrival.

5 Instinct, reason, and faith conducted the saving band along; and now they are at Glencoe, and at the door of the hut.

To life were brought the dead; and there, at midnight, sat they up like ghosts. Then, as if in holy 10 fear, they gazed in each other's faces, thinking that they had awakened in heaven. "Flora!" said Ronald; and that word, the first he had been able to speak, reminded him of all that had passed, and he knew that the God in whom they had put their trust had sent 15 them deliverance.

LEARNING BY HEART.

VERNON LUSHINGTON.

TILL he has fairly tried it, I suspect a reader does not know how much he would gain from committing to memory passages of real excellence; precisely because he does not know how much he overlooks in merely 20 reading. Learn one true poem by heart, and see if you do not find it so. Beauty after beauty will reveal itself, in chosen phrase, or happy music, or noble suggestion otherwise undreamed of. It is like looking at one of nature's wonders through a microscope.

Again, how much in such a poem that you really did feel admirable and lovely on a first reading passes away if you do not give it a further and much better reading! — passes away utterly, like a sweet sound, or an image on the lake, which the first breath of wind dispels. If you could only fix that image, as the photographers do theirs, so beautifully, so perfectly! And you can do so! Learn it by heart, and it is yours forever!

Poems and noble extracts, whether of verse or prose, once so reduced into possession and rendered truly our own, may be to us a daily pleasure — better far than a whole library unused. They may come to us in our dull moments, to refresh us as with spring flowers; in our selfish musings, to win us by pure delight from the tyranny of foolish castle-building, self-congratulations, and mean anxieties. They may be with us in the workshop, in the crowded streets, by the fireside; sometimes, perhaps, on pleasant hillsides, or by sounding shores — noble friends and companions, our own! never intrusive, ever at hand, coming at our call!

Shakespeare, Milton, Wordsworth, Tennyson — the words of such men do not stale upon us; they do not grow old or cold. Further, though you are young now, some day you will be old. Some day you may reach that time when a man lives in greater part for memory and by memory. I can imagine a chance renewal, chance visitation of the words long remembered, long garnered in the heart, and I think I see a gleam of rare joy in the eyes of the old man.

For those, in particular, whose leisure time is short, and precious as scant rations to beleaguered men, I believe there could not be a better expenditure of time than deliberately giving an occasional hour — it re-
5 quires no more — to committing to memory chosen passages from great authors. If the mind were thus daily nourished with a few choice words of the best English poets and writers ; if the habit of learning by heart were to become so general that, as a matter of course,
10 any person presuming to be educated amongst us might be expected to be equipped with a few good pieces, — I believe it would lead, far more than the mere sound of it suggests, to the diffusion of the best kind of literature and the right appreciation of it, and men would
15 not long rest satisfied with having a few stock pieces.

The only objection I can conceive to what I have been saying is, that it may be said that a relish for higher literature belongs only to the few ; that it is the result of cultivation ; and that there is no use in try-
20 ing to create what must be in general only a fictitious interest. But I do not admit that literature, even the higher literature, must belong to the few. Poetry is, in the main, addressed to all men ; and though some poetry requires particular knowledge and superior
25 culture, much, and that the noblest, needs only natural feeling and the light of common experience.

To abandon all recitation is to give up a custom which has given delight and instruction to all the races of articulately speaking men. If our faces are set against vain display, and set towards rational enjoyment of one another, each freely giving his best, and freely receiving what his neighbor offers, we need not fear that our social evenings will be marred by an occasional recitation, or that the fine passages will wither. And, moreover, 5 it is not for reciting's sake that I chiefly recommend this most faithful form of reading — learning by heart.

I come back, therefore, to this, that learning by heart is a good thing, and is neglected amongst us. Why is it neglected? Partly because of our indolence, but partly, 10 I take it, because we do not sufficiently consider that it is a good thing, and needs to be taken in hand. We need to be reminded of it; I here remind you. Like a town-crier, ringing my bell, I would say to you, "O-yes, o-yes! Lost, stolen, or strayed, a good ancient prac- 15 tice — the good ancient practice of learning by heart. Every finder should be handsomely rewarded." . . .

If any ask, "What shall I learn?" the answer is, "Do as you do with tunes; begin with what you sincerely like best, what you would most wish to remem- 20 ber, what you would most enjoy saying to yourself or repeating to another." You will soon find the list inexhaustible. Every one has spare ten minutes; one of the problems of life is how to employ them usefully. You may well spend some in looking after and securing 25 this good property you have won.

A COURT LADY.

ELIZABETH BARRETT BROWNING.

ELIZABETH BARRETT was born in England on the 6th of March, 1806. Her father was a wealthy Englishman, and shortly after the birth of this daughter he built a country house in Herefordshire — "a luxurious home standing in a

park, among trees, and sloping hills all sprinkled with sheep."

Elizabeth, a slender little maiden with dark eyes, soft curls, and a smile like a sunbeam, occupied a room in the upper part of the house, where she could look out upon the tree-tops and listen to the soft notes of the birds.

Each of the children of the family had a garden of his own, and Elizabeth was so fond of white roses that she had a bower overgrown with them.

Her tutor found in her a remarkable pupil, and at eight years
20 of age the little girl was reading Greek, often holding her book in one hand while she nursed her doll on her arm.

Her father was very proud of his little daughter, and when she was between eleven and twelve he had one of her poems, "The Battle of Marathon," published for his own library.

25 But her time was not all spent in study. She loved to play with her brothers and sisters, and ride her black pony, Moses, about the country. One day in trying to saddle him in the field, she fell and injured her back, so that for years she was a helpless invalid. This trial did not prevent her from living as
30 she had dreamed and hoped to live, and she continued to read and write in her seclusion.

Her mother died when Elizabeth was twenty, and her father

was unfortunate in business, so that he was obliged to sell his beautiful home, and the family went to London.

Elizabeth was seldom able to leave her room, but continued to write. Her name soon became known to the world. One of her first works to attract attention was "Prometheus," which was published when she was twenty-six years old. 5

Many a sweet and tender poem came from her pen, and she always wrote on the side of truth and freedom.

She became acquainted with Robert Browning, another of England's great poets, and they were married in 1846. Mr. Browning took his wife to Florence, Italy, and the sunny skies of that country partially restored her health. 10

"Casa Guidi Windows," one of Mrs. Browning's strongest poems, was written during her life in Florence, as she looked from her windows upon the Italian people struggling for freedom. 15

"Aurora Leigh" is Mrs. Browning's most famous work. Every page is filled with beauty. This most gifted of women-poets died at Florence in 1861.

HER hair was tawny with gold, her eyes with purple
        were dark,
Her cheeks' pale opal burnt with a red and restless spark.

Never was lady of Milan nobler in name and in race;
Never was lady of Italy fairer to see in the face.

Never was lady on earth more true as woman and wife,
Larger in judgment and instinct, prouder in manners
        and life.

She stood in the early morning, and said to her maidens,
        "Bring
That silken robe made ready to wear at the court of
        the King.

"Bring me the clasps of diamond, lucid, clear of the
    mote,
Clasp me the large at the waist, and clasp me the small
    at the throat."

Gorgeous she entered the sunlight which gathered her
    up in a flame,
While, straight in her open carriage, she to the hospital
    came.

In she went at the door, and gazing from end to
    end,
"Many and low are the pallets, but each is the place
    of a friend."

Up she passed through the wards, and stood at a young
    man's bed :
Bloody the band on his brow, and livid the droop of
    his head.

"Art thou a Lombard, my brother?   Happy art thou,"
    she cried,
And smiled like Italy on him : he dreamed in her face
    and died.

Down she stepped to a pallet where lay a face like a
    girl's,
Young, and pathetic with dying, — a deep black hole
    in the curls.

"Art thou from Tuscany, brother? and seest thou,
  dreaming in pain,
Thy mother stand in the piazza, searching the list of
  the slain?"

Kind as a mother herself, she touched his cheeks with
  her hands:
"Blessed is she who has borne thee, although she should
  weep as she stands."

On she passed to a Frenchman, his arm carried off by
  a ball:
Kneeling, "O more than my brother! how shall I thank
  thee for all?

"Each of the heroes around us has fought for his land
  and line,
But thou hast fought for a stranger, in hate of a wrong
  not thine.

"Happy are all free peoples, too strong to be dis-
  possest;
But blessed are those among nations who dare to be
  strong for the rest."

Ever she passed on her way, and came to a couch
  where pined
One with a face from Venitia, white with a hope out
  of mind.

Long she stood and gazed, and twice she tried at the
name,
But two great crystal tears were all that faltered and
came.

Only a tear for Venice? She turned as in passion and
loss,
And stooped to his forehead and kissed it, as if she
were kissing the cross.

Faint with that strain of heart she moved on then to
another,
Stern and strong in his death. "And dost thou suffer,
my brother?"

Holding his hands in hers: "Out of the Piedmont
lion
Cometh the sweetness of freedom! sweetest to live or
to die on."

Holding his cold rough hands, "Well, oh, well have ye
done
In noble, noble Piedmont, who would not be noble
alone?"

Back he fell while she spoke. She rose to her feet
with a spring,
"That was a Piedmontese! and this is the Court of the
King."

THE STAG OF CLANRUADH.

GEORGE MacDONALD.

For a sketch of the life of George MacDonald see "Cyr's Fourth Reader."

AMONG the peasantry assembled at the feast were two that had neither danced nor seated themselves at the long table where all were welcome. The elder was a man about five and fifty, tall and lean, with a wiry frame, dark grizzled hair, and a shaven face. His eyes 5 were remarkably clear and keen, and the way he used them could hardly fail to attract attention. Although everybody spoke to him, he never spoke in reply — only made signs, sometimes with his lips, oftener with hand or head; the man was deaf and dumb. 10

His companion was a youth whose age it would have been difficult to guess. He looked a lad, and was not far from thirty. The relation between the two was strangely interesting. Day and night they were inseparable. Because the father was deaf, the son gave all 15 his attention to the sounds of the world; his soul sat in his ears, ever awake, ever listening.

What his people thought of him came out in the name they gave him: "Rob of the Angels." Some said he always looked cold; but I think that came of 20 the wonderful peace on his face, like the quiet of a lake over which lies a thin mist. Never was stronger nor fuller devotion manifested by son to father than by Rob of the Angels to Hector of the Stags.

The father trusted his son's hearing as implicitly as
his own sight. When he saw a certain look come on
his face he would drop on the instant and crouch as
still as if he had ears, watching Rob's face for news of
some sound wandering through the vast of night.

He had the keenest eyes in Clanruadh and was a
dead shot. Even the Chief was not his equal. Yet he
never stalked a deer, never killed anything for mere
sport. What the two wanted for food they would kill;
but it was not much they needed, for seldom can two
men have lived on less.

  . . . .

Two young men of wealth, named Sercombe and
Palmer, had come to the country to hunt. They had
neither experience nor trustworthy attendants; none
of the Chief's men would hunt with them. Neither
had shot a single stag and the time was drawing near
when they should return. To have no proof of prowess
to display was humbling to Sercombe; he must show
a stag's head or hide his own! He resolved, by himself, one of the next moonlit nights, to stalk a certain
great, wide-horn stag of whose habits he had received
information.

His sole attendant when shooting was a clever vaga-
bond lad, called Christian. From him he heard of the
great stag and the spots in the valley which he frequented, often scraping away the snow with his feet to
get the grass. The lad did not inform him that the
animal was a special favorite with the Chief of Clan-

ruadh, or that the clan looked upon him as their live symbol, the very stag represented upon their coat of arms.

Christian and Sercombe had stalked him day after day, but without success. And now, with one poor remaining hope, the latter had determined to stalk him by night. To despoil him of his life, his glorious rush over the mountain-side, to see that ideal of strength, suppleness, and joyous flight lie nerveless and placid at his feet, was for the time the ambition of Halary Sercombe.

There was, however, a reason for the failure of the young hunters beyond lack of skill and what they called their ill luck. Hector of the Stags was awake; his keen eye was upon them, seconded by the all-hearing ears of Rob of the Angels. They had discovered that the two men had set their hearts on the big stag, and every time they were out after him Hector, too, was out with his spyglass, the gift of an old seafaring friend, searching the billowy hills.

While the hunters would be toiling along to get wind of him unseen, for the old stag's eyes were as keen as his velvety nose, the father and son would be lying, perhaps close at hand, perhaps far away, on some hill-side of another valley, watching now the hunters, now the stag.

For love of the Chief and for love of the stag they had constituted themselves his guardians. Again and again, when one of the hunters had him within range,

quietly feeding, naught between the great pumping of his big joyous heart and the hot bullet but the brown skin, a distant shot would forestall the nigh one, a shot for life, not death; and the stag, knowing instantly, by
5 wondrous combination of sense and judgment, in what quarter lay the danger, would, without once looking around him, measure a hundred yards of hillock and rock between the sight-taking and the pulling of the trigger.

10 Another time it would be no shot, but the bark of a dog, the cry of a moor fowl, or a signal from some watching hind that started him.

The sounds that warned the stag were by no means always uttered by other animals. They were often but
15 imitations by Rob of the Angels. Not a moment did the stag neglect any warning, but from peaceful feeder was changed to wind-like fleer, his great horns thrown back upon his shoulders, and his four legs just touching the ground with elastic hoof.

20 One night Hector of the Stags could not sleep. It was not for cold, for the night was for the season a mild one. Raising himself on his elbow, Hector learned that Rob was not by his side. He, too, had been unable to sleep, and at last discovered that he was
25 uneasy about something; what, he could not tell. He rose and went out. The moon was shining, and, as there was much snow, the night was brighter than many a day. Hector soon joined his son. He had brought his telescope and immediately began to sweep

the moonlight on the opposite hill. In a moment he
touched Rob on the shoulder and handed him the telescope. Rob looked and saw a dark speck on the snow
moving along the hillside. It was the big stag. Now
and then he would stop to snuff and search for a mouth- 5
ful, but was evidently making for one of his feeding
places—most likely that on the Chief's land. They
did not stop for more than a glance, however, but made
for the valley as fast as they could walk; the noise of
running feet would be heard too far on such a clear 10
night. The whole way, without sound uttered, father
and son kept interchanging ideas on the matter.

From thorough acquaintance with the habits of the
animal, they were quite certain he was on his way to
his favorite haunt. If he reached there, he would be 15
safe; it was the Chief's ground and no one would dare
to touch him. But he was not yet upon it and was in
danger. If they found him at his usual feed, and danger threatening, they must scare him eastward; if no
peril was at hand, they would watch him awhile, that 20
he might feed in safety.

They approached the castle; immediately beyond that
they would be in sight of the feeding ground. But they
were still behind it when Rob of the Angels bounded
forward in terror at the sound of a gun. His father, 25
however, who was in front, was off before him. Neither
hearing anything, nor seeing Rob, he knew that a shot
had been fired, and, caution being now useless, was in
a moment at full speed.

The smoke of the shot hung white in the moonlight over the end of the ridge. No red bulk shadowed the green pasture, no thicket of horns went shaking over the sod. No lord of creation, but an enemy of life, stood regarding his work, a tumbled heap of death, yet saying to himself, "It is good."

Rage filled the heart of Hector of the Stags. He gave a roar like a wild beast and raised his gun. But Rob of the Angels caught it ere it reached his shoulder. He yielded, and with another roar like a lion bounded bare-handed upon the enemy.

It was not merely that the enemy had killed the great stag of their love; he had killed him on the Chief's own ground, under the eyes of the man whose business it was to watch over him. It was an insult as well as a wrong to his Chief. In the fierce majesty of his wrath he threw himself upon the poacher. Sercombe met him with a blow straight from the shoulder, and he dropped.

Rob of the Angels, close behind him, dropped his gun, his knife flashed pale in the moonlight, and he darted upon the enemy. It would have gone ill with the bigger man, for Rob was as lithe as a snake — not only swift to parry and dodge, but to strike. Sercombe's arm would have had at least one terrible gash, had not at that moment, from the top of the ridge, come the stern voice of the Chief. Rob's knife "made lightnings in the splendor of the moon," as he threw it from him and sank down by his father. Then Hector came to

himself and rose, trembling with excitement, for he saw
the stalwart form of his Chief on the ridge above him.

The Chief had been wakened by the gun, and, at the
roar of his friend Hector, sprang from his bed. But
when he saw his beloved stag dead on his pasture, he 5
came down the ridge like an avalanche. He gazed
speechless for a moment on the slaughtered stag and
heaved a great sigh. " Mr. Sercombe," he said, " I
would rather you had shot my best horse. Are you
aware, sir, that you are a poacher?" 10

" I had supposed the term inapplicable to a gentleman," answered Sercombe with entire coolness. " I will
pay whatever you choose to set on the brute." It would
be hard to say which was less agreeable to the Chief, to
have his stag called a brute, or be offered blood money. 15

"Stag Ruadh priced like a bullock," he said with a
slow smile, full of sadness; "the pride of every child in
the glen! Not a gentleman in the county would have
shot Clanruadh's deer."

Sercombe was by this time feeling uncomfortable, 20
and it made him angry. He muttered something
about superstition.

"He was taken when a calf," the Chief went on,
"and given to a great-aunt of mine ; but when he grew
up he took to the hills again, and was known by his 25
silver collar till he managed to rid himself of it. He
shall be buried where he lies, and his monument shall
tell how the stranger served the stag of Clanruadh."

From " What's Mine's Mine."

PINE TREES.

JOHN RUSKIN.

JOHN RUSKIN was born in London in 1819. He was a bright, active boy and learned to read when he was four years old. He amused himself by making little books, printing them by hand, and illustrating them with his own drawings.

His parents spent several summers in driving about England enjoying the sights and historical places. John went with them, and as soon as he could write he kept a journal.

Several years later he traveled with his father through Germany, sailed across the Italian lakes, and saw the Alps.

Ruskin was educated at Oxford. When he was graduated he had already become well known as a writer, gained the most popular university prize, and was considered a clever artist.

20 He became deeply interested in the artists of his time, and published a number of volumes entitled "Modern Painters." He has also written many other works, each containing common sense and truth, as well as beauty and imagination.

Mr. Ruskin is still living in his delightful home at Brantwood.

25 THE pine is trained to need nothing and to endure everything. Tall or short, it will be straight. Small or large, it will be round. It may be permitted to the soft, lowland trees that they should make themselves gay with the show of blossom and glad with pretty

charities of fruitfulness. We builders with the sword
have harder work to do for man, and must do it in
close-set troops.

To stay the sliding of the mountain snows, which
would bury him; to hold in divided drops, at our 5
sword points, the rain, which would sweep away him
and his treasure fields; to nurse in shade among our
brown, fallen leaves the tricklings that feed the brooks
in drought; to give massive shield against the winter
wind, which shrieks through the bare branches of the 10
plain, — such service must we do him steadfastly while
we live.

Our bodies also are at his service; softer than the
bodies of other trees, though our service is harder than
theirs. Let him take them as he pleases for his houses 15
and ships. So also it may be well for these timid, lowland trees to tremble with all their leaves, or turn their
paleness to the sky, if but a rush of rain passes by
them; or to let fall their leaves at last, sick and sere.
But we pines must live amidst the wrath of clouds. 20

We only wave our branches to and fro when the
storm pleads with us, as men toss their arms in a
dream.

And, finally, these weak, lowland trees may struggle
fondly for the last remnant of life, and send up feeble 25
saplings again from their roots when they are cut
down. But we builders with the sword perish boldly;
our dying shall be perfect and solemn, as our warring;
we give up our lives without reluctance, and forever.

I wish the reader to fix his attention for a moment
on these two great characters of the pine, its straightness and rounded perfectness ; both wonderful, and in
their issue lovely. I say first its straightness. Because
5 we see it in the wildest scenery, we are apt to remember only as examples of it those which have been dis-
turbed by violent accident or disease.

Of course such instances are frequent. The soil of
the pine is subject to continual change ; perhaps the
10 rock in which it is rooted splits in frost and falls forward, throwing the young stems aslope, or the whole
mass of earth around it is undermined by rain, or a
huge boulder falls on its stem from above, and forces
it for twenty years to grow with weight of several tons
15 leaning on its side.

Nevertheless this is not the truest or universal
expression of the pine's character. The pine rises in
serene resistance, self-contained ; nor can I ever without awe stay long under a great Alpine cliff, looking
20 up to its great companies of pine.

You cannot reach them ; those trees never heard
human voice ; they are far above all sound but that of
the winds. No foot ever stirred fallen leaf of theirs.

Then note, farther, their perfectness. The pine
25 stands compact, like one of its own cones, slightly
curved on its sides, and instead of being wild in its
expression, forms the softest of all forest scenery. For
other trees show their trunks and twisting boughs ;
but the pine, growing either in luxuriant mass or in

happy isolation, allows no bough to be seen. Lowland forests arch overhead and chequer the ground with darkness; but the pine, growing in scattered groups, leaves the glades between emerald bright. Its gloom is all its own; narrowing to the sky, it lets the sun- 5 shine strike down to the dew.

And then I want you to notice in the pine its exquisite fineness. Other trees rise against the sky in dots and knots, but this in fringes.

You never see the edges of it, so subtle are they; 10 and for this reason it alone of trees, so far as I know, is capable of the fiery changes noticed by Shakespeare.

When the sun rises behind a ridge crested with pine, provided the ridge be at a distance of about two miles, and seen clear, all the trees for about three or four 15 degrees on each side of the sun become trees of light, seen in clear flame against the darker sky, and dazzling as the sun itself.

I thought at first this was owing to the actual luster of the leaves; but I believe now it is caused by the 20 cloud-dew upon them, every minutest leaf carrying its diamond. It seems as if these trees, living always among the clouds, had caught part of their glory from them.

From " Modern Painters."

ASPECT OF THE PINES.

PAUL HAMILTON HAYNE.

PAUL HAMILTON HAYNE, a well-known Southern poet, was born in Charleston, S. C., in 1830.

His verses are filled with pictures of nature in the South and the lessons revealed to his poetic mind. He died in 1886.

TALL, somber, grim, against the morning sky
They rise, scarce touched by melancholy airs,
Which stir the fadeless foliage dreamfully,
As if from realms of mystical despairs.

Tall, somber, grim, they stand with dusky gleams
Brightening to gold within the woodland's core,
Beneath the gracious noontide's tranquil beams —
But the weird winds of morning sigh no more.

A stillness strange, divine, ineffable,
Broods round and o'er them in the wind's surcease,
And in each tinted copse and shimmering dell
Rests the mute rapture of deep-hearted peace.

Last sunset comes — the solemn joy — and night
Born from the nest when cloudless day declines —
Low, flutelike breezes sweep the waves of light,
And lifting dark green tresses of the pines,

Till every lock is luminous, gently float,
Fraught with pale odors up the heavens afar,
To faint when twilight on her virginal throat
Wears for a gem the tremulous vesper star.

WORK.

JOHN RUSKIN.

IT is physically impossible for a well-educated, intellectual, or brave man to make money the chief object
of his thoughts; as physically impossible as it is for
him to make his dinner the principal object of them.
All healthy people like their dinners, but their dinner 5
is not the main object of their lives. So all healthily
minded people like making money — ought to like it,
and to enjoy the sensation of winning it; but the main
object of their life is not money; it is something better
than money. 10

A good soldier, for instance, mainly wishes to do his
fighting well. He is glad of his pay — very properly
so, and justly grumbles when you keep him ten years
without it; still, his main notion of life is to win
battles, not to be paid for winning them. 15

So of doctors. They like fees no doubt — ought to
like them; yet if they are brave and well educated, the
entire object of their lives is not fees. They, on the
whole, desire to cure the sick; and — if they are good
doctors, and the choice were fairly put to them — 20
would rather cure their patient and lose their fee than
kill him and get it. And so with all other brave and
rightly trained men; their work is first, their fee
second; very important always, but still *second*.

But in every nation, as I said, there are a vast class 25

who are cowardly, and more or less stupid. And with these people, just as certainly the fee is first and the work second, as with brave people the work is first and the fee second.

5 And this is no small distinction. It is the whole distinction in a man. You cannot serve two masters; you *must* serve one or other. If your work is first with you, and your fee second, work is your master.

Observe then, all wise work is mainly threefold in 10 character. It is honest, useful, and cheerful. I hardly know anything more strange than that you recognize honesty in play, and you do not in work. In your lightest games you have always some one to see what you call "fair play." In boxing, you must hit fair; 15 in racing, start fair. Your watchword is fair play; your hatred, foul play. Did it ever strike you that you wanted another watchword also, fair work, and another hatred also, foul work?

THE MARCH OF THE MARSEILLAIS.

WHAT an uproar! The whole square, blazing with sunlight, was crammed full of people, all talking and shouting and gesticulating at once, while the National Guard was forming in line. No one seemed to know what had happened. 5

"What is it all about?" I asked.

"What is it all about?" repeated one of the soldiers. "The King of France is a traitor. We are betrayed by our king. The Marseilles battalion is on its way to Paris. It will pass through Avignon. We are going 10 to welcome these brave patriots."

Scarcely were we in line when a number of children came running towards us screaming: "Here they are! Here they are!"

And then, around the turn of the road, brave in their 15 red plumed cocked hats, appeared the leaders of the Marseilles battalion, while all the men together burst forth with: —

> "Forward, forward, countrymen!
> The glorious day has come!" 20

It was the "Marseillais" that they were singing; and that magnificent hymn, heard then for the first time, stirred us down to the very marrow of our bones.

On they came, and what a sight it was! Five hundred men sunburnt as locust beans, with black eyes 25 blazing like live coals under bushy eyebrows, all white with the dust of the road. They wore green cloth coats turned back with red like mine. Some wore cocked hats with waving feathers ; some, red liberty caps with the strings flying back over their shoulders.

5 Each man had stuck in the barrel of his gun a willow or a poplar branch to shelter him from the sun, and all this shrubbery cast dancing shadows over their faces that made them look still more fantastic and strange.

10 And when from all those red mouths — wide open as a wolf's jaws, with teeth gleaming white like a wild beast's teeth — burst forth the chorus, "To arms, citizens!" it fairly made a shiver run down one's spine.

The whole battalion passed onward and was swal-
15 lowed up in the city gate. Then came four men, hauling after them a rusty truck, on which was a cannon. These men were harnessed to the truck as oxen to the plough, and, like oxen, pulled from head and shoulders. With every muscle at full stretch they bent forward
20 to their heavy task. Following the truck came another and still another. Gasping though the men were for breath, yet they too raised their heads and shouted as they passed through our ranks: —

"To arms, citizens, to arms!"

25 Day was dawning as we began our march with the battalion, and soon we were on the highroad under a blazing sun, kicking up the dust like twenty flocks of sheep and making our throats as dry as limekilns.

In spite of heat and dust, in spite of thirst and weariness, no one complained as we tramped steadily on; one body and one soul, with one will and one aim —and that to make the traitor king and those Parisians who were traitors with him cry mercy.

At midday we reached Orange, where the whole town came to meet us. I can tell you I was a proud boy as I entered that town! From my shoes to my eyebrows I was white with dust. My red cap was cocked over one ear. I kept my eyes glaringly wide open, so as to look fierce and dangerous. I howled the "Marseillais" at the top of my voice as I marched —and I was sure no one saw or heard anybody but me!

Hours went by; onward we marched through the black night. Oh, how long was that night and how weary that road! We were too tired to talk. The only sounds we heard were the rumbling of the cannon on the road and the chirping of the crickets in the fields.

At last we came to a village just as the dawn began to whiten the sky. On the straw of some threshing-floors we laid ourselves down for an hour's sleep. At sunrise we were in line again.

This time I stationed myself in the rear, beside the cannon. A tremendous longing to help pull the guns had taken hold of me; for I thought that if only I could be harnessed up with the others I would not seem so young. I fancied to myself how I would look as we passed through the towns and villages — bending over and tugging at the straps, my eyes wide open and rolling ferociously, and all the while shouting in a voice as hoarse as I could make it, "Liberty forever!"

5 "Your turn will come in good time, little man," I was told. "We are not in Paris yet, and before we reach there you will have quite enough to do to carry your bundle and your gun and your sword, which is a good deal longer than you are!"

This setback made me turn red with shame, but 10 suddenly the drum beat the quickstep and we steadied our lines. We were entering the town beyond which we were to rest.

How delicious it was to go down on one's elbows and stretch out at full length on the soft grass in the 15 shade of the poplars and willows! I let my head fall between my hands and watched with great interest an ant who was carrying through the grass a crumb of bread bigger than himself. The little creature would lose its way in a thick tangle of grass blades, or 20 would slip down from a tall stem. In pity for him I would take a twig and help him on his way; putting the twig under him very gently so as not to hurt him, and so lifting him over a hard pass that would have cost him an hour of climbing to cross alone. And so 25 the afternoon wore away.

We marched all night. Now we were coming to the frontiers of the north. There were no more olive trees, and the soft sea wind of the Mediterranean was far away. But this was only the beginning of the march.

We went steadily on, drinking the water of brooks and ditches, and taking only snatches of sleep as the chance came.

The endless road was always the same long, weary way. Footsore, hungry, weary, still we toiled on. Some of the men began to drag behind, limping on bleeding feet; but they struggled bravely along. To drown the murmurs of pain, which even the best of them could not wholly stifle, we sang the "Marseillais."

And at last, after days of weariness and hunger and thirst, we saw on the edge of the green plain the towers and spires of Paris.

A great crowd followed us into the city, drawn on partly by the steady roll of the drums, but more strongly by the terrible chant of the "Marseillais," which all the five hundred men of the battalion sang in one tremendous voice. Soon the crowd caught the words of the chorus and sang with us — and then it was no longer five hundred, but a thousand, ten thousand, twenty thousand singers, singing with one voice.

I sang as if I would tear my throat open. From time to time I would look back to see the overwhelming, howling, terrible flood of people pouring in close behind us. Our weeks and weeks of marching were over. It seemed as if a great mountain were galloping after us with its peaks and valleys and forests shaken and riven by the avalanche, the tempest, the earthquake of God!

Adapted from Janvier's translation from the
"Provençal of Félix Gras."

THE LADY OF SHALOTT.

ALFRED TENNYSON.

For a sketch of the life of Alfred Tennyson, see "Cyr's Fourth Reader."

PART I.

On either side the river lie
Long fields of barley and of rye,
That clothe the wold and meet the sky;
And through the field the road runs by
      To many-towered Camelot;
And up and down the people go,
Gazing where the lilies blow
Round an island there below,
      The island of Shalott.

Willows whiten, aspens quiver,
Little breezes dusk and shiver,
Through the wave that runs forever,
By the island in the river
   Flowing down to Camelot.
Four gray walls and four gray towers,
Overlook a space of flowers,
And the silent isle embowers
   The Lady of Shalott.

By the margin, willow-veiled,
Slide the heavy barges trailed
By slow horses ; and unhailed,
The shallop flitteth silken-sailed,
   Skimming down to Camelot :
But who hath seen her wave her hand ?
Or at the casement seen her stand ?
Or is she known in all the land,
   The Lady of Shalott ?

Only reapers, reaping early
In among the bearded barley,
Hear a song that echoes cheerly
From the river winding clearly,
   Down to towered Camelot :
And by the moon the reaper weary,
Piling sheaves in uplands airy,
Listening, whispers, " 'T is the fairy
   Lady of Shalott."

Part II.

There she weaves by night and day
A magic web with colors gay.
She has heard a whisper say,
A curse is on her if she stay
        To look down to Camelot.
She knows not what the curse may be,
And so she weaveth steadily,
And little other care hath she,
        The Lady of Shalott.

And moving through a mirror clear
That hangs before her all the year,
Shadows of the world appear.
There she sees the highway near
        Winding down to Camelot:
There the river eddy whirls,
And there the surly village-churls,
And the red cloaks of market-girls,
        Pass onward from Shalott.

Sometimes a troop of damsels glad,
An abbot on an ambling pad,
Sometimes a curly shepherd-lad,
Or long-haired page in crimson clad,
        Goes by to towered Camelot;
And sometimes through the mirror blue
The knights come riding two and two:

She hath no loyal knight and true,
      The Lady of Shalott.

But in her web she still delights
To weave the mirror's magic sights,
For often through the silent nights
A funeral, with plumes and lights,
      And music, went to Camelot:
Or when the moon was overhead
Came two young lovers lately wed;
"I am half sick of shadows," said
      The Lady of Shalott.

PART III.

A bow-shot from her bower-eaves,
He rode between the barley-sheaves,
The sun came dazzling through the leaves,
And flamed upon the brazen greaves
      Of bold Sir Lancelot.
A red-cross knight forever kneeled
To a lady in his shield,
That sparkled on the yellow field,
      Beside remote Shalott.

The gemmy bridle glittered free,
Like to some branch of stars we see
Hung in the golden Galaxy.
The bridle bells rang merrily,
      As he rode down to Camelot:

And from his blazoned baldric slung
A mighty silver bugle hung,
And as he rode his armor rung,
      Beside remote Shalott.

His broad clear brow in sunlight glowed;
On burnished hooves his war-horse trode;
From underneath his helmet flowed
His coal black curls as on he rode,
      As he rode down to Camelot.
From the bank and from the river
He flashed into the crystal mirror,
"Tirra lirra," by the river
      Sang Sir Lancelot.

She left the web, she left the loom,
She made three paces through the room,
She saw the water-lily bloom,
She saw the helmet and the plume,
      She looked down to Camelot.
Out flew the web and floated wide;
The mirror cracked from side to side;
"The curse is come upon me!" cried
      The Lady of Shalott.

Part IV.

In the stormy east wind straining,
The pale yellow woods were waning,
The broad stream in his banks complaining,

Heavily the low sky raining
      Over towered Camelot;
Down she came and found a boat
Beneath a willow left afloat,
And round about the prow she wrote
      The Lady of Shalott.

And down the river's dim expanse —
Like some bold seer in a trance,
Seeing all his own mischance —
With a glassy countenance,
      Did she look to Camelot.
And at the closing of the day
She loosed the chain, and down she lay;
The broad stream bore her far away,
      The Lady of Shalott.

Lying, robed in snowy white
That loosely flew to left and right —
The leaves upon her falling light —
Through the noises of the night
      She floated down to Camelot:
And as the boat-head wound along
The willowy hills and fields among,
They heard her singing her last song,
      The Lady of Shalott.

Heard a carol, mournful, holy,
Chanted loudly, chanted lowly,
Till her blood was frozen slowly,

And her eyes were darkened wholly,
      Turned to towered Camelot.
For ere she reached upon the tide
The first house by the water-side,
Singing in her song she died,
      The Lady of Shalott.

Under tower and balcony,
By garden-wall and gallery,
A gleaming shape she floated by,
Dead-pale between the houses high,
      Silent into Camelot.
Out upon the wharves they came,
Knight and burgher, lord and dame,
And round the prow they read her name,
      The Lady of Shalott.

Who is this? and what is here?
And in the lighted palace near
Died the sound of royal cheer;
And they crossed themselves for fear :
      All the knights at Camelot :
But Lancelot mused a little space;
He said, " She has a lovely face;
God in his mercy lend her grace,
      The Lady of Shalott."

JOHN LOTHROP MOTLEY.

John Lothrop Motley was born in Dorchester, now a part of Boston, Mass., on the 15th of April, 1814. His parents belonged to old New England families, and John never tired of hearing their stories of the early settlers. His great-grandfather was killed 5 by the Indians, and his grandmother, who was a little child at the time of the attack, would have lost her life or been taken prisoner, if the maid servant had not hidden her under a large tub in the cellar.

John was a bright boy, truthful, and with a quick sense of honor. He was very fond of reading and was seldom seen without a book in his hand. He had a talent for declaiming, and one of his younger brothers 20 remembers being wrapped in a shawl, and kept quiet with sweetmeats, to represent the dead Cæsar, while John delivered the speech of Antony over his body.

His father's house was a large, homelike dwelling, and the children were allowed the freedom of the garret 25 and garden. Many a treasure was stowed away in trunks under the eaves, and John and his playfellows, among them Wendell Phillips, who afterward became a famous orator, often arrayed themselves in long cloaks and plumed hats, and acted plays or scenes from history.

John was sent to school at Northampton when he
5 was about ten years old. He was a brilliant scholar and gained a great reputation among the boys because of his ability to declaim. One of his teachers was George Bancroft, the historian, who little thought that his clever pupil would some day rank with himself as
10 an author.

At the age of thirteen, the future historian entered Harvard College. He was the youngest member of his class, and his reputation as a scholar and his handsome person attracted much attention. During his first year
15 in college, young Motley held the second or third rank in his class. He led a very pleasant life, receiving his friends in his handsomely furnished room, roaming about the old, historic town, and spending his leisure time in reading and writing sketches and poems for his own
20 amusement.

After completing his college course, he went to Germany and spent two years at the Universities of Berlin and Göttingen. One of the friends made at this time was Prince Bismarck, who was one of his fellow-
25 students at Göttingen. The two young men lodged in the same house and spent much time together.

On his return to America, Motley studied law. He was married when he was twenty-three to Mary Benjamin, and two years later his first work, a novel called

"Morton's Hope," was published. This book contains many scenes drawn from the life of the author.

In 1841 Mr. Motley was sent by the government to fill an office in Russia. He spent several months in St. Petersburg, but found the climate so trying that he was unwilling to take his family to that country, so resigned his position and returned to America.

Mr. Motley's first historical work was an article on "Russia" and "Peter the Great," which appeared in the "North American Review." It was a brilliant essay and gave the author a place among the foremost writers of the day.

After the success of this article, Mr. Motley determined to devote his time to historical writing, and he began reading for a history of the Dutch Republic. Meanwhile his second novel, "Merry-Mount," had been published. This was a romance of the Massachusetts Colony, and received more attention than the story of "Morton's Hope."

After working for several years on the Dutch history, Mr. Motley decided that in order to make his work complete he must consult the libraries of Europe.

He took his family abroad, and started his work anew, visiting the scenes which he was describing, and searching in the libraries for old letters and documents. He so lived in his work that to his imagination, Brussels seemed peopled with the kings and heroes of bygone days.

For ten years he labored upon this history, and then

published it at his own expense, for he could find no publisher willing to undertake so large a work.

The book was widely read and highly praised. It was reprinted in New York and translated into several languages, and the author, who had almost forgotten living men in his close study of historical characters, found himself the object of every attention.

Motley was forty years of age when "The Rise of the Dutch Republic" was published. He spent the next winter in this country, enjoying its social life, and then returned to England, where he was received with every attention. He was a welcome guest in the best houses, and the kindness and pleasure with which he was received added much to his happiness.

He again devoted himself to study, and in four years the first part of his second historical work, "The History of the United Netherlands," was published. It increased the reputation gained by the first history. The last volumes of this work were not published until eight years later.

Mr. Motley was a true American. When the Civil War broke out he was deeply interested in the welfare of his country and returned to the United States. He was appointed Minister to Austria, which position he held for six years, making his home in Vienna. During this time he met his old friend, Bismarck. Motley's daughter writes of their meeting: —

"Bismarck dined with us twice during his short stay, and was most delightful and agreeable. When he and my father were together they seemed to live over the youthful days they had spent together as students, and many were the anecdotes of their boyish frolics which Bismarck related."

After resigning his office in Vienna, Motley returned to America, and two years later was sent as Minister to England, remaining there one year.

He then devoted his time to literary work, and wrote the life of John of Barneveld, Advocate of Holland. In order to search for material for this work he took his family to The Hague, where the Queen of Holland had made ready a house for him. He completed this work; but it was his last, for his health was failing, and after the death of his wife in 1874 he laid aside his pen.

Mr. Motley's last days were spent in England. He died in that country in May, 1877.

THE ABDICATION OF CHARLES V.

JOHN LOTHROP MOTLEY.

ON the twenty-fifth day of October, 1555, the estates of the Netherlands were assembled in the great hall of the palace at Brussels. They had been summoned to be the witnesses and the guarantees of the abdication
5 which Charles V. had long before resolved upon, and which he was that day to execute.

The palace where the states-general were upon this occasion convened was a spacious and convenient building. In front was a large, open square, enclosed by an
10 iron railing; in the rear an extensive and beautiful park, filled with forest trees, and containing gardens and labyrinths, fish ponds and game preserves, fountains and promenades, race courses and archery grounds.

15 The main entrance to this edifice opened upon a spacious hall, connected with a beautiful chapel. The hall was celebrated for its size, harmonious proportions, and the richness of its decorations. At the western end a spacious platform, or stage, with six or seven steps,
20 had been constructed. In the center of the stage was a splendid canopy, decorated with the arms of Burgundy, beneath which were placed three gilded armchairs. The theater was filled — the audience was eager with expectation — the actors were yet to arrive.

25 As the clock struck three, the hero of the scene appeared. Cæsar, as he was always designated in the

classic language of the day, entered, leaning on the shoulder of William of Orange. They came from the chapel and were immediately followed by Philip II. and Queen Mary of Hungary, and other great personages came afterward, accompanied by a glittering throng. 5

All the company present had risen to their feet as the Emperor entered. By his command all immediately afterward resumed their places. The benches at either end of the platform were accordingly filled with the royal and princely personages invited, with the Fleece 10 Knights, with the members of the three great councils, and with the governors. The Emperor, the King, and the Queen of Hungary were left conspicuous in the center of the scene.

Charles V. was then fifty-five years old, but he was 15 already decrepit with premature old age. Broad in the shoulders, deep in the chest, very muscular in the arms and legs, he had been able to match himself with all competitors in the tourney and the ring, and to vanquish the bull with his own hand in the favorite national 20 amusement of Spain. He had been able in the field to do the duty of captain and soldier, to endure fatigue and exposure, and every privation except fasting.

These personal advantages were now departed. Crippled in hands, knees, and legs, he supported 25 himself with difficulty upon a crutch, with the aid of an attendant's shoulder. In face he had always been extremely ugly. His hair was white with age, close-clipped and bristling; his beard was gray, coarse, and shaggy. His forehead was spacious and commanding ; the eye was dark blue, with an expression both majestic and benignant.

So much for the father. The son, Philip II., was a 5 small, meager man, much below the middle height, with thin legs, a narrow chest, and the shrinking, timid air of an habitual invalid.

In face he was the living image of his father, having the same broad forehead and blue eye, with the same 10 aquiline but better proportioned nose. His demeanor in public was still, silent, almost sepulchral.

Such was the personal appearance of the man who was about to receive into his single hand the destinies of half the world ; whose single will was, for the future, 15 to shape the fortunes of every individual then present, of many millions more in Europe, America, and at the ends of the earth, and of countless millions yet unborn.

The three royal personages being seated upon chairs placed triangularly under the canopy, such of the audi- 20 ence as had seats provided for them now took their places and the proceedings commenced. Philibert de Bruxelles, a member of the council of the Netherlands, arose at the Emperor's command and made a long ora- tion. He spoke of the Emperor's warm affection for 25 the provinces, of his deep regret that his broken health and failing powers compelled him to resign his sover- eignty and to seek relief for his shattered frame in a more genial climate. He rejoiced, however, that his son was both vigorous and experienced, and that his

recent marriage with the Queen of England had furnished the provinces with a most valuable alliance. He
concluded with a tremendous exhortation to Philip on
the necessity of maintaining religion in its purity.

After this the councilor proceeded to read the deed 5
of cession by which Philip, already sovereign of Sicily,
Naples, Milan, and titular king of England, France,
and Jerusalem, now received all the Burgundian
property, including, of course, the seventeen Netherlands.   10

The Emperor then rose to his feet. Supported upon
his crutch and upon the shoulder of William of Orange,
he proceeded to address the states.

As long as God granted him health, he continued,
only enemies could have regretted that Charles was 15
living and reigning; but now that his strength was but
vanity, and life fast ebbing away, his love for dominion,
his affection for his subjects, and his regard for their
interests required his departure.

Turning toward Philip, he observed that for a father 20
to bequeath so magnificent an empire to his son was a
deed worthy of gratitude; but that when the father
thus descended into his grave before his time, and by
an anticipated and living burial sought to provide for
the welfare of his realms and the grandeur of his son, 25
the benefit thus conferred was surely far greater.

Posterity would applaud his abdication should his son
prove worthy of his bounty; and that could only be by
living in the fear of God, and by maintaining law and

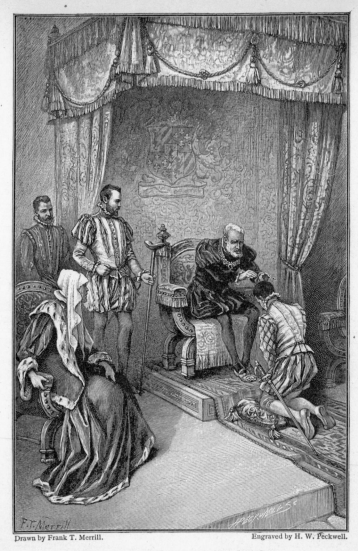

Drawn by Frank T. Merrill.

Engraved by H. W. Peckwell.

CHARLES V. BLESSING HIS SON PHILIP II.

justice in all their purity as the true foundation of the realm.

In conclusion he entreated the estates, and through them the nation, to render obedience to their new prince; begging them at the same time to pardon him all errors or offenses which he might have committed toward them during his reign, and assuring them that he should unceasingly remember their obedience and affection in his every prayer to that Being to whom the remainder of his life should be dedicated.

Sobs were heard throughout every portion of the hall, and tears poured profusely from every eye. As for the Emperor himself, he sank almost fainting upon his chair as he concluded his address. An ashy paleness overspread his countenance, and he wept like a child.

Even the icy Philip was almost softened as he rose to perform his part in the ceremony. Dropping upon his knees before his father's feet, he reverently kissed his hand. Charles placed his hands solemnly upon his son's head and blessed him. Then raising him in his arms he tenderly embraced him, saying as he did so, to the great potentates around him, that he felt a sincere compassion for the son on whose shoulders so heavy a weight had just devolved.

Philip now uttered a few words expressive of his duty to his father and his affection for his people. Turning to the orders, he signified his regret that he was unable to address them either in the French or Flemish language, and was obliged to ask their atten-

tion to the Bishop of Arras, who would act as his interpreter. Antony Perrenot accordingly arose, and in smooth, fluent, and well-turned commonplaces expressed at great length the gratitude of Philip toward
5 his father, with his firm determination to walk in the path of duty, and to obey his father's counsels and example in the future administration of the provinces.

This address was responded to by Jacob Maas, who had been selected to reply on the behalf of the states-
10 general. Queen Mary of Hungary, the regent of the Netherlands during the past twenty-five years, then rose to resign her office, making a brief address expressive of her affection for the people. Again Maas responded, asserting in terms of fresh compliment and
15 elegance the uniform satisfaction of the provinces with her conduct during her whole career.

The orations and replies having now been brought to a close, the ceremony was ended. The Emperor, leaning on the shoulders of the Prince of Orange and
20 of the Count de Buren, slowly left the hall, followed by Philip, the Queen of Hungary, and the whole court; all in the same order in which they had entered, and by the same passage into the chapel.

From " The Rise of the Dutch Republic."

MAZEPPA'S RIDE.

[Abridged.]

LORD BYRON.

Lord Byron was born in London in 1788. When he was ten years old he inherited a title of nobility and took possession of Newstead Abbey, the ancient family seat near Nottingham.

His early education was received at private schools, and he entered Trinity College, Cambridge, when he was seventeen years of age.

Two years later his first volume of verses, "Hours of Idleness," was published. It was severely criticised, and the young poet replied in so savage a poem that he attracted much attention.

After leaving college, Byron traveled along the shores of the Mediterranean, visiting Greece and Turkey. On his return he published the first part of "Childe Harold," which is generally considered his greatest work. After the publication of this poem he was recognized as one of the leading poets of England.

Byron took final leave of England when he was twenty-eight, and lived for several years in Switzerland and Italy, where he wrote some famous poems.

The cause of Greek independence appealed so strongly to him that he raised a large sum of money, and in the summer of 1823 he sailed to the assistance of the Greeks. He was made commander-in-chief of an expedition, but was taken ill and died on the 19th of April, 1824.

" ' Bring forth the horse ! '   The horse was brought ;
 In truth he was a noble steed,
 A Tartar of the Ukraine breed,
Who look'd as though the speed of thought
Were in his limbs ; but he was wild,
 Wild as the wild deer, and untaught,
With spur and bridle undefiled —
 'T was but a day he had been caught ;
And snorting, with erected mane,
And struggling fiercely, but in vain,
In the full foam of wrath and dread
To me the desert-born was led ;
They bound me on, that menial throng,
Upon his back with many a thong ;
Then loosed him with a sudden lash —
Away ! — away ! — and on we dash ! —
Torrents less rapid and less rash.

  . . . . . .

" Away, away, my steed and I,
 Upon the pinions of the wind,
 All human dwellings left behind ;
We sped like meteors through the sky ;
Town — village — none were on our track,
 But a wild plain of far extent,
And bounded by a forest black ;
 And, save the scarce seen battlement
On distant heights of some strong hold,

Against the Tartars built of old,
No trace of man.

. . . .

"We near'd the wild wood — 'twas so wide,
I saw no bounds on either side;
'Twas a wild waste of underwood,
And here and there a chestnut stood,
The strong oak, and the hardy pine;

. . . . .

We rustled through the leaves like wind,
Left shrubs, and trees, and wolves behind;
Where'er we flew they followed on,
Nor left us with the morning sun;
Behind I saw them, scarce a rood,
At daybreak winding through the wood,
And through the night had heard their feet
Their stealing, rustling step repeat.
Oh! how I wish'd for spear or sword,
At least to die amidst the horde,
And perish — if it must be so —
At bay, destroying many a foe!

. . . . .

"Up rose the sun; the mists were curl'd
Back from the solitary world.
The very air was mute;

And not an insect's shrill small horn,
Nor matin bird's new voice, was borne
From herb nor thicket.   Many a werst,
Panting as if his heart would burst,
The weary brute still stagger'd on;
And still we were — or seem'd — alone.
At length, while reeling on our way,
Methought I heard a courser neigh,
From out yon tuft of blackening firs.
Is it the wind those branches stirs?
No, no! from out the forest prance
    A trampling troop; I see them come!
In one vast squadron they advance!

    I strove to cry — my lips were dumb.
The steeds rush on in plunging pride;
But where are they the reins to guide?
A thousand horse — and none to ride!
With flowing tail, and flying mane,
Wide nostrils, never stretch'd by pain,
Mouths bloodless to the bit or rein,
And feet that iron never shod,
And flanks unscarr'd by spur or rod,
    Came thickly thundering on,
As if our faint approach to meet;
The sight re-nerved my courser's feet,
A moment staggering, feebly fleet,
A moment, with a faint low neigh,
    He answer'd, and then fell;
With gasps and glazing eyes he lay,

And reeking limbs immovable,
   His first and last career is done!
On came the troop — they saw him stoop,
  They saw me strangely bound along
  His back with many a bloody thong:
They stop — they start — they snuff the air,
Gallop a moment here and there,
Approach, retire, wheel round and round,
Then plunging back with sudden bound,
Headed by one black mighty steed,
Who seem'd the patriarch of his breed,
  Without a single speck or hair
Of white upon his shaggy hide;
They snort — they foam — neigh — swerve aside,
And backward to the forest fly,
By instinct, from a human eye.

  They left me there to my despair,
Link'd to the dead and stiffening wretch,
Whose lifeless limbs beneath me stretch,
Relieved from that unwonted weight,
From whence I could not extricate
Nor him, nor me — and there we lay,
  The dying on the dead!
I little deem'd another day
  Would see my houseless, helpless head.

   .   .   .   .

"I woke — Where was I? — Do I see
A human face look down on me?

And doth a roof above me close?
Do these limbs on a couch repose?
Is this a chamber where I lie?
And is it mortal, yon bright eye,
That watches me with gentle glance?
   I closed my own again once more,
As doubtful that the former trance
   Could not as yet be o'er.
A slender girl, long-hair'd, and tall,
Sate watching by the cottage wall;
The sparkle of her eye I caught,
Even with my first return of thought;
For ever and anon she threw
   A prying, pitying glance on me
   With her black eyes so wild and free;
I gazed, and gazed, until I knew
   No vision it could be, —
But that I lived, and was released."

From " Mazeppa."

THE GENIUS OF A GREAT ARCHITECT.

PHILLIPS BROOKS.

PHILLIPS BROOKS was born in Boston, December 13, 1835. His college education was received at Harvard, after which he studied theology at the seminary in Alexandria, Va.

After preaching for several years in Philadelphia he removed to Boston and filled the office of rector of Trinity Church, a 5 beautiful edifice which was designed by the famous architect, Henry H. Richardson.

Mr. Brooks was one of the most brilliant pulpit orators of his denomination, and his printed sermons are widely read.

He was offered the position of preacher and professor at Har- 10 vard University, but declined. In 1891 he was made Bishop of Massachusetts. His death occurred in January, 1893.

Bishop Brooks was loved and honored throughout England and America; and memorials to him have been placed in London, at Harvard University, and in several churches. 15

FROM 1872 to 1886 — fourteen years — was the great full period of Henry H. Richardson's life and work. And what years they were! He had realized his powers. The fire of distinct genius, indefinable and unmistakable, was burning brightly. His buildings 20 opened like flowers out of his life. It is not in my purpose now to name even his greatest works, or to describe the order in which they came, but rather to characterize some of the qualities, both of the man and of his work, as they showed themselves in those glori- 25 ous years when — all over the country, in Albany and Washington and Boston and Cincinnati and Chicago, and in quiet villages, where he made the town hall and library a perpetual inspiration, and along the railroads, where he made the station houses bear witness to the power of art to beautify the most prosaic uses, and in 5 dwellings, which he filled with dignity and grace — everywhere the man genuinely and spontaneously blended his own nature with the purposes and material of the structures which he built.

The first quality of true genius certainly was in all 10 that he did. It was instinctive and spontaneous. Based upon thorough study, genuinely expressing great ideas, it yet was true that there was much in Richardson's work of which he gave and could give to himself little or no account as to how it came to pass. He was not 15 a man of theories. His life passed into his buildings by ways too subtle even for himself to understand.

And so he has done a larger work than he ever deliberately resolved to do. He simply did his work in his own way, and the style was there.

20 It is a style of breadth and simplicity that corresponds with his whole nature. Never somber, because the irrepressible buoyancy and cheerfulness of his life are in it; never attaining the highest reach of spirituality and exaltation, for his own being had its strong 25 association with the earth, and knew no mystic raptures or transcendental aspirations; healthy and satisfying within its own range, and suggesting larger things as he himself always suggested the possession of powers which he had never realized and used — something like

this is the character of the buildings which he has left behind him.

He grew simpler as he grew older and greater. He often seemed to disregard and almost despise detail of ornament. He loved a broad, unbroken stretch of wall. He seemed to count, with Ruskin, "a noble surface of stone a fairer thing than most architectural features which it is caused to assume." And yet out of this simplicity could burst a sumptuousness of design or decoration all the more captivating and overwhelming for the simplicity out of which it sprang. I have heard one of his own profession call him "barbaric." It was that which made his work delightful. Whoever came in contact with it felt that the wind blew out of an elemental simplicity, out of the primitive life and fundamental qualities of man. And this great simplicity, the truthfulness with which he was himself, made him the real master of all that his art had ever been, made it possible for him, without concealment, to take some work of other days and appropriate it into work of his own, as Shakespeare took an Italian tale and turned it into Shylock or Othello.

These are the moral qualities of his architecture. But these qualities every one must feel who stands in front of one of Richardson's great buildings; and the same qualities every man felt who came to know him. That is another note of genius. The man and his work are absolutely one. The man is in the work, and the work is in the man. So Richardson possessed in himself that solidity without stolidity, that joyousness without frivolity, which his best art expresses.

Nowhere does this identity of Richardson and his work seem more impressive than in that unique house at Brookline which was at once his workshop and his home. No one who saw it when it was filled with his vitality will ever lose the feeling of how it was all vital, like a thing that had grown.

His life was like a great picture full of glowing color. The canvas on which it was painted was immense. It lighted all the room in which it hung. It warmed the chilliest air. It made, and it will long make, life broader, work easier, and simple strength and courage dearer to many men.

HONEST WORK.

" MEN said the old smith was foolishly careful, as he wrought on the great chain he was making in his dingy shop in the heart of the great city. But he heeded not their words, and only wrought with greater pains-taking. Link after link he fashioned and welded and 5 finished, and at last the great chain was completed.

" Years passed. One night there was a terrible storm, and the ship was in sore peril of being dashed upon the rocks. Anchor after anchor was dropped, but none of them held. The cables were broken like threads. At 10 last the mighty sheet anchor was cast into the sea, and the old chain quickly uncoiled and ran out till it grew taut. All watched to see if it would bear the awful strain. It sang in the wild storm as the vessel's weight surged upon it. It was a moment of intense anxiety. 15 The ship with its cargo of a thousand lives depended *upon this one chain.* What now if the old smith had wrought carelessly even *one link* of his chain ! But he had put honesty and truth and invincible strength into *every part of it ;* and it stood the test, holding the ship 20 in safety until the storm was over."

SONG OF THE FORGE.

CLANG, clang! the massive anvils ring;
Clang, clang! a hundred hammers swing;
Like the thunder rattle of a tropic sky,
The mighty blows still multiply;
      Clang, clang!
Say, brothers of the dusky brow,
What are your strong arms forging now?

Clang, clang! We forge the colter now, —
The colter of the kindly plough;
Prosper it, Heaven, and bless our toil!
  May its broad furrow still unbind
   To genial rains, to sun and wind,
The most benignant soil!

Clang, clang! Our colter's course shall be
On many a sweet and sunny lea,
  By many a streamlet's silver tide,
Amid the song of morning birds,
Amid the low of sauntering herds,
Amid soft breezes which do stray
Through woodbine hedges and sweet may,
  Along the green hill's side.

When regal Autumn's bounteous hand
With widespread glory clothes the land, —
When to the valleys, from the brow
  Of each resplendent slope, is rolled
  A ruddy sea of living gold, —
We bless — we bless the Plough.

Clang, clang! Again, my mates, what glows
Beneath the hammer's potent blows? —
Clink, clank! We forge the giant chain
Which bears the gallant vessel's strain,
'Mid stormy winds and adverse tides;
   Secured by this, the good ship braves
   The rocky roadstead, and the waves
Which thunder on her sides.

Anxious no more, the merchant sees
The mist drive dark before the breeze,
The storm-cloud on the hill;
   Calmly he rests, though far away
   In boisterous climes his vessel lay,
Reliant on our skill.

Say on what sands these links shall sleep,
Fathoms beneath the solemn deep;
By Afric's pestilential shore, —
By many an iceberg, lone and hoar, —
   By many a palmy Western isle,
   Basking in Spring's perpetual smile, —
By stormy Labrador.

Say, shall they feel the vessel reel,
When to the battery's deadly peal
The crashing broadside makes reply?
   Or else, as at the glorious Nile,
   Hold grappling ships, that strive the while
For death or victory?

Hurrah! Cling, clang! Once more, what glows,
   Dark brothers of the forge, beneath
The iron tempest of your blows,
   The furnace's red breath?
Clang, clang! A burning torrent, clear
   And brilliant, of bright sparks, is poured
Around and up in the dusky air,
   As our hammers forge the sword.

The sword! — a name of dread; yet when
   Upon the freeman's thigh 't is bound,
While for his altar and his hearth,
While for the land that gave him birth,
   The war-drums roll, the trumpets sound,
How sacred is it then!

Whenever, for the truth and right,
It flashes in the van of fight, —
Whether in some wild mountain pass,
As that where fell Leonidas, —
Or on some sterile plain, and stern,
A Marston or a Bannockburn, —
Or 'mid fierce crags and bursting rills,
The Switzer's Alps, gray Tyrol's hills, —
Or, as when sank the Armada's pride,
It gleams above the stormy tide, —
Still, still, whene'er the battle-word
   Is Liberty, when men do stand
   For justice and their native land,
Then Heaven bless the Sword!

ROBERT BURNS.

ROBERT BURNS was born near the town of Ayr, Scotland, on the 25th day of January, 1759. William Burns, "the brave father, a silent hero and poet," was a humble farmer, but he had a thirst for knowledge, and longed to give his family an education. He often spent his noon hour in pointing out the wonders of nature and imparting to his children what little knowledge he had gained.

Robert was sent to school at Mt. Oliphant in his sixth year; but his father's poverty gave him little opportunity for education, and at the age of thirteen he was assisting in threshing the corn, and at sixteen was the principal laborer on the farm.

There was an old woman named Betty Davidson who lived in the family. She had a store of tales and songs of fairies, ghosts, witches, dragons, and enchanted towers. Robert used to listen to these weird stories, which had a strong effect upon his imagination. They fostered his love of poetry, so that when his hands were busy with the farm work, his mind was galloping off on deeds of chivalry or indulging in flights of fancy.

The Sabbath was the only time for rest in this busy
5 household, and upon that day Robert Burns would be found wandering alone beside the river Ayr and listening to the songs of the birds:

> "The simple Bard, rough at the rustic plough,
>   Learning his tuneful trade from ev'ry bough;
> 10   The chanting linnet, or the mellow thrush,
>   Hailing the setting sun, sweet, in the green thorn bush."

A storm always filled his heart with reverence. He wrote:

"There is scarcely any earthly object gives me more
15 — I do not know if I should call it pleasure, but something that exalts me — than to walk in the sheltered side of a wood or high plantation in a cloudy winter day and hear the stormy wind howling among the trees and raving over the plain. . . . I listened to
20 the birds, and frequently turned out of my path lest I should disturb their little songs or frighten them to another station."

In spite of his long hours of hard work, Burns became a great reader. He carried some volume, usually a
25 book of poems, in his pocket to study during his spare moments, and wrote: "I pored over them driving my cart, or walking to labor, song by song, verse by verse, carefully noting the true, tender, sublime, or fustian."

While whistling along behind the plough or swinging the scythe, he was humming the songs of his country, or changing the forms of the ballads which he wrote at night in his cheerless room. It was while ploughing in the field that he composed   5

> "That I for puir auld Scotland's sake
> Some useful plan or book could make
> Or sing a song at least."

Burns had a tender heart and ready sympathy. One day his plough turned up a field mouse in her nest. 10 The frightened little creature started to run, and one of the boys was about to kill her when Burns interfered. The thought that he had broken up this home where Mousie thought herself safe from the cold of winter filled him with regret, and he wrote his celebrated 15 poem, "To a Mouse," on this occasion. Another poem, "To a Mountain Daisy," was composed while he was ploughing a field where he had uprooted a daisy which was just springing up through the soil.

His first poem of note, "Behind Yon Hills where 20 Lugar Flows," was written when Burns was twenty-two years old. During that year he went to Irvine to learn the flax dresser's trade. "It was," he writes, "an unlucky affair. As we were giving a welcome to the New Year, the shop took fire and burned to 25 ashes, and I was left, like a true poet, without a six-pence." His father's failing health and misfortunes made it necessary for him to return to the farm.

Burns began to be known in the neighborhood as a writer of verses, but some of his poems were received with disapproval, and other circumstances increased the feeling against him, so that he decided
5 to leave Scotland and sail for Jamaica. To raise the needful funds, he had six hundred copies of a volume of his poems printed at Kilmarnock. The little book sold rapidly, and the poet had twenty guineas left after paying all expenses. Burns was
10 now ready to leave Scotland, but a letter from a friend changed the current of his life and kept him in his native land.

The poet was received with the highest honor at Edinburgh, where he was invited into the society of the
15 men of letters, rank, and fashion. Surely his dream had come true. He had reached the heart of "Bonnie Scotland"! Burns has taken the humblest pictures of Scottish life and breathed a deeper meaning into them than has ever been dreamed of by poet or
20 artist. He has compared himself to an Æolian harp strung to every wind of Heaven, and there seems to be nothing from the "wee, modest, crimson-tipped flower" to Scotland, his dear native land, that he has not clothed in verse. A second edition of his
25 poems was published during the following year, and the proceeds of their sale brought the author five hundred pounds. Soon afterwards Burns married Jean Armour, to whom he had long been attached, and settled on a farm at Ellisland, not far from Dumfries.

When he took possession of the farm Burns asked little Betty, the servant, to take the family Bible and a
bowl of salt, and, placing the one on the other, to walk
into the house. This was one of the old customs, and
the poet delighted in such observances. He and his 5
wife followed Betty and began life on this farm.

While here he was appointed Excise officer for the
district, and spent much of his time riding about the

BIRTHPLACE OF BURNS.

hills and vales of Nithsdale searching for smugglers,
and murmuring his wayward fancies as he rode along. 10
He often had a half dozen pieces in his mind, and
thought of one or the other as suited his mood. At
this time Burns wrote about a hundred Scottish songs,
for which he received a shawl for his wife, a picture
representing "The Cotter's Saturday Night," and about 15
five pounds.

In a short time he was obliged to leave the pleasant
farm and remove to a small house at Dumfries, where

he hoped to support his family on his small increase of salary as Excise man of that district; but certain political views made him unpopular. He became intemperate, and his health failed. He decided to try sea bathing and at first imagined that the sea had benefited him, but on his return home on the 18th of July, 1796, he became very ill and died within a few days.

The inhabitants of Dumfries started a subscription for the support of the widow and children of their beloved poet, which was increased by contributions from all over Scotland, and from England also. In the old churchyard at Dumfries is the mausoleum built over the poet's tomb, and a monument was erected to his memory beside the banks of "Bonnie Doon"; but he still lives in the hearts and memories of the Scottish people, who sing his songs and reverence the very walks where he loved to muse.

PLEASURES.

ROBERT BURNS.

But pleasures are like poppies spread,
You seize the flow'r, its bloom is shed;
Or like the snow falls in the river,
A moment white — then melts for ever;
Or like the borealis race,
That flit ere you can point their place;

Or like the rainbow's lovely form
Evanishing amid the storm.

From " Tam O' Shanter."

FLOW GENTLY, SWEET AFTON.

ROBERT BURNS.

FLOW gently, sweet Afton, among thy green braes,
Flow gently, I'll sing thee a song in thy praise;
My Mary's asleep by thy murmuring stream,
Flow gently, sweet Afton, disturb not her dream.

Thou stock-dove whose echo resounds thro' the glen,
Ye wild whistling blackbirds in yon thorny den,
Thou green-crested lapwing, thy screaming forbear,
I charge you disturb not my slumbering fair.

How lofty, sweet Afton, thy neighboring hills,
Far mark'd with the courses of clear, winding rills;
There daily I wander as noon rises high,
My flocks and my Mary's sweet cot in my eye.

How pleasant thy banks and green valleys below,
Where wild in the woodlands the primroses blow;
There oft, as mild ev'ning weeps over the lea,
The sweet-scented birk shades my Mary and me.

Thy crystal stream, Afton, how lovely it glides,
And winds by the cot where my Mary resides;

How wanton thy waters her snowy feet lave,
As gathering sweet flow'rets she stems thy clear wave.

Flow gently, sweet Afton, among thy green braes,
Flow gently, sweet river, the theme of my lays;
My Mary's asleep by thy murmuring stream,
Flow gently, sweet Afton, disturb not her dream.

BONNIE DOON.

ROBERT BURNS.

Ye flowery banks o' bonnie Doon,
　　How can ye blume sae fair?
How can ye chant, ye little birds,
　　And I sae fu' o' care?

Thou 'll break my heart, thou bonnie bird,
　　That sings upon the bough;
Thou minds me o' the happy days,
　　When my fause[1] luve was true.

Thou 'll break my heart, thou bonnie bird,
　　That sings beside thy mate;
For sae I sat, and sae I sang,
　　And wist na o' my fate.

[1] *fause* = false.

Aft hae I rov'd by bonnie Doon
    To see the wood-bine twine,
And ilka [2] bird sang o' its luve,
    And sae did I o' mine.

Wi' lightsome heart I pu'd a rose
    Frae aff its thorny tree;
And my fause luver staw [3] my rose
    But left the thorn wi' me.

[2] *ilka* = every.   [3] *staw* = stole.

O Scotia! my dear, my native soil!
    For whom my warmest wish to Heaven is sent!
Long may thy hardy sons of rustic toil
    Be blest with health, and peace, and sweet content!
    And, oh! may Heaven their simple lives prevent
From luxury's contagion, weak and vile!
    Then, howe'er crowns and coronets be rent,
A virtuous populace may rise the while,
And stand a wall of fire around their much-lov'd isle.

From " The Cotter's Saturday Night."

HISTORY OF OUR FLAG.

THE history of our glorious old flag is of exceeding
interest, and brings back to us a throng of sacred and
thrilling associations. The banner of St. Andrew was
blue, charged with a white saltire or cross, in the form
5 of the letter X, and was used in Scotland as early as
the eleventh century. The banner of St. George was
white, charged with the red cross, and was used in
England as early as the first part of the fourteenth
century. By a royal proclamation, dated April 12,
10 1700, these two crosses were joined together upon the
same banner, forming the ancient national flag of
England.

It was not until Ireland, in 1801, was made a part of
Great Britain, that the present national flag of England,
15 so well known as the "Union Jack," was completed.
But it was the ancient flag of England that constituted

the basis of our American banner. Various other flags had indeed been raised at sundry times by our colonial ancestors. But they were not particularly associated with, or, at least, were not incorporated into and made a part of, the destined "Stars and Stripes." It was 5 after Washington had taken command of the fresh army of the Revolution, at Cambridge, that, January 2, 1776, he unfolded before them the new flag of thirteen stripes of alternate red and white, having upon one of its corners the red and white crosses of 10 St. George and St. Andrew, on a field of blue. And this was the standard which was borne into the city of Boston when it was evacuated by the British troops and was entered by the American army.

Uniting, as it did, the flags of England and America, 15 it showed that the colonists were not yet prepared to sever the tie that bound them to the mother country. By that union of flags they claimed to be a vital and substantial part of the empire of Great Britain, and demanded the rights and privileges which such a rela- 20 tion implied. Yet it was by these thirteen stripes that they made known the union *also* of the thirteen colonies, the stripes of white declaring the purity and innocence of their cause, and the stripes of red giving forth defiance to cruelty and opposition. 25

On the 14th day of June, 1777, it was resolved by Congress, " That the flag of the thirteen United States be thirteen stripes, alternate red and white, and that the Union be thirteen white stars in the blue field."

This resolution was made public September 3, 1777, and the flag that was first made and used in pursuance of it was that which led the Americans to victory at Saratoga. Here the thirteen stars were arranged in a 5 circle, as we sometimes see them now, in order better to express the idea of the union of the states.

In 1794, there having been two more new states added to the Union, it was voted that the alternate stripes, as well as the circling stars, be fifteen in 10 number, and the flag, as thus altered and enlarged, was the one which was borne through all the contests of the War of 1812. But it was thought that the flag would at length become too large if a new stripe should be added with every freshly admitted state. 15 It was therefore enacted, in 1818, that a permanent return should be made to the original number of thirteen stripes, and that the number of stars should henceforth correspond to the growing number of states.

20 Thus the flag would symbolize the Union as it might be at any given period of its history, and also as it was at the very hour of its birth. It was at the same time suggested that these stars, instead of being arranged in a circle, be formed into a single star — a suggestion 25 which we occasionally see adopted. In fine, no particular order seems now to be observed with respect to the arrangement of the constellation. It is enough if only the whole number be there upon that azure field — the blue to be emblematical of perseverance, vigilance, and

justice, each star to signify the glory of the state it may represent, and the whole to be eloquent forever of a Union that must be "one and inseparable."

What precious associations cluster around our flag! Not alone have our fathers set up this banner in the name of God over the well-won battlefields of the Revolution, and over the cities and towns which they rescued from despotic rule; but think where also their descendants have carried it, and raised it in conquest or protection! Through what clouds of dust and smoke has it passed — what storms of shot and shell — what scenes of fire and blood! Not only at Saratoga, at Monmouth, and at Yorktown, but at Lundy's Lane and New Orleans, at Buena Vista and Chapultepec. It is the same glorious old flag which, inscribed with the dying words of Lawrence, — "Don't give up the ship!" — was hoisted on Lake Erie by Commodore Perry just on the eve of his great naval victory — the same old flag which our great chieftain bore in triumph to the proud city of the Aztecs and planted upon the heights of her national palace. Brave hands raised it above the eternal regions of ice in the arctic seas, and have set it up on the summits of the lofty mountains in the distant west.

Where has it not gone, the pride of its friends and the terror of its foes? What countries and what seas has it not visited? Where has not the American citizen been able to stand beneath its guardian folds and defy the world? With what joy and exultation sea-

men and tourists have gazed upon its stars and stripes,
read in it the history of their nation's glory, received
from it the full sense of security, and drawn from it
the inspirations of patriotism! By it how many have
5 sworn fealty to their country!

What bursts of magnificent eloquence it has called
forth from Webster and from Everett! What lyric
strains of poetry from Drake and Holmes! How
many heroes its folds have covered in death! How
10 many have lived for it, and how many have died for
it! How many, living and dying, have said, in their
enthusiastic devotion to its honor, like that young
wounded sufferer in the streets of Baltimore, "Oh, the
flag! the Stars and Stripes!" And wherever that flag
15 has gone it has been a herald of a better day; it has
been the pledge of freedom, of justice, of order, of
civilization, and of Christianity. Tyrants only have
hated it, and the enemies of mankind alone have
trampled it to the earth. All who sigh for the triumph
20 of truth and righteousness love and salute it.

*

THE AMERICAN FLAG.

JOSEPH RODMAN DRAKE.

JOSEPH RODMAN DRAKE was born in New York City, in 1795. He wrote a number of poems which gave promise of his gaining high rank as a poet; but he died at the age of twenty-four.

WHEN Freedom from her mountain height
   Unfurled her standard to the air,
She tore the azure robe of night,
   And set the stars of glory there;
She mingled with its gorgeous dyes
The milky baldric of the skies,
And striped its pure, celestial white
With streakings of the morning light;
Then from his mansion in the sun
She called her eagle-bearer down,
And gave into his mighty hand
The symbol of her chosen land.

Flag of the brave, thy folds shall fly,
The sign of hope and triumph high !
When speaks the signal trumpet tone,
And the long line comes gleaming on
(Ere yet the life-blood, warm and wet,
Has dimmed the glistening bayonet)
Each soldier eye shall brightly turn
To where thy sky-born glories burn,
And as his springing steps advance,

Catch war and vengeance from the glance.
And when the cannon-mouthings loud
Heave in wild wreaths the battle-shroud,
And gory sabers rise and fall
Like shoots of flame on midnight's pall,
Then shall thy meteor glances glow,
    And cowering foes shall sink beneath
Each gallant arm that strikes below
    That lovely messenger of death.

Flag of the seas, on ocean wave
Thy stars shall glitter o'er the brave ;
When death, careering on the gale,
Sweeps darkly round the bellied sail,
And frighted waves rush wildly back
Before the broadside's reeling rack,
Each dying wanderer of the sea
Shall look at once to Heaven and thee,
And smile to see thy splendors fly
In triumph o'er his closing eye.

Flag of the free heart's hope and home,
    By angel hands to valor given,
Thy stars have lit the welkin dome,
    And all thy hues were born in heaven.
Forever float that standard sheet !
    Where breathes the foe, but falls before us,
With Freedom's soil beneath our feet,
    And Freedom's banner streaming o'er us ?

DREAM-CHILDREN: A REVERIE.

CHARLES LAMB.

CHARLES LAMB was born in London on the 10th of February, 1775.

He was sent to school at Christ's Hospital when he was eight years old and remained there for seven years. Charles was a delicate, sensitive boy, and there was little in the dull, hard life of this school to make him happy.

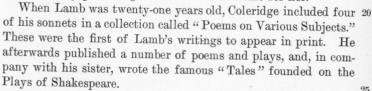

He was fortunate in having Coleridge for a companion, with whom he formed a lifelong friendship.

After leaving school Lamb held a clerkship for a short time, and then entered an accountant's office, where he remained for over thirty years.

A terrible sorrow shadowed his life. His sister Mary became violently insane and was placed in an asylum. After the recovery of her health her brother obtained her release by promising to watch over and care for her.

When Lamb was twenty-one years old, Coleridge included four 20 of his sonnets in a collection called "Poems on Various Subjects." These were the first of Lamb's writings to appear in print. He afterwards published a number of poems and plays, and, in company with his sister, wrote the famous "Tales" founded on the Plays of Shakespeare.

25

When Lamb was about forty-five years old, he wrote a number of essays, signing himself "Elia," and it is upon these that his literary fame rests. They are delicate in fancy and sparkle with wit and humor. He died on the 27th of December, 1834.

CHILDREN love to listen to stories about their elders 30 when *they* were children; to stretch their imagination

to the conception of a traditionary great-uncle, or a
grandame, whom they never saw. It was in this spirit
that my little ones crept about me the other evening
to hear about their great-grandmother Field, who lived
5 in a great house in Norfolk (a hundred times bigger
than that in which they and papa lived), which had
been the scene — so at least it was generally believed
in that part of the country — of the tragic incidents
which they had lately become familiar with from the
10 ballad of the "Children in the Wood." Certain it is
that the whole story of the children and their cruel
uncle was to be seen fairly carved out in wood upon
the chimney-piece of the great hall, the whole story
down to the Robin Redbreast; till a foolish rich per-
15 son pulled it down to set up a marble one of modern
invention in its stead, with no story upon it.

Here Alice put on one of her dear mother's looks, too
tender to be called upbraiding. Then I went on to
say how good their great-grandmother Field was; how
20 beloved and respected by everybody, though she was
not indeed the mistress of this great house, but had
only the charge of it (and yet in some respects she
might be said to be the mistress of it too) committed
to her by the owner, who preferred living in a newer
25 and more fashionable mansion which he had purchased
somewhere in the adjoining county; but still she lived
in it in a manner as if it had been her own, and kept
up the dignity of the great house in a sort while she
lived, which afterwards came to decay, and was nearly

pulled down, and all its old ornaments stripped and carried away to the owner's other house, where they were set up, and looked as awkward as if some one were to carry away the old tombs they had seen lately at the Abbey, and stick them up in Lady C.'s tawdry ₅ gilt drawing-room. Here John smiled, as much as to say, "That would be foolish indeed."

And then I told how, when she came to die, her funeral was attended by a concourse of all the poor, and some of the gentry too, of the neighborhood for ₁₀ many miles round, to show their respect for her memory, because she had been such a good woman; so good indeed that she knew all the Psalter by heart, ay, and a great part of the Testament besides. Here little Alice spread her hands. Then I told her what a tall, ₁₅ upright, graceful person their great-grandmother Field once was; and how in her youth she was esteemed the best dancer, — here Alice's little right foot played an involuntary movement, till, upon my looking grave, it desisted, — the best dancer in the country. ₂₀

Then I told how good she was to all her grandchildren, having us to the great house in the holidays, where I in particular used to spend many hours by myself in gazing upon the old busts of the twelve Cæsars that had been emperors of Rome, till the old marble heads would ₂₅ seem to live again or I to be turned into marble with them. How I never could be tired with roaming about that huge mansion with its vast empty rooms, with their wornout hangings, fluttering tapestry, and carved

oaken panels with the gilding almost rubbed out, —
sometimes in the spacious, old-fashioned gardens, which
I had almost to myself, unless when now and then a
solitary gardening man would cross me.

5   How the nectarines and peaches hung upon the
walls without my ever offering to pluck them, because
they were forbidden fruit, unless now and then, — and
because I had more pleasure in strolling about among
the old melancholy-looking yew trees, or the firs, and
10 picking up the red berries, and the fir apples, which
were good for nothing but to look at, — or in lying
about upon the fresh grass with all the fine garden
smells around me, — or basking in the orangery, till I
could almost fancy myself ripening too along with the
15 oranges and the limes in that grateful warmth, — or in
watching the dace that darted to and fro in the fish
pond at the bottom of the garden, with here and there
a great sulky pike hanging midway down the water
in silent state, as if it mocked at their impertinent
20 friskings. I had more pleasure in these busy-idle diversions than in all the sweet flavors of peaches, nectarines,
oranges, and such-like common baits of children.

  Here John slyly deposited back upon the plate a
bunch of grapes, which, not unobserved by Alice, he
25 had meditated dividing with her, and both seemed willing to relinquish them for the present as irrelevant.
Then, in somewhat a more heightened tone, I told how,
though their great-grandmother Field loved all her
grandchildren, yet in an especial manner she might be

said to love their uncle, John L——, because he was so handsome and spirited a youth, and a king to the rest of us. Instead of moping about in solitary corners, like some of us, he would mount the most mettlesome horse he could get, when but an imp no bigger than themselves, and make it carry him half over the county in a morning, and join the hunters when there were any out, — and yet he loved the old great house and gardens too, but had too much spirit to be always pent up within their boundaries, — and how their uncle grew up to man's estate as brave as he was handsome, to the admiration of everybody, but of their great-grand-mother Field most especially; and how he used to carry me upon his back when I was a lame-footed boy — for he was a good bit older than me — many a mile when I could not walk for pain.

In after life he became lame-footed too, and I did not always (I fear) make allowances enough for him when he was impatient and in pain, nor remember sufficiently how considerate he had been to me when I was lame-footed; and how when he died, though he had not yet been dead an hour, it seemed as if he had died a great while ago, such a distance there is betwixt life and death; and how I bore his death, as I thought pretty well at first, but afterwards it haunted and haunted me; and though I did not cry or take it to heart as some do, and as I think he would have done if I had died, yet I missed him all day long, and knew not till then how much I had loved him. I missed his kindness, and I missed his crossness, and wished him to be alive again.

Here the children fell a-crying and asked if their little mourning which they had on was not for Uncle John, and they looked up, and prayed me not to go on about their uncle, but to tell them some stories about their pretty dead mother.

Then I told how for seven long years, in hope sometimes, sometimes in despair, yet persisting ever, I courted the fair Alice W——n; and, as much as children could understand, I explained to them what coyness, and difficulty, and denial meant in maidens, — when suddenly, turning to Alice, the soul of the first Alice looked out at her eyes with such a reality of representment that I became in doubt which of them stood there before me, or whose that bright hair was. While I stood gazing, both the children gradually grew fainter to my view, receding, and still receding, till nothing at last but two mournful features were seen in the uttermost distance, which, without speech, strangely impressed upon me the effects of speech: "We are not of Alice, nor of thee, nor are we children at all. The children of Alice call Bartrum father. We are nothing; less than nothing, and dreams"; — and, immediately awaking, I found myself quietly seated in my bachelor armchair, where I had fallen asleep.

THE SHANDON BELLS.

FATHER PROUT.

FRANCIS SYLVESTER MAH'ONY, better known by his pen-name of Father Prout, was born in Ireland in 1804, and died in Paris in 1866.

He was a contributor of brilliant, witty, and fantastic productions to the leading periodicals of his time. His poem, "The 5 Shandon Bells," is the best known of his productions.

WITH deep affection
And recollection,
I often think of those Shandon bells,
Whose sounds so wild would,
In days of childhood,
Fling round my cradle their magic spells.

On this I ponder
Where'er I wander,
And thus grow fonder, sweet Cork, of thee;
With thy bells of Shandon,
That sound so grand on
The pleasant waters of the river Lee.

I 've heard bells chiming
Full many a clime in,
Tolling sublime in cathedral shrine,
While at a glib rate
Brass tongues would vibrate;
But all their music spoke naught like thine:

For memory dwelling
On each proud swelling
Of the belfry knelling its bold notes free,
Made the bells of Shandon
Sound far more grand on
The pleasant waters of the river Lee.

I 've heard bells tolling
Old Adrian's Mole in,
Their thunder rolling from the Vatican,
And cymbals glorious
Swinging uproarious
In the gorgeous turrets of Notre Dame;

But thy sounds were sweeter
Than the dome of Peter
Flings o'er the Tiber, pealing solemnly;—
O, the bells of Shandon
Sound far more grand on
The pleasant waters of the river Lee!

Such empty phantom
I freely grant them ;
But there is an anthem more dear to me,
'T is the bells of Shandon,
That sound so grand on
The pleasant waters of the river Lee.

DON QUIXOTE AND THE LIONS.

MIGUEL DE CERVANTES.

MIGUEL DE CERVANTES was born in the province of New Castile, Spain, in 1547.   He was descended from a noble family, his grandfather having been a knight of some distinction.

Cervantes received a good education and soon showed a talent for writing.   5

At the age of twenty-one he became a soldier and won glory, during a sea battle, by rising from a sick-bed and taking command of some soldiers at the post of greatest danger, declaring his resolve to die fighting for his God and his king, rather than to remain under shelter and take care of his health.   10

Some years later, Cervantes was captured by the Algerians and made a slave; but after five years of captivity, which he bore with wonderful heroism, he was ransomed and returned to Spain, where he rejoined his regiment and distinguished himself.   15

He left the army when he was about thirty-five years of age, and engaged in writing poems and plays.   Many years of hardship and poverty followed.

His great work "Don Quixote" was published in 1604, when he was fifty-seven years old.   It was intended to ridicule the 20 extravagant stories of chivalry which were popular at that time. This book has been translated into many languages, and although nearly three hundred years have passed since it was written, it still retains its popularity.

Cervantes died at Madrid in 1616, the same year in which 25 Shakespeare died in England.

THE history relates that when Don Quixote called out to Sancho Panza, his servant, he was buying some curds of the shepherds, and being summoned in such haste to his master he knew not what to do with them; 30

so to prevent their being wasted he poured them into the helmet and hurried away to receive the commands of his master.

"Sancho," said the knight, "give me my helmet; for either I know little of adventures, or that which I descry yonder is one that will oblige me to have recourse to arms."

He of the green riding coat, hearing this, looked on all sides and could see nothing but a cart coming towards them with two or three small flags, by which he thought it probable that it was conveying some of the King's money.

He mentioned his conjecture to Don Quixote, but his only reply was: "Forewarned, forearmed; to be prepared is half the victory. I know by experience that I have enemies both visible and invisible, and I know not when, nor from what quarter, nor at what time, nor in what shape they may attack me."

He then took his helmet from Sancho, and without perceiving the contents, clapped it hastily upon his head. The curds being squeezed and pressed, the whey began to run down the face and beard of the knight to his great consternation.

"What can this mean, Sancho?" said he; "methinks my skull is softening, or my brains melting, or I sweat from head to foot! If so, it is certainly not through fear, though I verily believe that this will prove a terrible adventure."

Sancho said nothing but gave him a cloth. Don

Quixote took off his helmet to see what was so cool to his head. "By my soul!" he exclaimed, "these are curds which thou hast put here, thou unmannerly squire!"

Sancho replied with much coolness and cunning: "If they are curds, sir, I should sooner have put them into my stomach than into your Worship's helmet."

"Well," said Don Quixote, "there may be something in that"; and after having wiped his head, face, beard, and helmet, again put it on, and fixing himself firm in his stirrups, adjusting his sword, and grasping his lance he exclaimed: "Now, come what may, I am prepared to encounter the enemy!"

They were soon overtaken by the cart with the flags, which was attended only by the driver, who rode upon one of the mules, and a man sitting upon the cart.

Don Quixote planted himself just before them and said: "Whither go ye, brethren? What carriage is this? What does it contain, and what are those banners?"

"The cart is mine," answered the carter, "and in it are two fierce lions, which the general of Oran is sending to court as a present to his Majesty; the flags belong to our liege, the King, to show that what is in the cart belongs to him."

"And are the lions large?" demanded Don Quixote.

"Larger never came from Africa to Spain," said the man on the front of the cart; "I am their keeper, and in my time have had charge of many lions, but never of any so large as these. Not having eaten to-day, they are now hungry; therefore, sir, stand aside, for we must make haste to the place where they are to be fed."

"What!" said Don Quixote with a scornful smile, 5 "lion whelps against me! Against me, your puny monsters! and at this time of day! By yon blessed sun! those that sent them hither shall see whether I am a man to be scared by lions. Alight, honest friend, and since you are their keeper, open the cages and turn 10 out your savages of the desert; for in the midst of this field I will make them know who Don Quixote is, in spite of the enchanters that sent them hither to me. I vow, Don Rascal, if thou dost not instantly open the cages, with this lance I will pin thee to the cart."

15 Whilst the keeper was unbarring the first grate, Don Quixote deliberated whether it would be better to engage on horseback or not; and finally determined it should be on foot, as Roxinante, his steed, might be terrified at sight of the lions. He therefore 20 leaped from his horse, flung aside his lance, braced on his shield, and drew his sword; then slowly advancing, with marvelous courage and an undaunted heart, he planted himself before the lion's cage.

The keeper, seeing that he could not avoid letting 25 loose the lions without incurring the resentment of the angry and daring knight, set wide open the door of the first cage where lay a monster, which appeared to be of an extraordinary size and of a hideous and frightful aspect.

The first thing the creature did was to turn himself round in the cage, reach out a paw, and stretch himself at full length. Then he opened his mouth and yawned very leisurely; after which he threw out some half yard of tongue, wherewith he licked and washed 5 his face. This done, he thrust his head out of the cage and stared round on all sides with eyes like redhot coals; a sight to have struck temerity itself with terror!

Don Quixote observed him with fixed attention, im- 10 patient for him to leap out of his den, that he might grapple with him and tear him to pieces.

But the generous lion, after having stared about him, turned his back upon Don Quixote, and calmly and quietly laid himself down again in his cage. 15

Upon which Don Quixote ordered the keeper to give him some blows, and provoke him to come forth. "That I will not do," answered the keeper; "for, should I provoke him, I shall be the first whom he will tear to pieces. The lion has the door open to 20 him, and the liberty to come forth; and since he has not done so, he will not come out to-day.

"The greatness of your Worship's courage is already sufficiently shown; no brave combatant is bound to do more than challenge his foe and wait his coming in the 25 field; and if the antagonist fails to meet him, the disgrace falls upon him, while the challenger is entitled to the crown of victory."

"That is true," answered Don Quixote; "shut the

door, friend, and give me a certificate, in the best form you can, of what you have seen me perform."

The keeper closed the door, and Don Quixote, having fixed the linen cloth with which he had wiped the
5 curds from his face, upon the end of his lance, began to hail the troop in the distance, who were still retiring, looking around at every step.

They all stopped, and saw that it was Don Quixote that made the sign; and their fear in some degree abat-
10 ing, they ventured to return slowly, till they could distinctly hear the words of Don Quixote, who continued calling to them.

When they had reached the cart again, Don Quixote said to the driver: "Now, friend, put on your mules
15 again and proceed on your journey; and, Sancho, give two crowns to him and the keeper to make them amends for this delay."

" That I will with all my heart," answered Sancho; "but what is become of the lions? Are they dead or
20 alive ? "

The keeper then gave an account of the conflict, enlarging to the best of his skill on the valor of Don Quixote, at sight of whom the daunted lion would not or durst not stir out of his cage, though he held open
25 the door a good while; and upon his representing to the knight that it was tempting God to provoke the lion and force him out, he had, at length, very reluctantly permitted him to close it.

Sancho gave the gold crowns; the carter yoked his

mules; the keeper thanked Don Quixote for his present, and promised to relate this valorous exploit to the King himself when he arrived at court.

"If, perchance, his Majesty," said Don Quixote, "should inquire who performed it, tell him the 5 knight of the lions; for henceforward I resolve that the title I have hitherto borne, of the knight of the sorrowful figure, shall be thus changed, and herein I follow the ancient practice of knights-errant, who changed their names at pleasure." 10

From " Don Quixote."

THE SIGNING OF THE DECLARATION.

GEORGE LIPPARD.

IT is a cloudless summer day; a clear blue sky arches and expands above a quaint edifice, rising among the giant trees in the center of a wide city. That edifice is built of plain red brick, with heavy
5 window frames and a massive hall door.

Such is the statehouse of Philadelphia in the year of our Lord 1776.

In yonder wooden steeple, which crowns the summit of that red brick statehouse, stands an old man with
10 snow-white hair and sunburnt face. He is clad in humble attire, yet his eye gleams as it is fixed on the ponderous outline of the bell suspended in the steeple there. By his side, gazing into his sunburnt face in wonder, stands a flaxen-haired boy with laughing eyes
15 of summer blue. The old man ponders for a moment upon the strange words written upon the bell, then, gathering the boy in his arms, he speaks: "Look here, my child. Will you do this old man a kindness? Then hasten down the stairs and wait in the hall
20 below till a man gives you a message for me; when he gives you that word, run out into the street and shout it up to me. Do you mind?" The boy sprang from the old man's arms and threaded his way down the dark stairs.

Many minutes passed. The old bell keeper was alone. "Ah," groaned the old man, "he has forgotten me!" As the word was upon his lips a merry ringing laugh broke on his ear. And there, among the crowd on the pavement, stood the blue-eyed boy, clapping his tiny hands, while the breeze blew his flaxen hair all about his face, and swelling his little chest he raised himself on tiptoe and shouted the single word "Ring!"

Do you see that old man's eye fire? Do you see that arm so suddenly bared to the shoulder? Do you see that withered hand grasping the iron tongue of the bell? That old man is young again. His veins are filling with a new life. Backward and forward, with sturdy strokes, he swings the tongue. The bell peals out; the crowds in the street hear it and burst forth in one long shout. Old "Delaware" hears it and gives it back on the cheers of her thousand sailors. The city hears it and starts up, from desk and workshop, as if an earthquake had spoken.

Under that very bell, pealing out at noonday, in an old hall, fifty-six traders, farmers, and mechanics had assembled to break the shackles of the world. The committee, who have been out all night, are about to appear. At last the door opens and they advance to the front. The parchment is laid on the table. Shall it be signed or not? Then ensues a high and stormy debate. Then the faint-hearted cringe in corners. Then Thomas Jefferson speaks his few bold words, and John Adams pours out his whole soul.

Still there is a doubt; and that pale-faced man, rising in one corner, squeaks out something about "axes, scaffolds, and a gibbet." A tall, slender man rises, and his dark eye burns, while his words ring
5 through the halls: "Gibbets! They may stretch our necks on every scaffold in the land. They may turn every rock into a gibbet, every tree into a gallows; and yet the words written on that parchment can never die. They may pour out our blood on a thou-
10 sand altars, and yet, from every drop that dyes the axe or drips on the sawdust of the block, a new martyr to freedom will spring into existence. What! are these shrinking hearts and faltering voices here, when the very dead upon our battlefields arise and call upon us
15 to sign that parchment or be accursed forever?

"Sign! if the next moment the gibbet's rope is around your neck. Sign! if the next moment this hall ring with the echo of the falling axe. Sign! by all your hopes in life or death, as husbands, as fathers,
20 as men! Sign your names to that parchment!

"Yes! were my soul trembling on the verge of eternity, were this voice choking in the last struggle, I would still, with the last impulse of that soul, with the last gasp of that voice, implore you to remember this
25 truth: God has given America to the free. Yes! as I sink down into the gloomy shadow of the grave, with my last breath I would beg of you to sign that parchment."

KING'S MOUNTAIN.

A Ballad of the Carolinas.

WILLIAM GILMORE SIMMS.

WILLIAM GILMORE SIMMS was born at Charleston, South
Carolina, in 1806, and died at Savannah in 1870.

He made verses when but seven years of age, and during the
War of 1812 wrote many a rhyme celebrating the victories of
the American army and navy.   5

His early education was received in the public schools of his
native city. At the age of eighteen he began the study of law,
and was afterwards admitted to the bar. After practicing law
for a year, he purchased an interest in a newspaper, but this
venture proved unsuccessful.   10

Mr. Simms then resolved to be an author, and from that time
was constantly at work. He wrote plays, poems, novels, and
historical romances.

What Cooper was to the North, Simms was to the South.
His writings are full of vivid and picturesque scenes, telling of 15
the brave and chivalrous deeds of the people in his section of
the country. He was a true American and a man of pleasant
and genial manners.

HARK! 't is the voice of the mountain,
　　And it speaks to our heart in its pride,
As it tells of the bearing of heroes,
　　Who compassed its summits and died!
How they gathered to strife as the eagles,
　　When the foemen had clambered the height!
How, with scent keen and eager as beagles,
　　They hunted them down for the fight!

Hark! through the gorge of the valley,
　'T is the bugle that tells of the foe;
Our own quickly sounds for the rally,
　And we snatch down the rifle and go.
As the hunters who hear of the panther,
　Each arms him and leaps to his steed,
Rides forth through the desolate antre,
　With the knife and the rifle at need.

From a thousand deep gorges they gather —
　From the cot lowly perched by the rill,
The cabin half hid in the heather,
　'Neath the crag where the eagle keeps still;
Each lonely at first in his roaming,
　Till the vale to the sight opens fair,
And he sees the low cot through the gloaming,
　When his bugle gives tongue to the air.

Thus a thousand brave hunters assemble
　For the hunt of the insolent foe;
And soon shall his myrmidons tremble
　'Neath the shock of the thunderbolt's blow.
Down the lone heights now wind they together,
　As the mountain brooks flow to the vale,
And now, as they group on the heather,
　The keen scout delivers his tale: —

"The British — the Tories are on us;
　And now is the moment to prove

To the women whose virtues have won us,
   That our virtues are worthy their love !
They have swept the vast valleys below us,
   With fire, to the hills from the sea ;
And here would they seek to o'erthrow us,
   In a realm which our eagle makes free ! "

No war council suffered to trifle
   With the hours devote to the deed ;
Swift followed the grasp of the rifle,
   Swift followed the bound to the steed ;
And soon, to the eyes of our yeomen,
   All panting with rage at the sight,
Gleamed the long wavy tents of the foeman,
   As he lay in his camp on the height.

Grim dashed they away as they bounded, —
   The hunters to hem in the prey, —
And with Deckard's long rifles surrounded,
   Then the British rose fast to the fray ;
And never, with arms of more vigor,
   Did their bayonets press through the strife,
Where, with every swift pull of the trigger,
   The sharpshooters dashed out a life !

'T was the meeting of eagles and lions,
   'T was the rushing of tempests and waves,
Insolent triumph 'gainst patriot defiance,
   Born freemen 'gainst sycophant slaves :

Scotch Ferguson sounding his whistle,
   As from danger to danger he flies,
Feels the moral that lies in Scotch thistle,
   With its " touch me who dare ! " and he dies.

An hour, and the battle is over ;
   The eagles are rending the prey ;
The serpents seek flight into cover,
   But the terror still stands in the way :
More dreadful the doom that on treason
   Avenges the wrongs of the state ;
And the oak tree for many a season
   Bears its fruit for the vultures of Fate.

TRAILING ARBUTUS.

HENRY WARD BEECHER.

HENRY WARD BEECHER was born in Litchfield, Conn., on the 24th of June, 1813. He was graduated from Amherst College and then studied theology with his father, the Rev. Lyman Beecher.

He became pastor of the Plymouth Church, Brooklyn, when he was thirty-four years of age and held this position until his death, in 1887. 5

Mr. Beecher was an author and orator as well as a preacher.

. . . THE ground was white in spots with half-melted snow. A few whirls of snow had come down in the night, and the air was too cold to change to rain. Some green leaves, in sheltered nooks, had accepted the advances of the sun and were preparing for the summer. But that which I came to search after was trailing arbutus, one of the most exquisite of all Nature's fondlings. 15

I did not seek in vain. The hills were covered with it. Its gay whorls of buds peeped forth from ruffles of snow in the most charming beauty. Many blossoms, too, quite expanded, did I find ; some pure white, and a few more deliciously suffused with pink. For nearly 20 an hour I wandered up and down, in pleasant fancies, searching, plucking, and arranging these most beautiful of all early blossoms.

Who would suspect by the leaf what rare delicacy was to be in the blossom ? Like some people of plain 25 and hard exterior, but of sweet disposition, it was all the more pleasant from the surprise of contrast. All winter long this little thing must have slumbered with dreams, at least, of spring. It has waited for no pioneer 5 or guide, but started of its own self and led the way for all the flowers on this hillside.

Its little viny stem creeps close to the ground, humble, faithful, and showing how the purest white may lay its cheek in the very dirt without soil or taint.

10 The odor of the arbutus is exquisite, and as delicate as the plant is modest. Some flowers seem determined to make an impression on you. They stare at you. They dazzle your eyes. If you smell them, they overfill your sense with their fragrance. They leave 15 nothing for your gentleness and generosity, but do everything themselves.

But this sweet nestler of the spring hills is so secluded, half covered with russet leaves, that you would not suspect its graces, did you not stoop to uncover 20 the vine, to lift it up, and then you espy its secluded beauty.

If you smell it, at first it seems hardly to have an odor. But there steals out of it at length the finest, rarest scent, that rather cites desire than satisfies your 25 sense. It is coy, without designing to be so, and its reserve plays upon the imagination far more than could a more positive way.

Without doubt there are intrinsic beauties in plants and flowers, and yet very much of pleasure depends upon their relations to the seasons, to the places where they grow, and to our own moods. No midsummer flower can produce the thrill that the earliest blossoms bring, which tell us that winter is gone, that growing days have come! 5

Indeed, it often happens that the air is cold and the face of earth is brown, so that we have no suspicion that it is time for anything to sprout, until we chance upon a flower. That reveals what our senses had failed to perceive — a warmth in the air, a warmth in the soil, 10 an advance in the seasons!

Strange that a silent white flower, growing on a hillside, measures the astronomic changes, and, more than all our senses, discerns that the sun is traveling back from his far southward flight! 15

Sometimes we admire flowers for their boldness, in places where that quality seems fit. When meadows and fields are gorgeous, we look for some flower that shall give the climax. An intensity often serves to reveal the nature of things in all their several grada- 20 tions.

A violet color in these early spring days would not please half so well as these pure whites or tender pinks. We like snowdrops and crocuses to come up pale colored, as if born of the snow and carrying 25 their mother's complexion. But later, when the eye is used to blossoms, we wish deeper effects and profusions of color, which, had they existed earlier, would have offended us.

Flowers seem to have a peculiar power over some natures. Of course they gratify the original faculties of form, color, odor ; but that is the least part of their effect. They have a mysterious and subtle influence upon the feelings, not unlike some strains of music. They relax the tenseness of the mind. They dissolve its rigor.

In their presence one finds an almost magnetic tremulousness, as if they were messengers from the spirit world, and conveyed an atmosphere with them in which the feelings find soothing, pleasure, and peacefulness.

Besides this, they are provocative of imagination. They set the mind full of fancies. They seem to be pretty and innocent jugglers that play their charms and incantations upon the senses and the fancy, and lead off the thoughts in gay analogies or curious medleys of fantastic dreaming.

From " Eyes and Ears."

THE CHRISTIAN KNIGHT AND THE SARACEN CAVALIER.

SIR WALTER SCOTT.

For a sketch of the life of Sir Walter Scott, see "Cyr's Fourth Reader."

THE burning sun of Syria had not yet attained its highest point in the horizon when a knight of the Red Cross, who had left his distant northern home and joined the host of the crusaders in Palestine, was pacing slowly along the sandy deserts which lie in the vicinity of the Dead Sea, where the waves of the Jordan pour themselves into an inland sea from which there is no discharge of waters.

The dress of the rider and the accouterments of his horse were peculiarly unfit for the traveler in such a country. A coat of linked mail, with long sleeves, plated gauntlets, and a steel breastplate, had not been esteemed a sufficient weight of armor; there was also his triangular shield suspended round his neck, and his barred helmet of steel, over which he had a hood and collar of mail, which was drawn around the warrior's shoulders and throat and filled up the vacancy between the hauberk and the headpiece. His lower limbs were sheathed, like his body, in flexible mail, securing the legs and thighs, while the feet rested in plated shoes, which corresponded with the gauntlets.

A long, broad, straight-shaped, double-edged falchion, with a handle formed like a cross, corresponded with a stout poniard on the other side. The knight also bore,

secured to his saddle, with one end resting on his stirrup, the long steel-headed lance, his own proper weapon,
which, as he rode, projected backwards and displayed
its little *pennoncelle*, to dally with the faint breeze or
5 drop in the dead calm. To this cumbrous equipment
must be added a surcoat of embroidered cloth, much
frayed and worn, which was thus far useful that it
excluded the burning rays of the sun from the armor,
which they would otherwise have rendered intolerable
10 to the wearer.

The surcoat bore in several places the arms of the
owner, although much defaced. These seemed to be
a couchant leopard with the motto: *"I sleep — wake me
not."* An outline of the same device might be traced on
15 his shield, though many a blow had almost defaced the
painting. The flat top of his cumbrous cylindrical
helmet was unadorned with any crest.

The accouterments of the horse were scarcely less
massive and unwieldy than those of the rider. The
20 animal had a heavy saddle plated with steel, uniting
in front with a species of breastplate, and behind with
defensive armor made to cover the loins. Then there
was a steel axe or hammer, called a mace-of-arms,
which hung to the saddlebow; the reins were secured
25 by chain work, and the front stall of the bridle was a
steel plate with apertures for the eyes and nostrils,
having in the midst a short, sharp pike projecting from
the forehead of the horse like the horn of the fabulous
unicorn.

As the Knight of the Couchant Leopard continued to fix his eyes attentively on the yet distant cluster of palm trees, it seemed to him as if some object were moving among them. The distant form separated itself from the trees, which partly hid its motions, and advanced toward the knight with a speed which soon showed a mounted horseman, whom his turban, long spear, and green caftan floating in the wind, on his nearer approach, proved to be a Saracen cavalier. "In the desert," saith an Eastern proverb, "no man meets a friend." The crusader was totally indifferent whether the infidel, who now approached on his gallant barb as if borne on the wings of an eagle, came as a friend or foe; perhaps as a vowed champion of the cross, he might rather have preferred the latter. He disengaged his lance from his saddle, seized it with the right hand, placed it in rest with its point half elevated, gathered up the reins in the left, waked his horse's mettle with the spur, and prepared to encounter the stranger with the calm self-confidence belonging to the victor of many contests.

The Saracen came on at the speedy gallop of an Arab horseman, managing his steed more by his limbs and the inflection of his body than by any use of the reins, which hung loose in his left hand; so that he was enabled to wield the light, round buckler of the skin of the rhinoceros, ornamented with silver loops which he wore on his arm, swinging it as if he meant to oppose its slender circle to the formidable thrust of the Western lance.

His own long spear was not couched or leveled like that of his antagonist, but grasped by the middle with his right hand and brandished at arm's length above his head. As the cavalier approached his enemy at full career, he seemed to expect that the Knight of the Leopard would put his horse to the gallop to encounter him.

But the Christian knight, well acquainted with the customs of Eastern warriors, did not mean to exhaust his good horse by any unnecessary exertion ; and, on the contrary, made a dead halt, confident that if the enemy advanced to the actual shock, his own weight and that of his powerful charger would give him sufficient advantage without the additional momentum of rapid motion.

Equally sensible and apprehensive of such a probable result, the Saracen cavalier, when he had approached within twice the length of his lance, wheeled his steed to the left with inimitable dexterity and rode twice around his antagonist, who, turning without quitting his ground, and presenting his front constantly to his enemy, frustrated his attempts to attack him on an unguarded point; so that the Saracen, wheeling his horse, was fain to retreat to the distance of a hundred yards.

A second time, like a hawk attacking a heron, the heathen renewed the charge, and a second time was fain to retreat without coming to a close struggle. A third time he approached in the same manner, when the

Christian knight, desirous to terminate this illusory
warfare, in which he might at length have been worn
out by the activity of his foeman, suddenly seized the
mace which hung at his saddlebow, and, with a strong
hand and unerring aim, hurled it against the head of 5
the Emir; for such, and not less, his enemy appeared.

The Saracen was just aware of the formidable missile in time to interpose his light buckler betwixt the
mace and his head; but the violence of the blow forced
the buckler down on his turban, and though that defense 10
also contributed to deaden its violence, the Saracen was
beaten from his horse.

Ere the Christian could avail himself of this mishap
his nimble foeman sprang from the ground, and, calling
on his steed, which instantly returned to his side, he 15
leaped into his seat without touching the stirrup and
regained all the advantage of which the Knight of the
Leopard had hoped to deprive him.

But the latter had in the meanwhile recovered his
mace, and the Eastern cavalier, who remembered the 20
strength and dexterity with which his antagonist had
aimed it, seemed to keep cautiously out of reach of that
weapon of which he had so lately felt the force; while
he showed his purpose of waging a distant warfare with
missile weapons of his own.   25

Planting his long spear in the sand at a distance
from the scene of combat, he strung with great address
a short bow which he carried at his back, and, putting
his horse to the gallop, once more described two or

three circles of a wider extent than formerly, in the course of which he discharged six arrows at the Christian with such unerring skill that the goodness of his harness alone saved him from being wounded in as
5 many places. The seventh shaft apparently found a less perfect part of the armor, and the Christian dropped heavily from his horse.

But what was the surprise of the Saracen, when, dismounting to examine the condition of his prostrate
10 enemy, he found himself suddenly within the grasp of the European, who had had recourse to this artifice to bring his enemy within his reach. Even in this deadly grapple the Saracen was saved by his agility and presence of mind. He unloosed the sword-belt in which the
15 Knight of the Leopard had fixed his hold, and thus eluding his fatal grasp, mounted his horse, which seemed to watch his motions with the intelligence of a human being, and again rode off.

But in the last encounter the Saracen had lost his
20 sword and his quiver of arrows, both of which were attached to the girdle, which he was obliged to abandon. He had also lost his turban in the struggle. These disadvantages seemed to incline the Moslem to a truce; he approached the Christian with his
25 right hand extended, but no longer in a menacing attitude.

"There is a truce betwixt our nations," he said in the language commonly used for the purpose of communication with the crusaders; "wherefore should there be war betwixt thee and me? Let there be peace betwixt us."

"I am well contented," answered he of the Couchant Leopard, "but what security dost thou offer that thou wilt observe the truce?" 5

"The word of a follower of the Prophet was never broken," answered the Emir. "It is thou, brave Nazarene, from whom I should demand security, did I not know that treason seldom dwells with courage."

The crusader felt that the confidence of the Moslem 10 made him ashamed of his own doubts.

"By the cross of my sword," he said, laying his hand on the weapon as he spoke, "I will be true companion to thee, Saracen, while our fortune wills that we remain in company together." 15

"By Mohammed, Prophet of God, and by Allah, God of the Prophet," replied his late foeman, "there is not treachery in my heart towards thee. And now wend we to yonder fountain, for the hour of rest is at hand, and the stream had hardly touched my lip when I was 20 called to battle by thy approach."

The Knight of the Couchant Leopard yielded a ready and courteous assent; and the late foes, without an angry look or gesture of doubt, rode side by side to the little cluster of palm trees. 25

From " The Talisman."

A MYSTERIOUS VISITOR.

THOMAS CARLYLE.

THOMAS CARLYLE was born in a little village in Scotland, in the year 1795.

His father, James Carlyle, was a poor mason, so poor that at times there was scarcely enough food in the house for his
5 family; but the father resolved that the boy should have an education, and saved, little by little, the money to pay for it.

When Thomas was ten years old, he and his father walked to the town of Annan, where Thomas was to enter the academy.

The father little dreamed, as they trudged along together, that one day his son would be famous as one of the world's greatest writers, so great that even the Queen of England would wish to talk with him.

He studied at the academy of Annan for three years. His father, dressed in his coarse workman's clothes, once visited him there. Thomas was afraid that the other boys would laugh at him, but the sturdy Scotchman was so dignified that he won their respect.

When Thomas reached the age of thirteen his parents decided to send him to the great University at Edinburgh. They walked
25 through the village streets with him and watched him start on the highway. It was a journey of a hundred miles, and he traveled all the way on foot.

These experiences made the boy brave and resolute. He was not afraid of the world.

30 A few years after leaving the University he began to earn his living by writing. For many years his income was small, as he

would only write what he thought would make the world better. He used to say that he would write his books as his father built his houses, so that they would last. He scolded the world for its faults, but he was very kind-hearted.

His "History of the French Revolution" is a wonderful work. 5 When the first volume of this history was written, Carlyle loaned it to a friend, and the manuscript was accidentally destroyed. Carlyle did not utter a word of reproach, although the loss meant months of study and thought, but set manfully to work and wrote it once more. 10

He was fond of German literature, and translated the "Wilhelm Meister" by Goethe. He wrote many other books, and became so famous that when Gladstone retired from office as Lord Rector of Edinburgh, Carlyle was made his successor. It was a great triumph for the mason's son; but in the midst of 15 his new honors his wife died, and there was no one to share his happiness.

Not long after this, Queen Victoria sent for Carlyle and granted him a personal interview. On his eightieth birthday he was honored by gifts from Scotland, England, and Germany. 20 He died in 1881.

In the village of Entepfuhl dwelt Andreas Futteral and his wife — childless, in still seclusion, and cheerful, though now verging toward old age.

Andreas had been grenadier sergeant and even regi- 25 mental schoolmaster under Frederick the Great ; but now, quitting the halbert and ferule for the spade and pruning hook, cultivated a little orchard, on the produce of which he lived not without dignity.

Fruits, the peach, the apple, the grape, with other 30 varieties came in their season, all of which Andreas knew how to sell. On evenings he smoked or read

(as beseemed a regimental schoolmaster), and talked
to the neighbors about the victory of Rossbach; and
how " Fritz the Only" had once with his own royal
lips spoken to him, and had been pleased to say,
5 when Andreas as camp sentinel demanded the password,
" Peace, hound!" before any of his staff adjutants could
answer. " There is what I call a king!" would Andreas
exclaim; "but the smoke of Kunersdorf was still
smarting his eyes."

10 Gretchen, the housewife, had been won by the deeds
rather than the looks of her husband, nevertheless she
at heart loved him both for his valor and wisdom.
Was not Andreas in very deed a man of order, courage,
downrightness, that understood Büsching's Geography,
15 had been in the victory of Rossbach, and left for dead
on the battlefield?

The good Gretchen, for all her fretting, watched
over him and hovered round him as only a true house-
mother can; she cooked and sewed and scoured for
20 him; so that not only his old regimental sword and
grenadier cap, but the whole habitation, where on pegs
of honor they hung, looked ever trim and gay; a
roomy cottage, embowered in fruit trees and forest
trees, evergreens and honeysuckles, rising many-colored
25 from amid shaven grass plots, flowers struggling in
through the very windows; under its long projecting
eaves nothing but garden tools and seats where, especially on summer nights, a king might have wished
to sit and smoke and call it his.

Into this home, one meek, yellow evening, it was that a stranger of reverend aspect entered, and, with grave salutation, stood before the two rather astonished housemates. He was closely muffled in a wide mantle, which without farther parley unfolding, he deposited therefrom what seemed some basket, overhung with green Persian silk, saying only: "Good Christian people, here lies for you an invaluable loan; take all heed thereof, in all carefulness employ it; with high recompense, or else with heavy penalty will it one day be required back." Uttering which singular words in a clear, bell-like, forever memorable tone, the stranger gracefully withdrew; and before Andreas and his wife, gazing in expectant wonder, had time to fashion either question or answer, was gone.

Neither out of doors could aught of him be seen or heard; he had vanished in the thickets, in the dusk; the orchard gate stood quietly closed; the stranger was gone once and always. So sudden had the whole transaction been in the autumn stillness and twilight, so gentle and noiseless, that the Futterals could have fancied it all a trick of imagination, or a visit from some spirit; only that green silk basket, such as neither imagination nor spirits are wont to carry, still stood visible and tangible on their little parlor table.

Toward this the astonished couple, now with lit candle, hastily turned their attention. Lifting the green veil to see what invaluable it hid, they descried there, amid down and rich white wrappings, no Pitt diamond or Hapsburg regalia, but in the softest sleep a little red-colored infant! Beside it lay a roll of gold, the exact amount of which was never publicly known; also a baptismal certificate, wherein, unfortunately, nothing but the name was decipherable.

To wonder and conjecture were unavailing then and thenceforth. Nowhere in Entepfuhl did tidings transpire of any such figure as the stranger. Meanwhile, for Andreas and his wife, the grand practical problem was what to do with this little sleeping infant! Amid amazements and curiosities which had to die away without satisfying, they resolved, as in such circumstances charitable, prudent people needs must, on nursing it, if possible, into manhood.

Young Diogenes, or rather young Gneschen, for by such diminutive had they in their fondness named him, traveled forward by quick but easy stages. I have heard him noted as a still infant, that kept his mind much to himself; above all, that he seldom cried. He already felt that time was precious; that he had other work cut out for him than whimpering.

Most graceful is the following little picture: "On fine evenings I was wont to carry forth my supper, bread crumbs boiled in milk, and eat it out of doors. On the coping of the orchard wall, which I could reach by climbing, or still more easily if Father Andreas would set up the pruning ladder, my porringer was placed; there many a sunset have I, looking at the western mountains, consumed my evening meal.

"Those hues of gold and azure, that hush of the world's expectation as day died, were still a Hebrew speech for me; nevertheless I was looking at the fair, illuminated letters, and had an eye for their gilding."

With the little one's friendship for cattle and poultry we shall not much intermeddle. It may be that hereby he acquired a certain deeper sympathy with animated nature. He says again: "Impressive enough was it to hear in early morning the swineherd's horn, and know that so many hungry quadrupeds were, on all sides, starting in hot haste to join him for breakfast on the heath. Or to see them at eventide, all marching in again with short squeak, almost in military order; and each trotting off in succession to the right or left, through its own lane, to its own dwelling."

Thus encircled by mystery, waited on by the four seasons, with their changing contributions, for even grim winter brought its skating matches, its snowstorms and Christmas carols, did the child sit and learn. These things were the alphabet whereby in after time he was to syllable and partly read the grand volume of the world; what matters it whether such alphabet be in large gilt letters or in small ungilt ones, so you have an eye to read it?

For Gneschen, eager to learn, the very act of looking thereon was a blessedness that gilded all; his existence was a bright, soft element of joy, out of which wonder after wonder bodied itself forth to teach by charming.

From " Sartor Resartus."

A SCENE FROM WILLIAM TELL.

SHERIDAN KNOWLES.

Scene I.

[WILLIAM TELL, ALBERT HIS SON, AND GESLER.]

Gesler.   What is thy name?

Tell.   My name?
It matters not to keep it from thee now:—
My name is Tell.

Ges.   Tell!— William Tell?

Tell.   The same.

Ges.   What! he so famed 'bove all his countrymen
For guiding o'er the stormy lake the boat?
And such a master of his bow, 't is said
His arrows never miss!—   Indeed—I 'll take
Exquisite vengeance!—   Mark! I 'll spare thy life—
Thy boy's too!—both of you are free—on one
Condition.

Tell.   Name it.

Ges.   I would see you make
A trial of your skill with that same bow
You shoot so well with.

Tell.   Name the trial you
Would have me make.

Ges.   You look upon your boy
As though instinctively you guessed it.

Tell.   Look upon my boy! What mean you? Look
upon

My boy as though I guessed it! —   Guessed the trial
You'd have me make! —   Guessed it
Instinctively! you do not mean — no — no —
You would not have me make a trial of
My skill upon my child! —   Impossible!
I do not guess your meaning.

 Ges. I would see
Thee hit an apple at the distance of
A hundred paces.

 Tell. Is my boy to hold it?

 Ges. No.

 Tell. No! —   I'll send the arrow through the
core!

 Ges. It is to rest upon his head.

 Tell. Great Heaven, you hear him!

 Ges. Thou dost hear the choice I give —
Such trial of the skill thou art master of,
Or death to both of you; not otherwise
To be escaped.

 Tell. O monster!

 Ges. Wilt thou do it?

 Albert. He will! he will!

 Tell. Ferocious monster! —   Make
A father murder his own child.

 Ges. Take off
His chains, if he consent.

 Tell. With his own hand!

 Ges. Does he consent?

 Alb. He does. [*Gesler signs to his officers, who pro-*

*ceed to take off Tell's chains. Tell all the time uncon-
scious what they do.*]

Tell.   With his own hand!
Murder his child with his own hand — This hand!
The hand I 've led him, when an infant, by!
'T is beyond horror — 't is most horrible.
Amazement! [*His chains fall off.*] What 's that you 've
done to me.
Villains! put on my chains again. My hands
Are free from blood, and have no gust for it,
That they should drink my child's! Here! here! I 'll not
Murder my boy for Gesler.
   Alb.   Father — father!
You will not hit me, father! —
   Tell.   Hit thee! — Send
The arrow through thy brain — or, missing that,
Shoot out an eye — or, if thine eye escape,
Mangle the cheek I 've seen thy mother's lips
Cover with kisses! — Hit thee — hit a hair
Of thee, and cleave thy mother's heart —
   Ges.   Dost thou consent?
   Tell.   Give me my bow and quiver.
   Ges.   For what?
   Tell.   To shoot my boy!
   Alb.   No, father — no!
To save me! — You 'll be sure to hit the apple —
Will you not save me, father?
   Tell.   Lead me forth —
I 'll make the trial!

Alb.   Thank you!

Tell.   Thank me!   Do
You know for what? —   I will not make the trial,
To take him to his mother in my arms,
And lay him down a corpse before her!

Ges.   Then he dies this moment — and you certainly
Do murder him whose life you have a chance
To save, and will not use it.

Tell.   Well — I'll do it: I'll make the trial.

Alb.   Father —

Tell.   Speak not to me:
Let me not hear thy voice —   Thou must be dumb;
And so should all things be —   Earth should be dumb
And Heaven — unless its thunders muttered at
The deed, and sent a bolt to stop it!   Give me
My bow and quiver! —

Ges.   When all's ready.

Tell.   Well! lead on!

Scene II.

PERSONS. — *Enter, slowly, People in evident distress —
Officers, Sarnem, Gesler, Tell, Albert, and soldiers —
one bearing Tell's bow and quiver, another with a
basket of apples.*

Ges.   That is your ground.   Now shall they measure
thence
A hundred paces.   Take the distance.

Tell.   Is the line a true one?

Ges.   True or not, what is 't to thee ?

Tell.   What is 't to me ?   A little thing,
A very little thing — a yard or two
Is nothing here or there — were it a wolf
I shot at !   Never mind.

Ges.   Be thankful, slave,
Our grace accords thee life on any terms.

Tell.   I will be thankful, Gesler ! —   Villain, stop !
You measure to the sun !

Ges.   And what of that ?
What matter whether to or from the sun ?

Tell.   I 'd have it at my back — the sun should shine
Upon the mark, and not on him that shoots.
I cannot see to shoot against the sun —
I will not shoot against the sun !

Ges.   Give him his way !   Thou hast cause to bless
  my mercy.

Tell.   I shall remember it.   I 'd like to see
The apple I 'm to shoot at.

Ges.   Stay ! show me the basket ! — there —

Tell.   You 've picked the smallest one.

Ges.   I know I have.

Tell.   O ! do you ? —   But you see
The color on 't is dark —   I 'd have it light,
To see it better.

Ges.   Take it as it is :
Thy skill will be the greater if thou hit'st it.

Tell.   True — true !   I did not think of that —   I
  wonder

I did not think of that — Give me some chance
To save my boy! [*Throws away the apple with all his force.*]
I will not murder him,
If I can help it — for the honor of
The form thou wearest, if all the heart is gone.

   Ges. Well, choose thyself.

   Tell. Have I a friend among the lookers on?

   Verner. [*Rushing forward.*] Here, Tell!

   Tell. I thank thee, Verner!

He is a friend runs out into a storm
To shake a hand with us. I must be brief:
When once the bow is bent, we cannot take
The shot too soon. Verner, whatever be
The issue of this hour, the common cause
Must not stand still. Let not to-morrow's sun
Set on the tyrant's banner! Verner! Verner!
The boy! — the boy! Thinkest thou he hath the courage
To stand it.

   Ver. Yes.

   Tell. How looks he?

   Ver. Clear and smilingly:
If you doubt it — look yourself.

   Tell. No — no — my friend:
To hear it is enough.

   Ver. He bears himself so much above his years —

   Tell. I know! — I know.

   Ver. With constancy so modest! —

   Tell. I was sure he would —

Ver.   And looks with such relying love
And reverence upon you —
    Tell.   Man! Man! Man!
No more!   Already I'm too much the father
To act the man! —   Verner, no more, my friend!
I would be flint — flint — flint.   Don't make me feel
I'm not —   Do not mind me! —   Take the boy
And set him, Verner, with his back to me.
Set him upon his knees — and place this apple
Upon his head, so that the stem may front me, —
Thus, Verner; charge him to keep steady — tell him
I'll hit the apple!   Verner, do all this
More briefly than I tell it thee.
    Ver.   Come, Albert!   [*Leading him out*.]
    Alb.   May I not speak with him before I go?
    Ver.   No.
    Alb.   I would only kiss his hand.
    Ver.   You must not.
    Alb.   I must! —   I cannot go from him without.
    Ver.   It is his will you should.
    Alb.   His will, is it?
I am content, then — come.
    Tell.   My boy!   [*Holding out his arms to him*.]
    Alb.   My father!   [*Rushing into Tell's arms*.]
    Tell.   If thou canst bear it, should not I? — Go, now,
My son — and keep in mind that I can shoot —
Go, boy — be thou but steady, I will hit
The apple —   Go! —   God bless thee — go. —   My
    bow! — .   [*The bow is handed to him*.]

Thou wilt not fail thy master, wilt thou?— Thou
Hast never failed him yet, old servant— No,
I 'm sure of thee— I know thy honesty.
Thou art stanch— stanch.— Let me see my quiver.

   Ges. Give him a single arrow.

   Tell. Do you shoot?

   Sol. I do.

   Tell. Is it so you pick an arrow, friend?
The point, you see, is bent ; the feather jagged:

                                        [Breaks it.]

That 's all the use 't is fit for.

   Ges. Let him have another.

   Tell. Why, 't is better than the first,
But yet not good enough for such an aim
As I 'm to take— 't is heavy in the shaft:
I 'll not shoot with it! *[Throws it away.]* Let me see
    my quiver.
Bring it!— 'T is not one arrow in a dozen
I 'd take to shoot with at a dove, much less
A dove like that.—

   Ges. It matters not.
Show him the quiver.

   Tell. See if the boy is ready.

                  [Tell here hides an arrow under his vest.]

   Ver. He is.

   Tell. I 'm ready, too! Keep silent for
Heaven's sake and do not stir— and let me have
Your prayers— your prayers— and be my witnesses
That if his life 's in peril from my hand,

'T is only for the chance of saving it.   [*To the people.*]

   Ges.   Go on.

   Tell.   I will.

O friends, for mercy sake, keep motionless

And silent.

     [*Tell shoots — a shout of exultation bursts from the crowd — Tell's head drops on his bosom; he with difficulty supports himself upon his bow.*]

   Ver.   [*Rushing in with Albert.*]   The boy is safe, — no hair of him is touched.

   Alb.   Father, I 'm safe! — your Albert 's safe, dear father, —

Speak to me!   Speak to me!

   Ver.   He cannot, boy!

   Alb.   You grant him life?

   Ges.   I do.

   Alb.   And we are free?

   Ges.   You are.   [*Crossing angrily behind.*]

   Alb.   Thank Heaven! — thank Heaven!

   Ver.   Open his vest,

And give him air.

     [*Albert opens his father's vest, and the arrow drops. Tell starts, fixes his eye upon Albert, and clasps him to his breast.*]

   Tell.   My boy! —   My boy!

   Ges.   For what

Hid you that arrow in your breast? —   Speak, slave!

   Tell.   To kill thee, tyrant, had I slain my boy!

ADDRESS TO THE SURVIVORS OF THE BATTLE OF BUNKER HILL.

DANIEL WEBSTER.

DANIEL WEBSTER, one of the greatest of American statesmen, was born at Salisbury, N. H., in 1782.

His father, Ebenezer Webster, was a farmer and Justice of the County Court. He had been an officer in the Revolutionary war.

Daniel received his early instruction from his mother, a woman 5 of rare intellectual powers, and from the country school which he attended during the winters.

Although he became a distinguished orator, he failed utterly in public speaking at school. He afterwards said: "There was one thing I could not do; I could not make a declamation. I could not speak before the school."

Daniel showed so great ability as a student that the family decided he must attend college, although this step called for additional hardship and sacrifice 20 on the part of those at home. He studied under the direction of a clergyman in a neighboring town, spent one year at Phillips Exeter Academy, and entered Dartmouth College when he was fifteen years old. During his vacations he taught school to pay his expenses. He also assisted his brother Ezekiel in 25 obtaining his education.

He finished his course at college with credit, and then studied law in Boston. He began his practice in Boscawen, a country town near his home; but after the death of his father he removed to Portsmouth, and was soon regarded as the leading 30 man in his profession.

After a time he removed to Boston, where he became known as one of the ablest lawyers of his time.

Webster was elected to Congress from Boston, and took his seat in December, 1823, and continued to serve in that position 5 till he was elected to the Senate, in which body he took his seat on the 4th of March, 1827.

The awkward village lad who could not declaim in the district school now ranked among the most eloquent orators of the country.

On the anniversary of the landing of the Pilgrim Fathers, 10 Webster delivered a stirring oration, which made him famous throughout the country; and at the laying of the corner stone of the Bunker Hill Monument he delivered an address which has not been equaled in this century. From that time Daniel Webster was sought after for every public occasion. He twice held the 15 office of Secretary of State. He resigned the latter office on account of failing health during the summer of 1852, and retired to his country seat at Marshfield, Mass., where he died in the following October.

You have come down to us from a former generation. 20 Heaven has bounteously lengthened out your lives that you might behold this joyous day. You are now where you stood fifty years ago this very hour, with your brothers and your neighbors, shoulder to shoulder in the strife of your country. Behold how altered! The 25 same heavens are indeed over your heads; the same ocean rolls at your feet; but all else, how changed! You hear now no roar of hostile cannon; you see no mixed volumes of smoke and flame rising from burning Charlestown. The ground strewed with the dead and 30 the dying; the impetuous charge; the steady and successful repulse; the loud call to repeated assault; the summoning of all that is manly to repeated resistance;

a thousand bosoms freely and fearlessly bared in an
instant to whatever of terror there may be in war and
death,— all these you have witnessed, but you witness
them no more. All is peace. The heights of yonder
metropolis, its towers and roofs, which you then saw 5
filled with wives and children and countrymen in distress and terror, and looking with unutterable emotions
for the issue of the combat, have presented you to-day
with the sight of its whole happy population, come out
to welcome and greet you with a universal jubilee. 10
Yonder proud ships, by a felicity of position appropri-
ately lying at the foot of this mount, and seeming
fondly to cling around it, are not means of annoyance
to you, but your country's own means of distinction
and defense. All is peace ; and God has granted you 15
this sight of your country's happiness ere you slumber
in the grave forever. He has allowed you to behold
and to partake the reward of your patriotic toils, and
he has allowed us, your sons and countrymen, to meet
you here, and, in the name of the present generation, 20
in the name of your country, in the name of liberty, to
thank you.

But, alas! you are not all here. Time and the sword
have thinned your ranks. Prescott, Putnam, Stark,
Brooks, Read, Pomeroy, Bridge! our eyes seek for you 25
in vain amidst this broken band. You are gathered
to your fathers and live only to your country in her
grateful remembrance and your own bright example.
But let us not too much grieve that you have met the

common fate of men. You lived at least long enough
to know that your work had been nobly and success-
fully accomplished. You lived to see your country's
independence established and to sheathe your swords
5 from war. On the light of liberty you saw arise the
light of peace, like

another morn,
Risen on mid-noon, —

and the sky on which you closed your eyes was cloudless.
10   Veterans of half a century! when, in your youthful
days, you put everything at hazard in your country's
cause, good as that cause was, and sanguine as youth
is, still your fondest hopes did not stretch onward to
an hour like this. At a period to which you could not
15 reasonably hope to arrive, at a moment of national
prosperity such as you could never have foreseen, you
are now met here to enjoy the fellowship of old
soldiers, and to receive the overflowings of a universal
gratitude.
20   But your agitated countenances and your heaving
breasts inform me that even this is not an unmixed
joy. I perceive that a tumult of contending feelings
rushes upon you. The images of the dead, as well as
the persons of the living, throng to your embraces.
25 The scene overwhelms you, and I turn from it. May
the Father of all mercies smile upon your declining
years and bless them! and when you shall here have
exchanged your embraces, when you shall once more
have pressed the hands which have been so often

extended to give succor in adversity or grasped in
the exultation of victory, then look abroad into this
lovely land, which your young valor defended, and
mark the happiness with which it is filled ; yea, look
abroad into the whole earth, and see what a name you 5
have contributed to give to your country, and what a
praise you have added to freedom, and then rejoice in
the sympathy and gratitude which beam upon your
last days from the improved condition of mankind.

THE AMERICAN UNION.

DANIEL WEBSTER.

I HAVE not allowed myself, sir, to look beyond the 10
Union, to see what might lie hidden in the dark recess
behind. Nor could I regard him as a safe counsellor
in the affairs of this government whose thoughts should
be mainly bent on considering, not how the Union may
be best preserved, but how tolerable might be the con- 15
dition of the people when it shall be broken up and
destroyed. While the Union lasts, we have high,
exciting, gratifying prospects spread out before us,
for us and our children. Beyond that I seek not to
penetrate the veil. God grant that, in my day at 20
least, that curtain may not rise ! God grant that on
my vision never may be opened what lies behind !
When my eyes shall be turned to behold for the last

time the sun in heaven, may they not see him shining
on the broken and dishonored fragments of a once
glorious Union ; on States dissevered, discordant, bel-
ligerent ; on a land rent with civil feuds, or drenched,
5 it may be, in fraternal blood. Let their last feeble
and lingering glance rather behold the gorgeous ensign
of the republic, now known and honored throughout
the earth, still full high advanced; its arms and tro-
phies streaming in all their original luster, not a stripe
10 erased or polluted, not a single star obscured ; bearing
for its motto no such miserable interrogatory as " What
is all this worth ?" nor those other words of delusion
and folly, of " Liberty first, and Union afterwards " ;
but everywhere, spread all over in characters of living
15 light, and blazing on all its ample folds, as they float
over the sea and over the land, and in every wind
under the whole heavens, that other sentiment dear
to every true American heart — " Liberty AND Union
— now and forever — one and inseparable ! "

RECESSIONAL.

A Victorian Ode.

RUDYARD KIPLING.

RUDYARD KIPLING was born in Bombay, India, in 1865.
His father and mother used to meet beside Lake Rudyard,
and gave its name to their son.   John Lockwood Kipling, the
father, was at the head of the
Lahore School of Art, and has
illustrated a recent edition of his
son's works.

On reaching the school age,
young Kipling was sent to England to be educated, as was the
custom among the English resi-
dents of India.   He was educated
in the United Services College,
returning home at the age of
eighteen.

It was his ambition to become
a writer and he secured employ-
ment on the "Civil and Military Gazette."   His work here famil-
iarized him with the life in the garrisons, which he afterwards
turned to good account in his ballads and short stories.   20

He was twenty-one years old when he became assistant editor
of the "Lahore Journal."   It was a strange newspaper office,
judging by accounts which he has given us of it.   There were
native type-setters and a queer Mohammedan foreman.   In a
story which he wrote, called "The Man Who Would be King," 25
Kipling tells how they worked in the stifling Indian heat.

From time to time Kipling published verses and stories in the
local paper, and when these had been gathered together and sent
out into the world in the form of a book called "Plain Tales

from the Hills," the name of the young author and poet became
famous.

He then went to England and made his home in London.
He wrote many stories and poems of the old life in India,
5 one of the best collections of which is the "Barrack-Room
Ballads."

In London he met Walcott Balestier, of Brattleboro, Vt., and
they wrote stories together until Balestier's death. Not long
after, Kipling married Caroline Balestier. They came to this
10 country and lived for a time in Vermont, where the poet surrounded himself with everything that would remind him of the
life in India.

Among other works of Kipling are "Soldiers Three," "The
Phantom 'Rickshaw, and Other Stories," the two Jungle Books,
15 and "The Day's Work."

At the time of Queen Victoria's jubilee, Kipling wrote what
was perhaps his greatest poem, the "Recessional," which was
published in "The London Times."

GOD of our fathers, known of old —
Lord of our far-flung battle line —
Beneath whose awful hand we hold
Dominion over palm and pine —
Lord God of Hosts, be with us yet,
Lest we forget — lest we forget!

The tumult and the shouting dies —
The Captains and the Kings depart —
Still stands Thine ancient sacrifice,
An humble and a contrite heart.
Lord God of Hosts, be with us yet,
Lest we forget — lest we forget!

Far-called our navies melt away —
On dune and headland sinks the fire —
Lo, all our pomp of yesterday
Is one with Nineveh and Tyre!
Judge of the Nations, spare us yet,
Lest we forget — lest we forget!

If, drunk with sight of power, we loose
Wild tongues that have not Thee in awe —
Such boasting as the Gentiles use,
Or lesser breeds without the Law —
Lord God of Hosts, be with us yet,
Lest we forget — lest we forget!

For heathen heart that puts her trust
In reeking tube and iron shard —
All valiant dust that builds on dust,
And guarding calls not Thee to guard.
For frantic boast and foolish word,
Thy Mercy on Thy People, Lord!

                              Amen.

WILLIAM HICKLING PRESCOTT.

WILLIAM HICKLING PRESCOTT was born in the quaint old town of Salem, Mass., on the 4th of May, 1796. His father was a successful lawyer, and his mother was

a lady of great ability who spent much time in educating and training her son. William was a bright, merry boy, who learned with ease, and was a great favorite among the boys. The first school he attended was taught by a gentle, old-fashioned lady, who was called the school mother. When he was seven years old he was sent to a more advanced school, taught by "Master Knapp," and remained there for five years.

Though strong and large of his age, he cared more
20 for books than he did for boyish sports. He never remembered a time when he did not love to read.

When he was twelve years old his father removed to Boston, and William was sent to the best classical school then known in New England. He had George Ticknor
25 the historian for a classmate and friend. The two boys progressed so rapidly in Latin and Greek that they out-distanced the rest of the class and recited by themselves.

Books and reading matter were then much more rare than now; but not far from the Prescott home there had been started a library, called the Boston Athenæum. The founder, Mr. William Shaw, who also acted as librarian, was fond of bright boys and allowed a few 5 of them to read there. William, who was one of his favorites, spent many an hour in these rooms, reading whatever pleased his fancy. He was especially fond of romances and tales of wild adventure.

His most intimate friend was a son of Dr. Gardiner, 10 his teacher, and the boys were constantly together. They used to invent stories to tell each other on their way to and from school. Prescott's tales were the wilder, for he had a vivid imagination and had read many books of adventure. 15

William's grandfather, Colonel Prescott, had commanded the American forces at Bunker Hill, and William often listened to the story of this battle, and gazed with awe upon the sword which the colonel wore during the contest. He and young Gardiner amused 20 themselves with fighting mock battles, dressing in some pieces of old armor which they found among the curiosities of the Athenæum, and imagining that they were Revolutionary heroes, Greeks or Romans, or knights of the olden time. 25

Prescott entered Harvard College at the age of fifteen, passing his examinations with credit. He wished to hold a high rank in his class, and as it was an effort for him to apply himself, he made rules devoting a

certain time to each study. He was of a happy, gay
disposition and enjoyed the college life ; but his course
was interrupted by a painful accident. He was passing
out of the dining hall one day when the sound of some
5 frolic attracted his attention and he turned his head to
see what it was. At that moment one of the students
threw a piece of bread, which struck him on the open
eye.

The shock of the blow was so great that he fell and
10 was taken to his home and placed in the charge of a
physician. After several weeks he returned to college,
but the sight of the injured eye was entirely destroyed.
He was graduated with honors in spite of this affliction,
and wrote a Latin poem for Commencement.

15 On leaving college Prescott entered his father's law
office, but continued reading Latin and Greek. After
several months his sound eye became affected and there
was fear of his becoming totally blind. He spent four
months in a darkened room and bore his suffering
20 bravely, always greeting the family with some word of
cheer, as though they were the sufferers and it was his
place to comfort them. As soon as he was able to
travel he was sent to visit his grandfather Hickling,
who was United States Consul at the Azores.

25 The passage was long and trying, and he was glad
to reach land and receive the hearty welcome of his
relatives. They lived in a delightful country house,
in the midst of a beautiful garden, and Prescott was
charmed with the tropical plants and orange groves.

He had been there but a fortnight when his eye again became affected, and he was obliged to spend three months in a darkened room. But he was so bright and patient that he won the hearts of all, and it was with sorrow that they finally saw him sail away.   5

After leaving the Azores, he spent several months in Europe, and then returned to America, spending the next winter at home. He was obliged to avoid the light; but his old school friend, Gardiner, read some of his favorite books to him each day, and his sister 10 spent the greater part of her time with him, reading to him for hours.

Prescott was now twenty-two years old, and his outlook for the future was discouraging. He did not know what profession to follow, for there was no hope 15 of his fully regaining his sight. There seemed no improvement in spite of his quiet life, and he began to go about and enjoy society.

He was married, when he was twenty-four years of age, to Miss Susan Amory, who was his devoted wife 20 and companion. Mrs. Prescott's grandfather had also been a commander at the Battle of Bunker Hill, and captain of a British sloop-of-war.

The swords worn by the soldier and the sailor on that day had been handed down in both families, and hung 25 for many years in Prescott's library, peacefully crossed above his books.

Prescott had now chosen a life of literary work, and persuaded himself that so long as his hearing was spared he would be able to succeed. He felt that he must make especial preparation in order to gain the place he desired, and began to study as if he were a schoolboy, reading the best English, Latin, French, and 5 Italian authors.

He intended to study. German, but he became interested in some lectures on Spanish literature, written by his friend Mr. Ticknor, and decided to write a history of the reign of Ferdinand and Isabella.

10 This was slow work, for although he learned the language, he was unable to use his eyes and depended on the reading of a man who could only pronounce the Spanish words. He finally secured a secretary and reader who understood Spanish and could copy his 15 notes for him. His own writing was done with the aid of an instrument used by the blind, which guided his hand upon the paper.

After ten years of labor his book was published. Its success was remarkable, and it was reprinted in 20 England, Germany, and Spain.

Mr. Prescott was then nearly forty-two years old, tall, handsome, and attractive in his manner. He led a regular life, planning his days carefully, rising at a fixed hour each morning, and taking exercise in the open air. 25 He was a good horseman and composed some of his most stirring battle scenes as he galloped along the country roads.

He divided his time among three residences — one in the city of Boston, another at Lynn, with a view of

the ocean, and a third at Pepperell, the old home of
Colonel Prescott.

The success of "Ferdinand and Isabella" led the
author to continue his writing, and after resting for
some months, he began to prepare the "History of the 5
Conquest of Mexico," which was published six years
after his first history. This work was greeted with
applause throughout the country. Four years later he
wrote the "History of the Conquest of Peru." He next
undertook the "History of Philip the Second," but it 10
was never finished.

In spite of his loss of sight, Prescott gained the first
place among our historians. He visited London in
1850, and received a most cordial welcome and many
attentions. On his return his health failed and he 15
spent less time in writing. His family were always
very dear to him, and he delighted in gathering his
children and grandchildren about him in the old home-
stead at Pepperell. Mr. Prescott died in 1859.

STORMING THE FORTRESS.

WILLIAM HICKLING PRESCOTT.

THE cheering words and courageous bearing of the 20
cavaliers went to the hearts of their followers. All
now agreed to stand by their leader to the last. But,
if they would remain longer in their present position,

it was absolutely necessary to dislodge the enemy from the fortress; and, before venturing on this dangerous service, Hernando Pizarro resolved to strike such a blow as should intimidate the besiegers from further attempts to molest his present quarters.

He communicated his plan of attack to his officers and formed his little troop into three divisions. The Indian pioneers were sent forward to clear away the rubbish, and the several divisions moved up the principal avenues towards the camp of the besiegers; and the three bodies, bursting impetuously on the disordered lines of the Peruvians, took them completely by surprise. For some moments there was little resistance, and the slaughter was terrible. But the Indians gradually rallied, and, coming into something like order, returned to the fight with the courage of men who had long been familiar with danger. They fought hand to hand with their copper-headed war clubs and poleaxes, while a storm of darts, stones, and arrows rained on the well-defended bodies of the Christians.

The barbarians showed more discipline than was to have been expected; for which it is said they were indebted to some Spanish prisoners, from several of whom the Inca, having generously spared their lives, took occasional lessons in the art of war. The Peruvians had also learned to manage with some degree of skill the weapons of their conquerors; and they were seen armed with bucklers, helmets, and swords of European workmanship, and even in a few instances mounted on the horses which they had taken from the white men. The young Inca in particular, accoutered in the European fashion, rode a war horse which he managed with considerable address, and, with a long lance in his hand, led on his followers to the attack.

After a gallant struggle, in which the natives threw themselves fearlessly on the horsemen, endeavoring to tear them from their saddles, they were obliged to give way before the repeated shock of their charges. Many were trampled under foot, others cut down by the Spanish broadswords, while the arquebusiers, supporting the cavalry, kept up a running fire that did terrible execution on the flanks and rear of the fugitives. At length, trusting that the chastisement he had inflicted on the enemy would secure him from further annoyance for the present, the Castilian general drew back his forces to their quarters in the capital.

His next step was the recovery of the citadel. It was an enterprise of danger. The fortress, which overlooked the northern section of the city, stood high on a rocky eminence, where it was defended only by a single wall. Towards the open country it was more easy of approach; but there it was protected by two semicircular walls, each about twelve hundred feet in length and of great thickness. Within the interior wall was the fortress, consisting of three strong towers, one of great height, which, with a smaller one, was now held by the enemy, under the command of an Inca noble, a warrior of well-tried valor, prepared to defend it to the last.

As the fortress was to be approached through the mountain passes, it became necessary to divert the enemy's attention to another quarter. A little while before sunset Juan Pizarro left the city with a picked 5 corps of horsemen, and took a direction opposite to that of the fortress, that the besieging army might suppose the object was a foraging expedition. But, secretly countermarching in the night, he fortunately found the passes undefended and arrived before the outer 10 wall of the fortress without giving the alarm to the garrison.

The entrance was through a narrow opening in the center of the rampart; but this was now closed up with heavy stones that seemed to form one solid work 15 with the rest of the masonry. It was an affair of time to dislodge these huge masses in such a manner as not to rouse the garrison. The Indian natives, who rarely attacked in the night, were not sufficiently acquainted with the art of war even to provide against surprise by 20 posting sentinels. When the task was accomplished, Juan Pizarro and his gallant troop rode through the gateway and advanced towards the second parapet.

But their movements had not been conducted so secretly as to escape notice, and they now found the 25 interior court swarming with warriors, who, as the Spaniards drew near, let off clouds of missiles that compelled them to come to a halt. Juan Pizarro, aware that no time was to be lost, ordered one-half of his corps to dismount, and, putting himself at their

head, prepared to make a breach as before in the fortifications. Leading on his men, he encouraged them in
the work of demolition in the face of such a storm of
stones, javelins, and arrows as might have made the
stoutest heart shrink from encountering it. The good 5
mail of the Spaniards did not always protect them; but
others took the place of such as fell, until a breach was
made, and the cavalry, pouring in, rode down all who
opposed them.

The parapet was now abandoned, and the Indians, 10
hurrying with disorderly flight across the enclosure,
took refuge on a kind of platform or terrace, commanded by the principal tower. Here, rallying, they
shot off fresh volleys of missiles against the Spaniards,
while the garrison in the fortress hurled down frag- 15
ments of rock and timber on their heads. Juan Pizarro,
still among the foremost, sprang forward on the terrace, cheering on his men by his voice and example;
but at this moment he was struck by a large stone on
the head, not then protected by his buckler, and was 20
stretched on the ground. The dauntless chief still continued to animate his followers by his voice till the terrace was carried and its miserable defenders were put
to the sword. His sufferings were then too much for
him, and he was removed to the town below, where, 25
notwithstanding every exertion to save him, he survived the injury but a fortnight. He had served in
the conquest of Peru from the first, and no name on
the roll of its conquerors is less tarnished by the

reproach of cruelty or stands higher in all the attributes of a true and valiant knight.

Though deeply sensible to his brother's disaster,

STORMING THE FORTRESS.

Hernando Pizarro saw that no time was to be lost in profiting by the advantages already gained. Committing the charge of the town to Gonzalo, he put himself at the head of the assailants and laid vigorous siege to the fortresses. One surrendered after a short resistance. The other and more formidable of the two still held out under the brave Inca noble who commanded it. He was a man of an athletic frame, and might be seen striding along the battlements, armed with a Spanish buckler and cuirass, and in his hand wielding a formidable mace, garnished with points or knobs of copper.

With this terrible weapon he struck down all who attempted to force a passage into the fortress. Some of his own followers who proposed a surrender he is said to have slain with his own hand. Ladders were planted against the walls; but no sooner did a 5 Spaniard gain the topmost round than he was hurled to the ground by the strong arm of the Indian warrior. His activity was equal to his strength; and he seemed to be at every point the moment that his presence was needed. 10

The Spanish commander was filled with admiration at this display of valor; for he could admire valor even in an enemy. He gave orders that the chief should not be injured, but be taken alive, if possible. This was not easy. At length, numerous ladders having been 15 planted against the tower, the Spaniards scaled it on several quarters at the same time, and, leaping into the place, overpowered the few combatants who still made a show of resistance. But the Inca chieftain was not to be taken; and, finding further resistance ineffectual, 20 he sprang to the edge of the battlements, and casting away his war club, wrapped his mantle around him and threw himself headlong from the summit. He died like an ancient Roman. He had struck his last stroke for the freedom of his country, and he scorned to survive 25 her dishonor. The Castilian commander left a small force in garrison to secure his conquest, and returned in triumph to his quarters.

From " History of the Conquest of Peru."

A COUNTRY SUNDAY.

JOSEPH ADDISON.

JOSEPH ADDISON was born in England in 1672. His father was a clergyman, well educated and of strong character. He was devoted to his family, and their home life was delightful.

Joseph first attended the schools in the neighborhood, and  was then sent to the Charterhouse, which was one of the best-known schools in England.

He entered Oxford when he was fifteen years old, and was looked upon as a promising scholar. After two years at this college a copy of some Latin verses written by him fell into the hands of Dr. Lancaster, a man of influence, and he was elected to a scholarship in Magdalen College.

His life there was quiet; he studied late at night, and went 20 on long, solitary walks. He continued to write Latin verses, and became so familiar with the Latin writers that he could recite many of their poems. Every little touch of beauty was appreciated by him and filled him with delight.

From his twenty-first to his thirty-second year Addison spent 25 his time in study, writing, and thought.

He spent several years in traveling about France and Italy. While in Paris he lived at the house of the ambassador, where he met the most brilliant society; and in Italy he studied the great works of art. These views of life, added to his natural grace 30 and love of refinement, made him a master of literary style and expression. On his return from his travels he held several offices for the government, and later became a member of Parliament.

Richard Steele, an old schoolfellow and writer of some note, started some periodicals — "The Tatler," followed by "The Spectator," and later by "The Guardian." Addison became interested in these publications and wrote a large number of essays for them — among them the "Sir Roger de Coverley 5 Papers." His characters were taken from life and he describes the manners and customs of the time in language which is cited by all critics as a model of pure English. He also wrote several dramas and poems.

Addison led a happy life. His position under the government 10 brought him a good income. He was looked upon as one of the foremost writers of the day. He loved truth, purity, and kindness, and his works are models of grace and beauty.

He died in 1719, and was buried in the Poets' Corner at Westminster Abbey.   15

I AM always very well pleased with a country Sunday, and think if keeping holy the seventh day were only a human institution, it would be the best method that could have been thought of for the polishing and civilizing of mankind. It is certain the country people 20 would soon degenerate into a kind of savages and barbarians, were there not such frequent returns of a stated time, in which the whole village meet together with their best faces, and in their cleanliest habits, to converse with one another upon indifferent subjects, hear their duties 25 explained to them, and join together in adoration of the Supreme Being.

·   ·   ·   ·   ·   ·   ·   ·   ·

My friend, Sir Roger, being a good churchman, has beautified the inside of his church with several texts of

his own choosing.   He has likewise given a handsome
pulpit cloth, and railed in the communion table at his
own expense.

He has often told me that at his
coming to his estate, he found his
parishioners very irregular; and that
in order to make them kneel and join
in the responses, he gave every one of
them a hassock and a Common Prayer
Book; and, at the same time, employed
an itinerant singing-master, who goes
about the country for that purpose, to

instruct them rightly
in the tunes of the
15 Psalms, upon which
they now very much
value themselves, and
indeed outdo most of
the country churches
20 that I have ever heard.

As Sir Roger is
landlord to the whole
congregation, he keeps them
in very good order, and will
25 suffer nobody to sleep in it

SIR ROGER MEETING HIS TENANTS
AT CHURCH.

besides himself; for, if by chance he has been surprised
into a short nap at sermon, upon recovering out of it
he stands up and looks about him, and, if he sees anybody else nodding, either wakes them himself, or sends
his servants to them.   Several other of the old knight's 5
particularities break out upon these occasions.   Sometimes he will be lengthening out a verse in the singing
Psalms, half a minute after the rest of the congregation have done with it; sometimes when he is pleased
with the matter of his devotion, he pronounces "Amen" 10
three or four times to the same prayer; and sometimes stands up when everybody else is upon their
knees, to count the congregation, or see if any of
his tenants are missing.   I was yesterday very much
surprised to hear my old friend, in the midst of the 15
service, calling out to one John Matthews to mind
what he was about, and not disturb the congregation.
This John Matthews, it seems, is remarkable for being
an idle fellow, and at that time was kicking his heels
for his diversion.
                                                                                  20

This authority of the knight, though exerted in that
odd manner which accompanies him in all circumstances of life, has a very good effect upon the parish,
who are not polite enough to see anything ridiculous in
his behavior; besides that, the general good sense and 25
worthiness of his character make his friends observe
these little singularities as foils that rather set off than
blemish his good qualities.

As soon as the sermon is finished, nobody presumes to

stir till Sir Roger is gone out of the church. The knight walks down from his seat in the chancel between a double row of his tenants, who stand bowing to him on each side, and every now and then inquires how such an one's 5 wife, or mother, or son, or father do, whom he does not see at church; which is understood as a secret reprimand to the person that is absent.

The chaplain has often told me that upon a catechising day, when Sir Roger has been pleased with a boy 10 that answers well, he has ordered a Bible to be given him next day for his encouragement, and sometimes accompanies it with a flitch of bacon to his mother.

Sir Roger has likewise added five pounds a year to the clerk's place; and, that he may encourage the young 15 fellows to make themselves perfect in the church service, has promised upon the death of the present incumbent, who is very old, to bestow it according to merit.

From " The Sir Roger de Coverley Papers."

THE KING OF GLORY.

THE earth is the Lord's, and the fulness thereof;
The world, and they that dwell therein.
For he hath founded it upon the seas,
And established it upon the floods.

Who shall ascend into the hill of the Lord?
Or who shall stand in his holy place?

He that hath clean hands, and a pure heart;
Who hath not lifted up his soul unto vanity,
Nor sworn deceitfully.
He shall receive the blessing from the Lord,
And righteousness from the God of his salvation.

Lift up your heads, O ye gates;
And be ye lifted up, ye everlasting doors;
And the King of Glory shall come in.

Who is this King of Glory?

The Lord strong and mighty,
The Lord mighty in battle.

Lift up your heads, O ye gates;
Even lift them up, ye everlasting doors;
And the King of Glory shall come in.

Who is this King of Glory?

The Lord of hosts, he is the King of Glory.

Lift up your heads, O ye gates;
Even lift them up, ye everlasting doors;
And the King of Glory shall come in.

THE MAN WITHOUT A COUNTRY.

[ABRIDGED.]

EDWARD EVERETT HALE.

EDWARD EVERETT HALE was born in Boston in 1822. He was named for his uncle, Edward Everett, the celebrated orator. When six years of age he had begun the study of Latin, and entered Har-

vard College when he was thirteen. Though young Hale was a diligent student, he excelled in athletic sports, and his great physical strength is shown even now in his large frame and powerful hands and arms.

The future author and preacher was graduated from Harvard with honors when he was seventeen years old. He assisted his father in newspaper work, and was able to write editorials, keep the books, or set type, as the occasion required. He afterwards studied theology.

His first pastorate was at Worcester, Mass. He remained there for ten years. He then settled in Boston. He was with the Massachusetts Rifle Corps when the Civil War broke out, and it was upon an incident of that war that he founded his story of "The Man without a Country." This is one of the strongest stories of patriotism ever written, and has been reprinted in several languages.

For many years Dr. Hale has been pastor of the South Congregational Church in Boston. He has written many books; among them the best known are "Ten Times One is Ten" and "In His Name."

One can hardly imagine a busier life than he leads. His daily tasks consist in aiding public and private charities, lecturing, editing, writing, and preparing his sermons.

He was once asked how he was able to accomplish so much, and he replied: " If you are working with Aladdin's lamp, or 5 with Monte Cristo's treasures, you are not apt to think you will fail. Far less is your risk with the omnipotence of the Lord God behind you."

PHILIP NOLAN was as fine a young officer as there was in the " Legion of the West," as the Western 10 division of our army was then called. When Aaron Burr made his first dashing expedition down to New Orleans, or somewhere above on the river, he met this gay, dashing, bright young fellow, at some dinner party, I think. Burr marked him, talked to him, 15 walked with him, took him a day or two's voyage in his flatboat, and, in short, fascinated him, and led him to turn traitor to his country.

Nolan was proved guilty; yet you and I would never have heard of him, reader, but that when the 20 president of the court asked him at the close whether he wished to say anything to show that he had always been faithful to the United States, he cried out in a fit of frenzy: " Curse the United States! I wish I may never hear of the United States 25 again! "

I suppose he did not know how the words shocked old Colonel Morgan, who was holding the court. Half the officers who sat in it had served through the Revo- lution, and their lives, not to say their necks, had been 30

risked for the very idea which he so cavalierly cursed
in his madness.

Morgan called the court into his private room, and
returned in fifteen minutes with a face like a sheet, to
5 say: "Prisoner, hear the sentence of the Court! The
Court decides, subject to the approval of the President,
that you never hear the name of the United States
again."

Nolan laughed; but nobody else laughed. Old
10 Morgan was too solemn, and the whole room was
hushed dead as night for a minute. Even Nolan lost
his swagger in a moment. Then Morgan added: "Mr.
Marshal, take the prisoner to Orleans in an armed
boat, and deliver him to the naval commander there."
15 The marshal gave his orders and the prisoner was
taken out of court.

"Mr. Marshal," continued old Morgan, "see that
no one mentions the United States to the prisoner.
Mr. Marshal, make my respects to Lieutenant Mitchell
20 at Orleans, and request him to order that no one shall
mention the United States to the prisoner while he is
on board ship."

Nolan had the freedom of the ship he was on, so
long as he heard nothing of his country. No mess
25 liked to have him permanently, because his presence
cut off all talk of home or of the prospect of return,
of politics or letters, of peace or of war — cut off
more than half the talk men liked to have at sea.

Sometimes, when the marines or sailors had any

special jollification, they were permitted to invite
" Plain-Buttons," as they called him. Then Nolan
was sent with some officer, and the men were forbidden to speak of home while he was there. I believe
the theory was that the sight of his punishment did 5
them good. They called him " Plain-Buttons," because,
while he always chose to wear a regulation army uniform, he was not permitted to wear the army button,
for the reason that it bore either the initials or the
insignia of the country he had disowned.   10

As he was almost never permitted to go on shore,
even though the vessel lay in port for months, his
time at the best hung heavy; and everybody was permitted to lend him books, if they were not published
in America and made no allusion to it. He had almost 15
all the foreign papers that came into the ship, sooner
or later; only somebody must go over them first, and
cut out any advertisement or stray paragraph that
alluded to America.

Among these books was the " Lay of the Last 20
Minstrel," which they had all of them heard of, but
which most of them had never seen. I think it could
not have been published long. Well, nobody thought
there could be any risk of anything national in that, so
Nolan was permitted to join the circle one afternoon 25
when a lot of them sat on deck smoking and reading
aloud. Well, so it happened that in his turn Nolan
took the book and read to the others; and he read
very well, as I know. Nobody in the circle knew a

line of the poem, only it was all magic and Border chivalry, and was ten thousand years ago. Poor Nolan read
steadily through the fifth canto, stopped a minute and
then began, without a thought of what was coming : —

5   " Breathes there the man, with soul so dead,
                    Who never to himself hath said."

It seems impossible to us that anybody ever heard this
for the first time, but all these fellows did then, and
poor Nolan himself went on, still unconsciously or
10 mechanically : —

                " 'This is my own, my native land ! ' "

Then they all saw something was to pay ; but he expected to get through, I suppose, turned a little pale,
but plunged on : —

15   " Whose heart hath ne'er within him burned,
                    As home his footsteps he hath turned,
                        From wandering on a foreign strand ?
                    If such there breathe, go, mark him well."

By this time the men were all beside themselves, wish-
20 ing there was any way to make him turn over two
pages ; but he had not quite presence of mind for
that ; he colored crimson and staggered on : —

                " For him no minstrel raptures swell ;
                    High though his titles, proud his name,
25   Boundless his wealth as wish can claim ;

> Despite those titles, power, and pelf,
> The wretch, concentered all in self," —

And here the poor fellow choked, could not go on, but started up, swung the book into the sea, vanished into his stateroom, and we did not see him for two months again. He never read aloud again unless it was the Bible or Shakespeare, or something else he was sure of. But it was not that merely. He never entered in with the other young men exactly as a companion again.

 . . . .

In one of the great frigate duels with the English, it happened that a round-shot from the enemy entered one of our ports square, and took right down the officer of the gun himself, and almost every man of the gun's crew. Now you may say what you choose about courage, but that is not a nice thing to see. But, as the men who were not killed picked themselves up, and as they and the surgeon's people were carrying off the bodies, there appeared Nolan, in his shirt sleeves, with the rammer in his hand, and, just as if he had been the officer, told them off with authority — who should go to the cockpit with the wounded men, who should stay with him — perfectly cheery, and with that way which makes men feel sure all is right and is going to be right. And he finished loading the gun with his own hands, aimed it, and bade the men fire. And there he stayed, captain of that gun, keeping those fellows in spirits, till the enemy struck, — sitting on the carriage

while the gun was cooling, though he was exposed all
the time, — showing them easier ways to handle heavy
shot, making the raw hands laugh at their own blun-
ders, and when the gun cooled again, getting it loaded
5 and fired twice as often as any other gun on the ship.
The captain walked forward by way of encouraging
the men, and Nolan touched his hat and said : " I am
showing them how we do this in the artillery, sir."

The commodore said : " I see you are, and I thank
10 you, sir ; and I shall never forget this day, sir, and
you never shall, sir."

And after the whole thing was over, and he had the
Englishman's sword, in the midst of the state and
ceremony of the quarter-deck, he said : " Where is Mr.
15 Nolan ? Ask Mr. Nolan to come here."

And when Nolan came he said : " Mr. Nolan, we
are all very grateful to you to-day ; you are one of us
to-day ; you will be named in the dispatches."

And then the old man took off his own sword of
20 ceremony and gave it to Nolan, and made him put it
on. The man told me this who saw it. Nolan cried
like a baby, and well he might. He had not worn a
sword since that day at Fort Adams. But always
afterwards, on occasions of ceremony, he wore that
25 quaint old French sword of the commodore's.

.   .   .   .

I first came to understand anything about " the man
without a country " one day when we overhauled a
dirty little schooner which had slaves on board. An

officer was sent to take charge of her, and after a few minutes he sent back his boat to ask that some one might be sent him who could speak Portuguese. Nolan stepped out and said he should be glad to interpret if the captain wished, as he understood the language. 5

"Tell them they are free," said Vaughan.

Then there was a yell of delight, clinching of fists, leaping and dancing, kissing of Nolan's feet.

"Tell them," said Vaughan, well pleased, "that I will take them all to Cape Palmas." 10

This did not answer so well. Cape Palmas was practically as far from the homes of most of them as New Orleans or Rio Janeiro was; that is, they would be eternally separated from home there. And their interpreters, as we could understand, instantly said: 15 "*Ah, non Palmas.*" The drops stood on poor Nolan's white forehead as he hushed the men down and said: "He says, 'Not Palmas.' He says, 'Take us home, take us to our own country, take us to our own house, take us to our own pickaninnies and our own women.' 20 He says he has an old father and mother who will die if they do not see him. And this one says he left his people all sick, and paddled down to Fernando to beg the white doctor to come and help them, and that these caught him in the bay just in sight of home; 25 and that he has never seen anybody from home since then. And this one says," choked out Nolan, "that he has not heard a word from his home in six months, while he has been locked up in a barracoon."

As quick as Vaughan could get words, he said:
"Tell them yes, yes, yes; tell them they shall go to
the mountains of the Moon, if they will. If I sail the
schooner through the Great White Desert, they shall
5 go home."

And after some fashion Nolan said so. And then
they all fell to kissing him again, and wanted to rub
his nose with theirs.

But he could not stand it long; and getting Vaughan
10 to say he might go back, he beckoned me down into
our boat. As we lay back in the stern sheets and the
men gave way, he said to me: "Youngster, let that
show you what it is to be without a family, without a
home, and without a country. And if you are ever
15 tempted to say a word or to do a thing that shall put
a bar between you and your family, your home and
your country, pray God in his mercy to take you that
instant home to his own heaven. Stick by your family,
boy; forget you have a self, while you do everything
20 for them. Think of your home, boy; write and send,
and talk about it. Let it be nearer and nearer to your
thought, the farther you have to travel from it; and
rush back to it when you are free, as that poor black
slave is doing now. And for your country, boy," and
25 the words rattled in his throat, "and for that flag,"
and he pointed to the ship, "never dream a dream but
of serving her as she bids you, though the service
carry you through a thousand hells. No matter what
happens to you, no matter who flatters you or who

abuses you, never look at another flag, never let a
night pass but you pray God to bless that flag. Remember, boy, that behind all these men you have to
do with, behind officers and government, and people
even, there is the Country Herself, your Country, and 5
that you belong to Her as you belong to your own
mother. Stand by Her, boy, as you would stand by
your mother."

I was frightened to death by his calm, hard passion;
but I blundered out that I would by all that was holy, 10
and that I had never thought of doing anything else.
He hardly seemed to hear me; but he did, almost in
a whisper, say: "Oh, if anybody had said so to me
when I was of your age!"

.   .   .   .

Extract from a letter written in 1863 : —   15

"DEAR FRED :   "LEVANT, 2° 2′ S. @ 131° W.

"I try to find heart and life to tell you that it is all over with
dear old Nolan. The doctor has been watching him very carefully, and yesterday morning came to me and told me that Nolan
was not so well, and he said he should like to see me. Well, I 20
went in, and there, to be sure, the poor fellow lay in his berth,
smiling pleasantly as he gave me his hand, but looking very
frail. I could not help a glance round, which showed me what
a little shrine he had made of the box he was lying in. The
stars and stripes were triced up above and around a picture of 25
Washington, and he had painted a majestic eagle, with lightnings blazing from his beak, and his foot just clasping the whole
globe, which his wings overshadowed. The dear old boy saw

my glance and said with a sad smile : 'Here, you see, I have a country !'

.   .   .   .

"An hour after I had left him, when the doctor went in gently, he found Nolan had breathed his life away with a smile.

5   "We looked in his Bible, and there was a slip of paper at the place where he had marked the text : 'They desire a country, even a heavenly : wherefore God is not ashamed to be called their God : for He hath prepared for them a city.'

"On this slip of paper he had written : 'Bury me in the sea ;

10 it has been my home, and I love it.   But will not some one set up a stone for my memory at Fort Adams, or at Orleans, that my disgrace may not be more than I ought to bear ?   Say on it :

In Memory of

PHILIP NOLAN,

Lieutenant in the Army of the United States.

He loved his country as no other man has
loved her ; but no man deserved
less at her hands.' "

LOVE OF COUNTRY.

SIR WALTER SCOTT.

BREATHES there the man, with soul so dead,
Who never to himself hath said,
  "This is my own, my native land!"
Whose heart hath ne'er within him burned,
As home his footsteps he hath turned,
  From wandering on a foreign strand?
If such there breathe, go, mark him well.
For him no minstrel raptures swell;
High though his titles, proud his name,
Boundless his wealth as wish can claim;
Despite those titles, power, and pelf,
The wretch, concentered all in self,
Living, shall forfeit fair renown,
And, doubly dying, shall go down
To the vile dust, from whence he sprung,
Unwept, unhonored, and unsung.

From " The Lay of the Last Minstrel."

THE HEROINE OF NANCY.

IN the year 1476, Charles the Bold, Duke of Burgundy, laid siege to the town of Nancy, capital of the duchy of Lorraine. In the absence of the young duke, René II., who had gone to raise troops among the enemies of Charles, the town and its little garrison were 5 left in charge of a brave and patriotic governor, who had an only daughter, named Télésile. It is with the noble conduct of this heroic young girl that our story has chiefly to do.

5 Charles the Bold — who ought rather to have been called the Rash, or the Furious, from his headlong and violent disposition — had sought to erect a kingdom within the dominions of his great rival, Louis XI. of France. To extend his power, he had overrun prov-
10 inces, which, as soon as his strong hand was withdrawn, took the first opportunity to revolt against him. Lorraine was one of these; and he now appeared before the walls of Nancy, resolved to punish its inhabitants, whom he regarded as rebels.

15 But, thanks to the governor and his heroic daughter, the city held out bravely, both against the assaults of his soldiers, and the threats and promises with which he tried to induce a surrender. While the governor directed and encouraged the defenders, Télésile inspired
20 their wives and daughters.

"Let us do," she cried, "as did the women of Beauvais when this same cruel Charles laid siege to their town. Mothers armed themselves, young girls seized whatever weapons they could find, — hatchets, broken
25 lances, which they bound together with their hair; and they joined their sons and brothers in the fight. They drove the invader from their walls; and so will we defeat and drive him back!"

"Put no trust in the tyrant!" said the intrepid

governor, addressing the people. "He is as faithless as he is cruel. He has promised to spare our lives and our property if we will accept him as our ruler; but be not deceived. Once within our walls, he will give up to massacre and pillage the city that has cost him so 5 dear.

"But if not for our own sakes," he went on, "then for the love of our rightful lord, Duke René, let us continue the glorious struggle. Already at the head of a brave Swiss army, he is hastening to our relief. He 10 will soon be at our gates. Let us hold out till then; or, sooner than betray our trust, let us fall with our defenses and be buried in the ruins of our beloved city!"

Thus defended, Nancy held out until Charles, maddened to fury by so unexpected and so prolonged a 15 resistance, made a final, desperate attempt to carry the town. By stratagem, quite as much as by force, he succeeded in gaining an entrance within the walls; and Nancy was at his mercy.

In the flush of vengeance and success, he was for 20 putting at once all the inhabitants — men, women, and children — to the sword. A young maiden was brought before him.

"Barbarian!" she cried, "if we are all to perish, over whom will you reign?" 25

"Who are you, bold girl! that dare to speak to me thus?" said the astonished Charles.

"Your prisoner, and one who would prevent you from adding to the list of your cruelties!"

Her beauty, her courage, and the prophetic tones in which she spoke, arrested Charles's fury.

"Give up to me your governor, whom I have sworn to punish," he said, "and a portion of the inhabitants
5 shall be spared."

But the governor was her own father, — for the young girl was no other than Télésile. Listening to the entreaties of his friends, he had assumed the dress of a private citizen; and all loved the good old man
10 too well to point him out to the tyrant.

When Télésile sorrowfully reported to her father the duke's words, he smiled. "Be of good cheer, my daughter!" he said. "I will see the Duke Charles, and try what I can do to persuade him."

15 When brought before the conqueror, he said, "There is but one man who can bring the governor to you. Swear on your sword to spare all the inhabitants of the town, and he shall be given up."

"That will I not!" cried the angry duke. "They
20 have braved my power too long; they have scorned my offers; they have laughed at my threats; now woe to the people of Nancy!"

Then, turning to his officers, he commanded that every tenth person in the town should be slain, and they at
25 once gave orders for the decimation. The inhabitants, young and old, women and infants, were assembled in a line which extended through the principal street of the city; while soldiers ransacked the houses, in order to drive forth or kill any that might remain concealed.

It was a terrible day for the doomed city. Families clung together, friends embraced friends; some weeping and lamenting, some trying to comfort and sustain those who were weaker than they, others calmly awaiting their fate. 5

Then, at a word from the conqueror, a herald went forth, and, waving his hand before the gathered multitude, began to count. Each on whom fell the fatal number *ten* was to be given at once to the sword. But at the outset a difficulty arose. 10

Near the head of the line Télésile and the governor were placed; and the devoted girl, watching the movements of the herald, and hearing him count aloud, saw by a rapid glance that the dreaded number was about to fall upon her father. Quick as thought, she slipped 15 behind him and placed herself at his other side. Before the old man was aware of her object, the doom which should have been his had fallen upon his daughter. He stood for a moment stupefied with astonishment and grief, then called out to the herald, "Justice! justice!" 20

"What is the matter, old man?" demanded the herald, before passing on.

"The count is wrong! there is a mistake! Not her!" exclaimed the father, as the executioners were laying hands upon Télésile; "take me, for I was the tenth!" 25

"Not so," said Télésile calmly. "You all saw that the number came to me."

"She put herself in my way, — she took my place, — on me! let the blow fall on me!" pleaded the old man;

while she as earnestly insisted that she was the rightly chosen victim.

Amazed to see two persons striving for the privilege of death at their hands, the butchers dragged them 5 before Charles the Bold, that he might decide the question between them.

Charles was no less surprised at beholding once more the maiden and the old man who had already appeared before him, and at learning the cause of their strange 10 dispute; for he knew not yet that they were parent and child. Notwithstanding his violent disposition, the conqueror had a heart which pity could sometimes touch, and he was powerfully moved by the sight that met his eyes.

15 " I pray you hear me ! " cried Télésile, throwing herself at his feet. " I am a simple maiden ; my life is of no account ; then let me die, my lord duke ! But spare, oh, spare him, the best, the noblest of men, whose life is useful to all our unhappy people ! "

20 " Do not listen to her ! " exclaimed the old man, almost too much affected to speak ; " or if you do, let her own words confute her argument. You behold her courage, her piety, her self-sacrifice ; and I see you are touched ! You will not, you cannot, destroy so precious 25 a life ! It is I who am now worthless to my people. My days are almost spent. Even if you spare me, I have but a little while to live."

Then Télésile, perceiving the eyes of Charles bent upon her with a look of mingled admiration and pity, said : " Do not think there is anything wonderful in my conduct; I do but my simple duty; I plead for my father's life ! "

" Yes, I am her father," said the old man, moved by a sudden determination. " And I am something more. My lord duke, behold the man on whom you have sworn to have revenge. I am he who defended the city so long against you. Now let me die ! "

At this a multitude of people broke from the line in which they had been ranged, and, surrounding the governor and his daughter, made a rampart of their bodies about them, exclaiming, " Let us die for him ! We will die for our good governor ! "

All the better part of the rude Charles's nature was roused. Tears were in his own eyes, his voice was shaken by emotion. " Neither shall die ! " he cried. " Old man ! fair maiden ! I spare your lives and, for your sake, the lives of all these people. Nay, do not thank me; for I have gained in this interview a knowledge which I could never have acquired through years of conquest — that human love is greater than kingly power, and that mercy is sweeter than vengeance ! "

Well would it have been for the rash Charles could he have gained that knowledge earlier, or have shaped his future life by it even then. Still fired by ambition and love of power, he went forth to fight Duke René, who now appeared with an army to relieve his fair city of Nancy. A battle ensued, in which Charles was defeated and slain; and in the midst of joy and thanksgiving, the rightful duke entered and once more took possession of the town.

Warmly as he was welcomed, there were two who shared with him the honors of that happy day — the old man who had defended Nancy so long and well, and the young girl whose heroic conduct had saved from massacre one-tenth of all its inhabitants.

***

HUMANITY.

WILLIAM COWPER.

I WOULD not enter on my list of friends
(Though graced with polished manners and fine sense,
Yet wanting sensibility) the man
Who needlessly sets foot upon a worm.
An inadvertent step may crush the snail
That crawls at evening in the public path;
But he that has humanity, forewarned,
Will tread aside, and let the reptile live.

AN ICEBERG.

RICHARD H. DANA, JR.

RICHARD HENRY DANA, JR., was born in Cambridge, Mass., in 1815, and died in 1882.

He was educated at Harvard College. During his course there his eyesight became affected, and he was obliged to leave college for a time. 5

Being advised to take a sea voyage, he shipped for California and spent two years as a common sailor. On his return he published an account of his adventures, entitled "Two Years before the Mast." This book became popular both in England and America. It is still widely read. 10

Mr. Dana was admitted to the bar when he was twenty-five years old, and always held a prominent position as a lawyer and writer.

THIS day the sun rose fair, but it ran too low in the heavens to give any heat, or thaw out our sails and 15 rigging; yet the sight of it was pleasant, and we had a steady " reef-topsail breeze " from the westward. The atmosphere, which had previously been clear and cold, for the last few hours grew damp and had a disagreeable, wet chilliness in it; and the man who came from 20 the wheel said he heard the captain tell " the passenger " that the thermometer had fallen several degrees since morning, which he could not account for in any other way than by supposing that there must be ice near us, though such a thing was rarely heard of in 25 this latitude at this season of the year.

At twelve o'clock we went below, and had just got
through dinner when the cook put his head down the
scuttle and told us to come on deck and see the finest
sight that we had ever seen. "Where away, doctor?"
5 asked the first man who was up. "On the larboard
bow." And there lay, floating in the ocean, several
miles off, an immense, irregular mass, its top and
points covered with snow, and its center of a deep
indigo color. This was an iceberg, and of the largest
10 size, as one of our men said who had been in the Northern Ocean. As far as the eye could reach, the sea in
every direction was of a deep blue color, the waves running high and fresh, and sparkling in the light; and in
the midst lay this immense mountain-island, its cavities
15 and valleys thrown into deep shade, and its points and
pinnacles glittering in the sun.

All hands were soon on deck looking at it, and admir-
ing, in various ways, its beauty and grandeur. But no
description can give any idea of the strangeness, splen-
20 dor, and really the sublimity of the sight. Its great
size, — for it must have been from two to three miles
in circumference, and several hundred feet in height, —
its slow motion, as its base rose and sank in the water
and its high points nodded against the clouds; the dash-
25 ing of the waves upon it, which, breaking high with
foam, lined its base with a white crust; and the thundering sound of the cracking of the mass, and the breaking and tumbling down of huge pieces, together with its
nearness and approach, which added to a slight element

of fear, all combined to give to it the character of true sublimity.

The main body of the mass was, as I have said, of an indigo color, its base crusted with foam, and, as it grew thin and transparent towards the edges and top, its color shaded off from a deep blue to the whiteness of snow. It seemed to be drifting slowly towards the north, so that we kept away and avoided it. It was in sight all the afternoon, and when we got to leeward of it the wind died away, so that we lay to quite near it for a greater part of the night.

Unfortunately there was no moon; but it was a clear night, and we could plainly mark the long, regular heaving of the stupendous mass, as its edges moved slowly against the stars, now revealing them and now shutting them in. Several times in our watch loud cracks were heard, which sounded as though they must have run through the whole length of the iceberg, and several pieces fell down with a thundering crash, plunging heavily into the sea. Towards morning a strong breeze sprang up, and we filled away, and left it astern, and at daylight it was out of sight.

From " Two Years before the Mast."

JOHN MILTON.

JOHN MILTON was born in 1608, in a house called
"The Spread Eagle," in the very heart of old London.
His father, also John Milton, was a scrivener or law-
yer, and was well known as a musical composer. He

had received a good
education and took
great pains with his
son, employing pri-
vate tutors for him,
and afterwards send-
ing him to St. Paul's
school, where he was
for some time a day
scholar.

The boy was as
desirous of an edu-
cation as his father
could wish, and be-
came so interested in his books that he would read and
20 study until after midnight.

His compositions and verses attracted attention during his early boyhood. Before he was sixteen years old
he had written two of the Psalms in verse.

While at St. Paul's he formed a close friendship
25 with Charles Diodati, the son of an exiled Italian physician. This friendship aroused Milton's interest in
Italian literature.

Milton entered Christ's College, Cambridge, when he was seventeen years old, remaining there seven years. The handsome, graceful young man, with his scorn of all that lacked refinement, was not popular during the first years of his college course, and the students called 5 him "The Lady." They soon learned to honor his high character and brilliant scholarship. He was regarded as the best student of the university.

He had at first intended to become a clergyman, but gave up this plan and was uncertain as to what he 10 should do. His father had taken a house at Horton, about twenty miles from London, and, after leaving Cambridge, Milton spent five years at home, studying Greek and Latin, taking solitary walks, and writing wonderful verses. He also continued the study of 15 music under his father's teaching, and took great delight in it. Some of his most famous poems were written during those years at Horton.

Milton had long desired to travel, and after the death of his mother he found his home so lonely that he per- 20 suaded his father to allow him to visit France, Italy, and Switzerland. This journey occupied nearly sixteen months, and was a season of delight to the young poet, who, by reading, had become familiar with these old cities and the famous men who had walked their 25 streets. He also became acquainted with many learned men and persons of rank, and was received everywhere with courteous attention. During his stay at Florence he met the astronomer, Galileo, then old and blind, and

recently released from prison, where he had been confined on account of his theories and discoveries.

The house at Horton was occupied but a short time
after Milton's return.   His father went to live with
5 his son Christopher, and the poet went to London.   He
hired a pretty " garden-house," large enough for himself
and his books, and lived there with his two nephews,
of whose education he took charge.   He was fond of
teaching, and gradually several other boys joined the
10 class, and his house became a small private school.

In the spring of his thirty-fifth year Milton went to
Oxford and returned a month later, bringing home a
bride and a party of her relatives.   After several days
spent in feasting, the young wife of seventeen summers
15 was left alone with her husband, who became once more
absorbed in his books.   Mrs. Milton cared nothing for
literature, and before the summer was over she went to
visit her father, promising to return during September.
She refused to go home at the appointed time and
20 remained away for two years.

During the meantime Milton's father had come to
live with him, and the number of his pupils had so
increased that he had taken a larger house.   After the
death of his father, Milton decided to devote more time
25 to writing, so he dismissed his pupils and removed to a
smaller house.   He became deeply interested in politics,
writing some bold and daring essays on the questions of
the day.   When he was forty years old he was appointed
Secretary of Foreign Tongues, with a large salary and

MILTON DICTATING "PARADISE LOST."

a residence in Whitehall Palace in Scotland Yard. His eyesight had begun to fail, and three years after accepting this office he became blind. He continued, however, to attend to his duties with the aid of two assistants. Shortly after he lost his sight his wife died, leaving three little daughters. Four years later he married a second time, but this wife lived but a short time.

In 1660, when Milton was fifty-two years old, there came another change in the government, and Milton's life was in danger. He was obliged to hide for several months. Life seemed very gloomy to the blind man. His friends were dead or in exile, he had lost a large share of his property, and his work during the last twenty years seemed thrown away.

Many years before, Milton had planned to write his great poem of " Paradise Lost." He now devoted himself to this work, dictating it to Dorothy, his youngest and favorite child, who bore some resemblance to her
5 father, and who was most in sympathy with him.

Milton married for the third time during his fifty-fifth year. This wife proved a blessing to him. She was a lover of music, and sang to him while he accompanied her upon the organ or bass viol. They walked
10 together and talked about his favorite books and men of learning. His poem " Paradise Lost " was finished during the next two years. He loaned a copy to a friend, who suggested his writing " Paradise Regained," which was published about four years later.

15 These poems rank as the grandest works of one of the greatest minds that the world has ever known. The poet's humble home became an attraction for many visitors, who wished to look upon and talk with the man whose genius was so great.

20 Milton died in 1674.

DEATH OF SAMSON.

JOHN MILTON.

Scene — In Gaza.

OCCASIONS drew me early to this city;
And, as the gates I entered with sunrise,
The morning trumpets festival proclaimed
Through each high street: little I had dispatched,
When all abroad was rumored that this day
Samson should be brought forth, to show the people
Proof of his mighty strength in feats and games;
I sorrowed at his captive state, but minded
Not to be absent at that spectacle.

The building was a spacious theater
Half-round, on two main pillars vaulted high,
With seats, where all the lords, and each degree
Of sort, might sit in order to behold;
The other side was open, where the throng
On banks and scaffolds under sky might stand;
I among these, aloof, obscurely stood.

The feast and noon grew high, and sacrifice
Had filled their hearts with mirth, high cheer, and wine,
When to their sports they turned.   Immediately
Was Samson as a public servant brought,
In their state livery clad; before him pipes
And timbrels, on each side went arm̈ed guards,

Both horse and foot; before him and behind
Archers and slingers, cataphracts and spears.
At sight of him the people with a shout
Rifted the air, clamoring their god with praise,
Who had made their dreadful enemy their thrall.

He, patient, but undaunted, where they led him,
Came to the place; and what was set before him,
Which without help of eye might be essayed,
To heave, pull, draw, or break, he still performed,
All with incredible, stupendous force,
None daring to appear antagonist.

At length, for intermission sake, they led him
Between the pillars; he his guide requested,
As over-tired, to let him lean awhile
With both his arms on those two massy pillars,
That to the archèd roof gave main support.

He, unsuspicious, led him; which when Samson
Felt in his arms, with head awhile inclined,
And eyes fast fixed he stood, as one who prayed,
Or some great matter in his mind revolved;
At last, with head erect, thus cried aloud:
"Hitherto, lords, what your commands imposed
I have performed, as reason was, obeying,
Not without wonder or delight beheld:
Now, of my own accord, such other trial
I mean to show you of my strength, yet greater,
As with amaze shall strike all who behold."

This uttered, straining all his nerves, he bowed;
As with the force of winds and waters pent,
When mountains tremble, those two massy pillars
With horrible convulsion to and fro
He tugged, he shook, till down they came, and drew
The whole roof after them, with burst of thunder,
Upon the heads of all who sat beneath, —
Lords, ladies, captains, counselors, or priests,
Their choice nobility and flower, not only
Of this, but each Philistian city round,
Met from all parts to solemnize this feast.
Samson, with these immixed, inevitably
Pulled down the same destruction on himself;
The vulgar only 'scaped who stood without.

From "Samson Agonistes."

MAY MORNING.

JOHN MILTON.

Now the bright morning star, Day's harbinger,
Comes dancing from the east, and leads with her
The flowery May, who from her green lap throws
The yellow cowslip and the pale primrose.
  Hail, bounteous May, that dost inspire
  Mirth, and youth, and warm desire!
  Woods and groves are of thy dressing;
  Hill and dale doth boast thy blessing.
Thus we salute thee with our early song,
And welcome thee, and wish thee long.

ON HIS BLINDNESS.

JOHN MILTON.

WHEN I consider how my light is spent,
　　Ere half my days, in this dark world and wide,
　　And that one talent which is death to hide
　　Lodged with me useless, though my soul more bent
To serve therewith my Maker, and present
　　My true account, lest He returning chide;
　　"Doth God exact day-labor, light denied?"
　　I fondly ask; but Patience, to prevent
That murmur, soon replies, "God doth not need
　　Either man's work or his own gifts; who best
　　Bear his mild yoke, they serve him best; his state
Is kingly: thousands at his bidding speed,
　　And post o'er land and ocean without rest;
　　They also serve who only stand and wait."

———————

How charming is divine philosophy!
Not harsh and crabbed, as dull fools suppose,
But musical as is Apollo's lute,
And a perpetual feast of nectared sweets,
Where no crude surfeit reigns.

A CHEERFUL SPIRIT.

SIR JOHN LUBBOCK.

Sir John Lubbock was born in England in 1834. He is a banker and has introduced great improvements into banking and custom-house business.

He has written a number of books on literary and scientific subjects.

5

Cheerfulness is a great moral tonic. As sunshine brings out the flowers and ripens the fruit, so does cheerfulness — the feeling of freedom and life — develop in us all the seeds of good — all that is best in us.

Cheerfulness is a duty we owe to others. There is 10 an old tradition that a cup of gold is to be found wherever a rainbow touches the earth, and there are some people whose smile, the sound of whose voice, whose very presence seems like a ray of sunshine, to turn everything they touch into gold.

15

Men never break down as long as they can keep cheerful. "A merry heart is a continual feast" to others besides itself. The shadow of Florence Nightingale cured more than her medicines; and if we share the burdens of others, we lighten our own.

20

All wish, but few know how, to enjoy themselves. They do not realize the dignity and delight of life.

Do not magnify small troubles into great trials. We often fancy we are mortally wounded when we are but scratched. A surgeon, says Fuller, "sent for to cure a 25 slight wound, sent off in a great hurry for a plaster.

'Why,' said the gentleman, 'is the hurt then so dangerous?' 'No,' said the surgeon, 'but if the messenger returns not in post-haste, it will cure itself.'" Time cures sorrow as well as wounds.

5 " A cultivated mind, I do not mean that of a philosopher, but any mind to which the fountains of knowledge have been opened, and which has been taught in any tolerable degree to exercise its faculties, will find sources of inexhaustible interest in all that surrounds it; in the
10 objects of Nature, the achievements of Art, the imagination of Poetry, the incidents of History, the ways of Mankind, past and present, and their prospects in the future."   *From " The Pleasures of Life."*

THE RELIEF OF LUCKNOW.

For eighty days the fort of Lucknow had held out
15 against fifty thousand rebel Sepoys. Disease, famine, and the fire of the enemy had thinned the ranks of the little garrison until but twenty remained. Day after day the garrison had hoped for relief, but now hope itself had died away. The Sepoys, grown desperate
20 by repulse, had decided to overwhelm the fort with their whole force. The engineers had said that within a few hours all would be over, and not a soul within Lucknow but was prepared for the worst.

A poor Scotch girl, Jessie Brown, had been in a
25 state of excitement all through the siege, and had

fallen away visibly within the last few days. A constant fever consumed her, and her mind wandered, especially on that day, when, as she said, she was "lukin far awa, far awa upon the craigs of Duncleuch as in the days of auld lang syne." At last, overcome 5 with fatigue, she sank on the ground too tired to wait.

As the Sepoys moved on to the attack, the women, remembering the horrible scenes of Cawnpore, besought the men to save them from a fate worse than death, by killing them with a volley from their guns. The 10 soldiers for the last time looked down the road whence the long-looked-for relief must come; but they saw no signs of Havelock and his troops. In despair they loaded their guns and aimed them at the waiting group; but suddenly all are startled by a wild, unearthly 15 shriek from the sleeping Scotch girl. Starting upright, her arms raised, and her head bent forward in the attitude of listening, with a look of intense delight breaking over her countenance, she exclaimed : "Dinna ye hear it ? Dinna ye hear it ? Ay, I'm no dreamin'; 20 it's the slogan o' the Highlanders! We're saved, we're saved!" Then, flinging herself upon her knees, she thanked God with passionate fervor.

The soldiers were utterly bewildered; their English ears heard only the roar of artillery, and they thought 25 poor Jessie still raving. But she darted to the batteries, crying incessantly to the men : "Courage ! Hark to the slogan — to the Macgregor, the grandest of them a'! Here's help at last!" For a moment

every soul listened in intense anxiety. Gradually, however, there was a murmur of bitter disappointment, and the wailing of the women began anew as the colonel shook his head. Their dull Lowland ears
5 heard nothing but the rattle of the musketry.

A few moments more of this deathlike suspense, of this agonizing hope, and Jessie, who had again sunk to the ground, sprang to her feet, and cried in a voice so clear and piercing that it was heard along the whole
10 line: "Will ye no believe it noo? The slogan has ceased, indeed, but the Campbells are comin'. D'ye hear? D'ye hear?"

At that moment they seem to hear the voice of God in the distance, as the bagpipes of the Highlanders
15 brought tidings of deliverance; for now there was no longer any doubt of their coming. That shrill, penetrating, ceaseless sound which rose above all other sounds could come neither from the advance of the enemy nor from the work of the sappers.

20 Yes! It was indeed the blast of the Scottish bagpipes, now shrill and harsh as the threatening vengeance of the foe, then in softer tones seeming to promise succor to their friends in need. Never, surely, was there such a scene as that which followed. Not a
25 heart in the residency of Lucknow but bowed itself before God. All by one simultaneous impulse fell upon their knees, and nothing was heard save bursting sobs and the murmured voice of prayer.

THE BIVOUAC OF THE DEAD.

THEODORE O'HARA.

THE muffled drum's sad roll has beat
   The soldier's last tattoo;
No more on life's parade shall meet
   That brave and fallen few.
On Fame's eternal camping-ground
   Their silent tents are spread,
And glory guards with solemn round,
   The bivouac of the dead.

No rumor of the foe's advance
   Now swells upon the wind;
No troubled thought at midnight haunts
   Of loved ones left behind;
No vision of the morrow's strife
   The warrior's dream alarms;
No braying horn or screaming fife
   At dawn shall call to arms.

The neighing troop, the flashing blade,
   The bugle's stirring blast,
The charge, the dreadful cannonade,
   The din and shout, are past.
Nor war's wild note, nor glory's peal,
   Shall thrill with fierce delight
Those breasts that nevermore may feel
   The rapture of the fight.

Like the fierce northern hurricane
    That sweeps his great plateau,
Flushed with the triumph yet to gain,
    Comes down the serried foe.
Who heard the thunder of the fray
    Break o'er the field beneath,
Knew well the watchword of that day
    Was "Victory or Death!"

Sons of the dark and bloody ground,
    Ye must not slumber there,
Where stranger steps and tongues resound
    Along the heedless air!
Your own proud land's heroic soil
    Shall be your fitter grave:
She claims from war its richest spoil, —
    The ashes of her brave.

Thus, 'neath their parent turf they rest,
    Far from the gory field,
Borne to a Spartan mother's breast
    On many a bloody shield.
The sunshine of their native sky
    Smiles sadly on them here,
And kindred eyes and hearts watch by
    The heroes' sepulcher.

Rest on, embalmed and sainted dead!
    Dear as the blood ye gave,

No impious footstep here shall tread
　　The herbage of your grave;
Nor shall your glory be forgot
　　While Fame her record keeps,
Or Honor points the hallowed spot
　　Where Valor proudly sleeps.

Yon marble minstrel's voiceless stone
　　In deathless song shall tell,
When many a vanished year hath flown,
　　The story how ye fell.
Nor wreck, nor change, nor winter's blight,
　　Nor Time's remorseless doom,
Can dim one ray of holy light
　　That gilds your glorious tomb.

ELEGY WRITTEN IN A COUNTRY CHURCH-YARD.

THOMAS GRAY.

THOMAS GRAY was born in London in 1716. His father neglected his family, and the boy was dependent upon his mother, who worked hard to provide her son with an education.

Through the influence of an uncle, who was an assistant at
5 Eton, the future poet was educated at that famous school, and

at Cambridge. He spent his vacations at his uncle's house. He cared nothing for the sports of the times, but loved nature. He would sit for hours in a quiet nook, surrounded by hills and cliffs, reading, dreaming, and watching the gambols of the hares and squirrels.

Gray was twenty-two years old when he left Cambridge. He spent the following six months at home, and then accepted the invitation of one of his college friends to accompany him, free of expense, on a tour through

France and Italy. His notes and letters written during this
20 trip show remarkable taste and learning.

After two and a half years of travel he returned to England. His father died during the next fall, after wasting his fortune. Gray began the study of law, but had not the means to finish the course. He began to devote his time to writing, left London,
25 where he had spent the winter, and went with his mother to visit an uncle who lived in a country hamlet called Stoke Poges. In this quiet village he wrote his "Ode on the Spring," "Ode on a Distant Prospect of Eton College," and began the "Elegy Written in a Country Church-Yard."

30 The "Elegy" is one of the most celebrated poems ever written. It was begun when Gray was twenty-six years old, but he did not

finish it until eight years later. Its fame spread over the world, and it still holds its rank as the most perfect of English poems.

The poet lived at Cambridge, where he devoted his time to study. The "Elegy" and a later work, "The Bard," placed him at the head of English poets. He was offered the office of poet laureate, which he refused. 5

In 1768 Gray accepted the chair of Modern History and Languages at Cambridge.

The last years of the poet's life were spent very quietly. He avoided society and was rarely seen in public. He died in London in 1771. 10

THE Curfew tolls the knell of parting day,
    The lowing herd wind slowly o'er the lea,
The plowman homeward plods his weary way,
    And leaves the world to darkness and to me.

Now fades the glimmering landscape on the sight,
    And all the air a solemn stillness holds,
Save where the beetle wheels his droning flight,
    And drowsy tinklings lull the distant folds;

Save that from yonder ivy-mantled tow'r
    The moping owl does to the moon complain
Of such, as wand'ring near her secret bow'r,
    Molest her ancient solitary reign.

Beneath those rugged elms, that yew-tree's shade,
    Where heaves the turf in many a mould'ring heap,
Each in his narrow cell forever laid,
    The rude Forefathers of the hamlet sleep.

CHURCH AT STOKE POGES.

The breezy call of incense-breathing Morn,
   The swallow twitt'ring from the straw-built shed,
The cock's shrill clarion, or the echoing horn,
   No more shall rouse them from their lowly bed.

For them no more the blazing hearth shall burn,
   Or busy housewife ply her evening care:
No children run to lisp their sire's return,
   Or climb his knees the envied kiss to share.

Oft did the harvest to their sickle yield,
   Their furrow oft the stubborn glebe has broke;
How jocund did they drive their team afield!
   How bow'd the woods beneath their sturdy stroke!

Let not Ambition mock their useful toil,
   Their homely joys, and destiny obscure;

With uncouth rhymes and shapeless sculpture deck'd,
   Implores the passing tribute of a sigh.

Their name, their years, spelt by th' unletter'd muse,
   The place of fame and elegy supply:
And many a holy text around she strews,
   That teach the rustic moralist to die.

For who to dumb Forgetfulness a prey,
   This pleasing anxious being e'er resign'd,
Left the warm precincts of the cheerful day,
   Nor cast one longing ling'ring look behind?

On some fond breast the parting soul relies,
   Some pious drops the closing eye requires;
Ev'n from the tomb the voice of Nature cries,
   Ev'n in our Ashes live their wonted Fires.

For thee, who mindful of th' unhonor'd Dead
   Dost in these lines their artless tale relate;
If chance, by lonely contemplation led,
   Some kindred Spirit shall inquire thy fate,

Haply some hoary-headed Swain may say,
   'Oft have we seen him at the peep of dawn
'Brushing with hasty steps the dews away
   'To meet the sun upon the upland lawn.

'There at the foot of yonder nodding beech
   'That wreathes its old fantastic roots so high,
'His listless length at noontide would he stretch,
   'And pore upon the brook that babbles by.

' Hard by yon wood, now smiling as in scorn,
  ' Mutt'ring his wayward fancies he would rove,
' Now drooping, woeful wan, like one forlorn,
  ' Or craz'd with care, or cross'd in hopeless love.

' One morn I miss'd him on the custom'd hill,
  ' Along the heath and near his fav'rite tree;
' Another came; nor yet beside the rill,
  ' Nor up the lawn, nor at the wood was he;

' The next with dirges due in sad array
  ' Slow thro' the church-way path we saw him borne.
' Approach and read (for thou can'st read) the lay,
  ' Grav'd on the stone beneath yon aged thorn.'

THE EPITAPH.

Here rests his head upon the lap of Earth
  A Youth to Fortune and to Fame unknown.
Fair Science frown'd not on his humble birth,
  And Melancholy mark'd him for her own.

Large was his bounty, and his soul sincere,
  Heav'n did a recompense as largely send:
He gave to Mis'ry all he had, a tear,
  He gain'd from Heav'n ('twas all he wish'd) a friend.

No farther seek his merits to disclose,
  Or draw his frailties from their dread abode,
(There they alike in trembling hope repose,)
  The bosom of his Father and his God.

BELSHAZZAR'S FEAST.

BELSHAZZAR the king made a great feast to a thousand of his lords, and drank wine before the thousand. Belshazzar, while he tasted the wine, commanded to bring the golden and silver vessels, which his father Nebuchadnezzar had taken out of the temple which 5 was in Jerusalem; that the king and his princes and his wives might drink therein.

Then they brought the golden vessels that were taken out of the temple of the house of God, which was at Jerusalem; and the king, his princes and his wives, 10 drank in them.

They drank wine, and praised the gods of gold, and of silver, of brass, of iron, of wood, and of stone.

In the same hour came forth fingers of a man's hand, and wrote over against the candlestick upon the 15 plaster of the wall of the king's palace: and the king saw the part of the hand that wrote.

Then the king's countenance was changed, and his thoughts troubled him, so that the joints of his loins were loosed, and his knees smote one against another. 20 The king cried aloud to bring in the astrologers, the Chaldeans, and the soothsayers. And the king spake and said to the wise men of Babylon: "Whosoever shall read this writing, and show me the interpretation thereof, shall be clothed with scarlet, and have a chain 25 of gold about his neck, and shall be the third ruler in the kingdom."

Then came in all the king's wise men: but they could not read the writing, nor make known to the king the interpretation thereof.

Then was King Belshazzar greatly troubled, and his
5 countenance was changed in him, and his lords were astonished.

Now the queen, by reason of the words of the king and his lords, came into the banquet house: and the queen spake and said: "O king, live for ever: let not
10 thy thoughts trouble thee, nor let thy countenance be changed:

"There is a man in thy kingdom in whom is the spirit of the holy gods; and in the days of thy father light and understanding and wisdom, like the wisdom
15 of the gods, was found in him; whom the king Nebuchadnezzar thy father, the king, I say, thy father, made him master of the magicians, astrologers, Chaldeans, and soothsayers;

"Forasmuch as an excellent spirit, and knowledge,
20 and understanding, interpreting of dreams, and showing of hard sentences, and dissolving of doubts, were found in the same Daniel, whom the king named Belteshazzar: now let Daniel be called, and he will show the interpretation."

25 Then was Daniel brought in before the king. And the king spake and said unto Daniel: "Art thou that Daniel, which art of the children of the captivity of Judah, whom the king, my father, brought out of Jewry?

"I have even heard of thee, that the spirit of the gods is in thee, and that light and understanding and excellent wisdom is found in thee.

"And now the wise men, the astrologers, have been brought in before me, that they should read this writing, and make known unto me the interpretation thereof: but they could not show the interpretation of the thing:

"And I have heard of thee, that thou canst make interpretations, and dissolve doubts: now if thou canst read the writing, and make known to me the interpretation thereof, thou shalt be clothed with scarlet, and have a chain of gold about thy neck, and shalt be the third ruler in the kingdom."

Then Daniel answered and said before the king: "Let thy gifts be to thyself, and give thy rewards to another; yet I will read the writing unto the king, and make known to him the interpretation.

"O thou king, the most high God gave Nebuchadnezzar thy father a kingdom, and majesty, and glory, and honor:

"And for the majesty that he gave him, all people, nations, and languages trembled and feared before him: whom he would he slew, and whom he would he kept alive; and whom he would he set up, and whom he would he put down.

"But when his heart was lifted up, and his mind hardened in pride, he was deposed from his kingly throne, and they took his glory from him:

"And he was driven from the sons of men; and his heart was made like the beasts, and his dwelling was with the wild asses : they fed him with grass like oxen, and his body was wet with the dew of heaven; till he
5 knew that the most high God ruled in the kingdom of men, and that he appointeth over it whomsoever he will.

"And thou his son, O Belshazzar, hast not humbled thine heart, though thou knewest all this ;

"But hast lifted up thyself against the Lord of
10 heaven ; and they have brought the vessels of his house before thee, and thou and thy lords and thy wives, have drunk wine in them ; and thou hast praised the gods of silver, and gold, of brass, iron, wood, and stone, which see not, nor hear, nor know : and the God
15 in whose hand thy breath is, and whose are all thy ways, hast thou not glorified :

"Then was the part of the hand sent from him ; and this writing was written.

"And this is the writing that was written : —

20   MENE, MENE, TEKEL, UPHARSIN.

This is the interpretation of the thing : —

MENE ;

God hath NUMBERED thy kingdom,
And finished it.

25   TEKEL ;

Thou art WEIGHED in the balances,
And art found wanting.

PERES ;

Thy kingdom is DIVIDED,
And given to the Medes and Persians."

Then commanded Belshazzar, and they clothed Daniel
with scarlet and put a chain of gold about his neck, 5
and made a proclamation concerning him, that he should
be the third ruler in the kingdom.

In that night was Belshazzar, the king of the Chaldeans, slain.

And Darius, the Median, took the kingdom, being 10
about threescore and two years old.

From " The Bible," Book of Daniel, Chap. V.

THE BATTLE OF QUEBEC.

FRANCIS PARKMAN.

FRANCIS PARKMAN was born in Boston in 1823. He was graduated from Harvard College when he was twenty-one. He visited

Europe and on his return went on a tour in the far West, across the prairies and among the Rocky Mountains. He became well acquainted with the Indians, sharing their camps and hunting buffaloes with them. His book, "The California and Oregon Trail," contains a vivid account of his explorations. This book was followed by "The History of the Conspiracy of Pontiac" and a novel called "Vassal Morton." Mr. Parkman devoted a number of years to writing histories of the attempts of the French and English to settle North America. His qualities as a writer were of a high order. His style is marked by uncommon vigor.
20 His pages are alive with thrilling adventure, brilliant description, and romantic episodes. He has left no room for a competitor in the same field. Mr. Parkman died in 1893.

THE eventful night of the 12th was clear and calm, with no light but that of the stars. Within two hours
25 before daybreak thirty boats, crowded with sixteen hundred soldiers, cast off from the vessels and floated downward, in perfect order, with the current of the ebb tide. To the boundless joy of the army, Wolfe's malady had abated, and he was able to command in person. His

ruined health, the gloomy prospects of the siege, and the disaster at Montmorenci had oppressed him with the deepest melancholy, but never impaired for a moment the promptness of his decisions or the impetuous energy of his action. He sat in the stern of one of the boats, pale and weak, but borne up to a calm height of resolution. Every order had been given, every arrangement made, and it only remained to face the issue. The ebbing tide sufficed to bear the boats along, and nothing broke the silence of the night but the gurgling of the river and the low voice of Wolfe, as he repeated to the officers about him the stanzas of Gray's "Elegy in a Country Churchyard," which had recently appeared and which he had just received from England. Perhaps, as he uttered those strangely appropriate words, —

"The paths of glory lead but to the grave,"

the shadows of his own approaching fate stole with mournful prophecy across his mind. "Gentlemen," he said as he closed his recital, "I would rather have written those lines than take Quebec to-morrow."

As they approached the landing-place, the boats edged closer in towards the northern shore, and the woody precipices rose high on their left, like a wall of undistinguished blackness.

They reached the landing-place in safety — an indentation in the shore about a league above the city, and now bearing the name of Wolfe's Cove. Here a narrow path led up the face of the heights, and a French guard was posted at the top to defend the pass. By the force of the current the foremost boats, including that which carried Wolfe himself, were borne a little below the spot. The general was one of the first on shore.

THE ASCENT TO THE PLAINS OF ABRAHAM.

Meanwhile the vessels had dropped downward with the current, and anchored opposite the landing-place. The remaining troops were disembarked, and, with the dawn of day, the whole were brought in safety to the shore.

The sun rose, and, from the ramparts of Quebec, the astonished people saw the Plains of Abraham glittering with arms, and the dark-red lines of the English forming in array of battle. Breathless messengers had borne the evil tidings to Montcalm, and far and near his wide-extended camp resounded with the rolling of alarm drums and the din of startled preparation. He, too, had his struggles and his sorrows. The civil power had thwarted him; famine, discontent, and disaffection were rife among his soldiers; and no small portion of the Canadian militia had dispersed from sheer starvation. In spite of all, he had trusted to hold out till the winter frosts should drive the invaders from before the town, when, on that disastrous morning, the news of their successful temerity fell like a cannon shot upon his ear. Still he assumed a tone of confidence. " They have got to the weak side of us at last," he is reported to have said, "and we must crush them with our numbers."

At a little before ten the English could see that Montcalm was preparing to advance, and in a few moments all his troops appeared in rapid motion. They came on in three divisions, shouting, after the manner of their nation, and firing heavily as soon as they came within range. In the British ranks not a trigger was pulled, not a soldier stirred; and their ominous composure seemed to damp the spirits of the assailants. It was not till the French were within forty yards that the fatal word was given, and the British muskets blazed forth at once in one crashing explosion. Like a ship at full career, arrested with sudden ruin on a sunken rock, the ranks of Montcalm staggered, shivered, and broke before that wasting storm of lead. The smoke, rolling along the field, for a moment shut out the view; but when the white wreaths were scattered on the wind, a wretched spectacle was disclosed; men and officers tumbled in heaps, battalions resolved into a mob, order and obedience gone; and

when the British muskets were leveled for a second
volley, the masses of the militia were seen to cower
and shrink with uncontrollable panic. For a few minutes the French regulars stood their ground, returning
5 a sharp and not ineffectual fire. But now, echoing
cheer on cheer, redoubling volley on volley, trampling
the dying and the dead, and driving the fugitives in
crowds, the British troops advanced and swept the field
before them. The ardor of the men burst all restraint.
10 They broke into a run and with unsparing slaughter
chased the flying multitude to the gates of Quebec.
Foremost of all, the light-footed Highlanders dashed
along in furious pursuit, hewing down the Frenchmen
with their broadswords, and slaying many in the very
15 ditch of the fortifications. Never was victory more
quick or more decisive; yet the triumph of the victors
was mingled with sadness as the tidings went from
rank to rank that Wolfe had fallen.

In the heat of the action, as he advanced at the head
20 of the grenadiers of Louisburg, a bullet shattered his
wrist; but he wrapped his handkerchief about the
wound and showed no sign of pain. A moment more
and a ball pierced his side. Still he pressed forward,
waving his sword and cheering his soldiers to the attack,
25 when a third shot lodged deep within his breast. He
paused, reeled, and, staggering to one side, fell to the
earth. Brown, a lieutenant of the grenadiers, Hender-
son, a volunteer, an officer of artillery, and a private
soldier raised him together in their arms, and, bearing

him to the rear, laid him softly on the grass. They
asked him if he would have a surgeon; but he shook
his head and answered that all was over with him.
His eyes closed with the torpor of approaching death,
and those around sustained his fainting form. Yet 5
they could not withhold their gaze from the wild turmoil before them and the charging ranks of their companions rushing through fire and smoke. "See how
they run!" one of the officers exclaimed as the French
fled in confusion before the leveled bayonets. "Who 10
run?" demanded Wolfe, opening his eyes, like a man
aroused from sleep. "The enemy, sir," was the reply;
"they give way everywhere." "Then," said the dying
general, "tell Colonel Burton to march Webb's regiment down to Charles River, to cut off their retreat 15
from the bridge. Now, God be praised! I will die in
peace," he murmured; and, turning on his side, he
calmly breathed his last.

From " Montcalm and Wolfe."

THE STARLING.

LAURENCE STERNE.

LAURENCE STERNE, an English novelist, was born in Ireland in 1713.

He was the son of an English officer, and the first ten years of his life were spent in traveling about with his father's regiment. 5 He then entered a school near Halifax, where he studied for eight or nine years, and completed his education at the University of Cambridge.

Mr. Sterne became a clergyman of the Church of England, but devoted a large portion of his time to the writing of fiction. He 10 died in London in 1768.

AND as for the Bastille, the terror is in the word. Make the most of it you can, said I to myself, the Bastille is but another word for a tower, and a tower is but another word for a house you can't get out of. Mercy 15 on the gouty! for they are in it twice a year. But with nine *livres* a day, and pen and ink and paper and patience, albeit a man can't get out, he may do very well within, at least for a month or six weeks, at the end of which, if he is a harmless fellow, his innocence appears 20 and he comes out a better and wiser man than he went in.

I had some occasion — I forget what — to step into the courtyard, as I settled this account, and remember I walked downstairs in no small triumph with the conceit of my reasoning. "Beshrew the *somber* pencil!" 25 said I vauntingly; "for I envy not its power, which paints the evils of life with so hard and deadly a color-

ing. The mind sits terrified at the objects she has mag-
nified herself and blackened. Reduce them to their
proper size and hue, she overlooks them. 'T is true,"
said I, correcting the proposition, "the Bastille is not
an evil to be despised. But strip it of its towers, fill 5
up the fosse, unbarricade the doors, call it simply a confinement, and suppose 't is some tyrant of a distemper,
and not of a man, which holds you in it, the evil van-
ishes and you bear the other half without complaint."

I was interrupted in the heyday of this soliloquy with 10
a voice which I took to be that of a child, which complained it could not get out. I looked up and down the
passage, and, seeing neither man, woman, nor child, I
went out without further attention.

In my return back through the passage, I heard the 15
same words repeated twice over; and, looking up, I saw
it was a starling, hung in a little cage. "I can't get
out — I can't get out," said the starling.

I stood looking at the bird; and to every person who
came through the passage it ran fluttering to the side 20
towards which they approached it, with the same lamen-
tation of its captivity. "I can't get out," said the starling. "God help thee!" said I; "but I 'll let thee out,
cost what it will." So I turned about the cage to get
the door. It was twisted and double twisted so fast 25
with wire there was no getting it open without pulling
the cage to pieces. I took both hands to it.

The bird flew to the place where I was attempting
his deliverance, and, thrusting his head through the

trellis, pressed his breast against it, as if impatient.
" I fear, poor creature," said I, " I cannot set thee at
liberty." " No," said the starling ; " I can't get out —
I can't get out."

5 I never had my affections more tenderly awakened,
nor do I remember an incident in my life where
the dissipated spirits to which my reason had been a
bubble were so suddenly called home. Mechanical as
the notes were, yet so true in tune to nature were they
10 chanted, that in one moment they overthrew all my
systematic reasonings upon the Bastille ; and I heavily
walked upstairs, unsaying every word I had said in
going down them.

" Disguise thyself as thou wilt, still, Slavery," said I,
15 " still thou art a bitter draught ; and though thousands
in all ages have been made to drink of thee, thou art
no less bitter on that account. 'T is thou, thrice sweet
and gracious goddess," — addressing myself to Liberty,
— " whom all, in public or in private, worship, whose
20 taste is grateful, and ever will be so, till Nature herself
shall change. No *tint* of words can spot thy snowy
mantle, nor chymic power turn thy scepter into iron.
With thee to smile upon him as he eats his crust, the
swain is happier than his monarch, from whose court
25 thou art exiled. Gracious Heaven ! " cried I, kneeling
down upon the last step but one in my ascent, " grant
me but health, thou great Bestower of it, and give me
but this fair goddess as my companion, and shower
down thy miters, if it seem good unto thy divine

providence, upon those heads which are aching for them."

The bird in his cage pursued me into my room. I sat down close by my table, and, leaning my head upon my hand, I began to figure to myself the miseries of 5 confinement. I was in a right frame for it, and so I gave full scope to my imagination.

I was going to begin with the millions of my fellow-creatures born to no inheritance but slavery; but finding, however affecting the picture was, that I could not 10 bring it near me, and that the multitude of sad groups in it did but distract me, I took a single captive, and, having first shut him up in his dungeon, I then looked through the twilight of his grated door to take his picture. 15

I beheld his body half wasted away with long expectation and confinement, and felt what kind of sickness of the heart it was which arises from hope deferred. Upon looking nearer, I saw him pale and feverish. In thirty years the western breeze had not once fanned his 20 blood. He had seen no sun, no moon in all that time, nor had the voice of friend or kinsman breathed through his lattice. His children! —

But here my heart began to bleed, and I was forced to go on with another part of the portrait. 25

He was sitting upon the ground, upon a little straw, in the farthest corner of his dungeon, which was alternately his chair and bed. A little calendar of small sticks was laid at the head, notched all over with the

dismal days and nights he had passed there. He had one of these little sticks in his hand, and with a rusty nail he was etching another day of misery to add to the heap. As I darkened the little light he had, he lifted
5 up a hopeless eye towards the door, then cast it down, shook his head, and went on with his work of affliction. I heard his chains upon his legs as he turned his body to lay his little stick upon the bundle. He gave a deep sigh. I saw the iron enter into his soul. I burst into
10 tears. I could not sustain the picture of confinement which my fancy had drawn.

From " The Sentimental Journey."

THE BELFRY PIGEON.

NATHANIEL PARKER WILLIS.

NATHANIEL PARKER WILLIS was born in Portland, Me., in 1807, and died near Cornwall-on-the-Hudson, N. Y., in 1867. His. father was an editor and founded "The Youth's Companion." His sister was an authoress who wrote under the name of " Fanny Fern." 5

Nathaniel was graduated at Yale College, and wrote poems and literary essays during his college course. He spent several years in traveling about Europe, and wrote a series of letters for the newspapers during this time.

Mr. Willis published a number of poems, books of travel, and 10 novels. He possessed great natural gifts and there is much beauty in his prose and verse.

ON the cross-beam, under the Old South bell,
The nest of a pigeon is builded well.
In summer and winter that bird is there,
Out and in with the morning air;
I love to see him track the street,
With his wary eye and active feet;
And I often watch him as he springs,
Circling the steeple with easy wings,
Till across the dial his shadow has passed,
And the belfry edge is gained at last.
'Tis a bird I love, with its brooding note,
And the trembling throb in its mottled throat;
There's a human look in its swelling breast,
And the gentle curve of its lowly crest;
And I often stop with the fear I feel —
He runs so close to the rapid wheel.

Whatever is rung on that noisy bell —
Chime of the hour, or funeral knell —
The dove in the belfry must hear it well.
When the tongue swings out to the midnight moon
When the sexton cheerily rings for noon,
When the clock strikes clear at morning light,
When the child is waked with "nine at night,"
When the chimes play soft in the Sabbath air,
Filling the spirit with tones of prayer, —
Whatever tale in the bell is heard,
He broods on his folded feet unstirred,
Or, rising half in his rounded nest,
He takes the time to smooth his breast,
Then drops again, with filméd eyes,
And sleeps as the last vibration dies.
Sweet bird, I would that I could be
A hermit in the crowd like thee!
With wings to fly to wood and glen,
Thy lot, like mine, is cast with men;
And daily, with unwilling feet,
I tread, like thee, the crowded street;
But unlike me, when day is o'er,
Thou canst dismiss the world and soar,
Or, at a half-felt wish for rest,
Canst smooth the feathers on thy breast,
And drop, forgetful, to thy nest.

LADY UNA AND THE LION.

EDMUND SPENSER.

EDMUND SPENSER was a famous English poet who lived in the time of Queen Elizabeth. He was born in London in 1553 and received his education at Cambridge, where he was a sizar. There is a mulberry tree which Spenser is said to have planted still standing in the garden of the college.

His early boyhood was passed in London, with frequent visits among the glens of northern England.

Spenser left Cambridge when he was twenty-four years old, and spent several years with his relations in the north of England. On his return to London, he published a series of twelve poems named after the months, and called "The Shephearde's Calender." This gained him a name as the first poet of the day. The next summer he went to Ireland as secretary to Lord Grey.

Several years later he was awarded the Castle of Kilcolman 20 for his services. Here he was visited by Sir Walter Raleigh. Spenser had written three books of "The Faerie Queene," his greatest poem, and Raleigh listened to them as the two poets sat beneath the alder trees beside the River Mulla, which flowed through the castle grounds. Raleigh was delighted with the 25 poem, and persuaded Spenser to accompany him to England, where he was presented to the Queen.

The first three books of "The Faerie Queene" were dedicated to Queen Elizabeth. It was the first great allegorical poem that England had produced, and it has never lost its power. 30

Spenser possessed a wonderful imagination, and had but to close his eyes and he was in an enchanted land.

"The Faerie Queene" is the story of noble knights fighting against wrong, and a beautiful lady rescued from danger. 5 Only six books of the twelve which Spenser planned were published.

The last years of Spenser's life were filled with sadness. During a rebellion his castle was burnt, and he and his family fled to England.

10 He died in London in 1599, at the age of forty-six, and was buried in Westminster Abbey.

Nought is there under heaven's wide hallowness
That moves more dear compassiön of mind,
Than beauty brought t' unworthy wretchedness
Through envy's snares, or fortune's freaks unkind.
I, whether lately through her brightness blind,
Or through allegiance and fast feälty,
Which I do owe unto all womankind,
Feel my heart pierced with so great agony,
When such I see, that all for pity I could die.

And now it is empassionèd so deep,
For fairest Una's sake, of whom I sing,
That my frail eyes these lines with tears do steep,
To think how she through guileful handëling,
Though true as touch, though daughter of a king,
Though fair as ever living wight was fair,
Though nor in word nor deed ill meriting,
Is from her Knight divorcèd in despair,
And her due loves derived to that vile Witch's share.

Yet she, most faithful Lady all this while,
Forsaken, woeful, solitary maid,
Far from all people's press, as in exile,
In wilderness and wasteful deserts stray'd
To seek her Knight; who, subtilly betray'd
Through that late vision which th' Enchanter wrought,
Had her abandon'd: she, of nought affray'd,
Through woods and wasteness wide him daily sought;
Yet wishèd tidings none of him unto her brought.

One day, nigh weary of the irksome way,
From her unhasty beast she did alight;
And on the grass her dainty limbs did lay
In secret shadow, far from all men's sight;
From her fair head her fillet she undight,
And laid her stole aside: her angel's face,
As the great eye of heaven, shinèd bright,
And made a sunshine in the shady place:
Did never mortal eye behold such heavenly grace.

It fortunèd, out of the thickest wood
A ramping lion rushèd suddenly,
Hunting full greedy after savage blood:
Soon as the royal Virgin he did spy,
With gaping mouth at her ran greedily,
To have at once devour'd her tender corse;
But to the prey when as he drew more nigh,
His bloody rage assuagèd with remorse,
And, with the sight amazed, forgat his furious force.

Instead thereof, he kiss'd her weary feet,
And lick'd her lily hands with fawning tongue,
As he her wrongèd innocence did weet.
O, how can beauty master the most strong,
And simple truth subdue avenging wrong!
Whose yielded pride and proud submissiön,
Still dreading death, when she had markèd long,
Her heart 'gan melt in great compassiön;
And drizzling tears did shed for pure affectiön.

"The lion, lord of every beast in field,"
Quoth she, "his princely puissance doth abate,
And mighty proud to humble weak does yield,
Forgetful of the hungry rage which late
Him prick'd, in pity of my sad estate:—
But he, my lion, and my noble lord,
How does he find in cruel heart to hate
Her that him loved, and ever most adored
As the god of my life? why hath he me abhorr'd?"

Redounding tears did choke th' end of her plaint,
Which softly echo'd from the neighbor wood;
And, sad to see her sorrowful constraint,
The kingly beast upon her gazing stood;
With pity calm'd, down fell his angry mood.
At last, in close heart shutting up her pain,
Arose the Virgin born of heavenly brood,
And to her snowy palfrey got again,
To seek her strayèd Champion if she might attain.

The lion would not leave her desolate,
But with her went along, as a strong guard
Of her chaste person, and a faithful mate
Of her sad troubles and misfortunes hard :
Still, when she slept, he kept both watch and ward ;
And, when she waked, he waited diligent,
With humble service to her will prepared :
From her fair eyes he took commandëment,
And ever by her looks conceivèd her intent.

From " The Faerie Queene."

Una is the heroine of the first Book of Spenser's "Faerie Queene." She appears to have been intended, at least in part, as a poetical impersonation of Truth. At all events, she is one of the sweetest and loveliest visions that ever issued from a poet's brain.

l. 2. In Spenser's time the endings *sion*, *tion*, as also *cian*, and various others, were often used as two syllables.

l. 13. That is, *handling*, in the sense of *treatment*. Here, again, we have a relic of ancient usage. So, too, in *commandement*, in the last stanza of this piece. And in many other like words the old poets often make two syllables where we now make but one.

l. 18. An old witch named Duessa, painted and dressed up into a false show of beauty, and dealing in magic arts. She had lied and cheated the red-cross Knight, the hero of the story, out of his faith in Una and beguiled him with her mighty spells.

l. 32. *undight*, took off. l. 33. *stole*, a long, loose garment reaching to the feet. l. 48. *weet*, understand. l. 64. *Redounding*, flowing.

PURITY OF CHARACTER.

Over the plum and apricot there may be seen a bloom and beauty more exquisite than the fruit itself — a soft delicate flush that overspreads its blushing cheek. Now, if you strike your hand over that, and it
5 is once gone, it is gone forever; for it never grows but once.

The flower that hangs in the morning impearled with dew, arrayed with jewels, once shake it so that the beads roll off, and you may sprinkle water over it
10 as you please, yet it can never be made again what it was when the dew fell lightly upon it from heaven.

On a frosty morning you may see the panes of glass covered with landscapes, mountains, lakes, and trees, blended in a beautiful fantastic picture. Now lay
15 your hand upon the glass, and by the scratch of your fingers, or by the warmth of the palm, all the delicate tracery will be immediately obliterated.

So in youth there is a purity of character which when once touched and defiled can never be restored
20 — a fringe more delicate than frost-work, and which, when torn and broken, will never be reëmbroidered.

When a young man leaves his father's house, with the blessing of his mother's tears still wet upon his forehead, if he once loses that early purity of character,
25 it is a loss he can never make whole again.

DELIGHTS OF READING.

SIR JOHN LUBBOCK.

BOOKS are to mankind what memory is to the individual. They contain the history of our race, the discoveries we have made, the accumulated knowledge and experience of ages; they picture for us the marvels and beauties of nature; help us in our difficulties, comfort 5 us in sorrow and in suffering, change hours of weariness into moments of delight, store our minds with ideas, fill them with good and happy thoughts, and lift us out of and above ourselves.

There is an Oriental story of two men: one was a 10 king, who every night dreamt he was a beggar; the other was a beggar, who every night dreamt he was a prince and lived in a palace. I am not sure that the king had very much the best of it. Imagination is sometimes more vivid than reality. But, however this 15 may be, when we read we may not only (if we wish it) be kings and live in palaces, but, what is far better, we may transport ourselves to the mountains or the seashore, and visit the most beautiful parts of the earth, without fatigue, inconvenience, or expense. 20

Many of those who have had, as we say, all that this world can give, have yet told us they owed much of their purest happiness to books. Ascham, in "The Schoolmaster," tells a touching story of his last visit to Lady Jane Grey. He found her sitting in an oriel 25

window reading Plato's beautiful account of the death
of Socrates. Her father and mother were hunting in
the park, the hounds were in full cry and their voices
came in through the open window. He expressed his
5 surprise that she had not joined them. But, said she,
"I wist that all their pleasure in the park is but a
shadow to the pleasure I find in Plato."

Macaulay had wealth and fame, rank and power, and
yet he tells us in his biography that he owed the hap-
10 piest hours of his life to books. In a charming letter
to a little girl he says: "Thank you for your very pretty
letter. I am always glad to make my little girl happy,
and nothing pleases me so much as to see that she likes
books, for when she is as old as I am she will find that
15 they are better than all the tarts and cakes, toys and
plays, and sights in the world. If any one would make
me the greatest king that ever lived, with palaces and
gardens and fine dinners, and wines and coaches, and
beautiful clothes, and hundreds of servants, on condi-
20 tion that I should not read books, I would not be a
king. I would rather be a poor man in a garret
with plenty of books than a king who did not love
reading."

Books, indeed, endow us with a whole enchanted pal-
25 ace of thoughts. There is a wider prospect, says Jean
Paul Richter, from Parnassus than from the throne. In
one way they give us an even more vivid idea than the
actual reality, just as reflections are often more beautiful than real nature. All mirrors, says George Mac-

Donald, " are magic mirrors. The commonest room is a room in a poem when I look in the glass."

English literature is the birthright and inheritance of the English race. We have produced and are producing some of the greatest of poets, of philosophers, of men of science. No race can boast a brighter, purer, or nobler literature — richer than our commerce, more powerful than our arms. It is the true pride and glory of our country, and for it we cannot be too thankful.

Precious and priceless are the blessings which the books scatter around our daily paths. We walk, in imagination, with the noblest spirits, through the most sublime and enchanting regions, — regions which, to all that is lovely in the forms and colors of earth,

> " Add the gleam,
> The light that never was on sea or land,
> The consecration and the poet's dream."

Without stirring from our firesides we may roam to the most remote regions of the earth, or soar into realms where Spenser's shapes of unearthly beauty flock to meet us, where Milton's angels peal in our ears the choral hymns of Paradise. Science, art, literature, philosophy, — all that man has thought, all that man has done, — the experience that has been bought with the sufferings of a hundred generations, — all are garnered up for us in the world of books.

From " The Use of Life."

BREAK, BREAK, BREAK.

ALFRED TENNYSON.

For a sketch of the life of Tennyson, see "Cyr's Fourth Reader."

BREAK, break, break,
 On thy cold gray stones, O Sea!
And I would that my tongue could utter
 The thoughts that arise in me.

O well for the fisherman's boy
 That he shouts with his sister at play!
O well for the sailor lad
 That he sings in his boat on the bay!

And the stately ships go on
 To their haven under the hill:
But O for the touch of a vanished hand,
 And the sound of a voice that is still!

Break, break, break,
 At the foot of thy crags, O Sea!
But the tender grace of a day that is dead
 Will never come back to me.

WILLIAM SHAKESPEARE.

WILLIAM SHAKESPEARE was born in the year 1564, at Stratford-on-Avon, in England. Queen Elizabeth was on the throne then, and it was one of the most brilliant periods in all English history. The poems and plays that Shakespeare wrote are the greatest in the English language, and one cannot appreciate the best there is in literature unless he has studied them. It is strange that no one thought, in the time  that he lived, of writing his history, so that we might know as much about him and his boyhood as we do of most other great men.

Stratford is in the heart of England, and the stream 20 of Avon winds through a beautiful country. There were two famous old castles near by, which had been peopled by knights in armor, and out of whose great stone gateways they had ridden to battle.

We are sure that Shakespeare loved to listen to the 25 tales of these old battles, for in later years he based several of his great historical plays upon them.

One of these plays is called " Richard III.," and part
of the scenes are laid in the old Warwick Castle, near
his home. He tells how the young son of the Duke
of Clarence was kept a prisoner in one of the great
5 gloomy towers, by the wicked Duke of Gloucester,
who afterward became King Richard III. ; and the
play ends with the Battle of Bosworth Field, where
King Richard is slain.

We know that Shakespeare was fond of the woods
10 and the fields, for his plays are filled with charming
descriptions of their beauty. The forest of Arden was
near Stratford, and its streams and woods filled him
with such delight that when he became a man he made
them forever famous by writing a play called " As
15 You Like It," the most beautiful scenes of which are
laid in this forest.

He liked to imagine that fairies dwelt in the Arden
woods, and though he could not see them in their
frolics, he could picture them in his brain. When he
20 saw the grass and flowers wet with dew, it pleased him
to think that this had been a task set by the Queen of
the Fairies in the night for her tiny subjects. So in
his play, " A Midsummer Night's Dream," he makes a
fairy say : —

25
> " Over hill, over dale,
> Thorough brush, thorough brier,
>
> I do wander everywhere,
> Swifter than the moony sphere;
> And I serve the Fairy Queen."

Then the fairy tells its companion it must hasten
away to its task : —

> "I must go seek some dewdrops here
> And hang a pearl in every cowslip's ear."

Shakespeare must have been in the forest of Arden 5
often in the summer mornings and seen the dewdrops

BIRTHPLACE OF SHAKESPEARE.

clinging to the cowslips and glistening in the sunlight
like pearls.

The exact day that Shakespeare was born is not certain, but it was about the 23d of April, and many men 10
who have made a study of the poet's life accept that
as his birthday. The house in which he was born is
still standing, although it has, of course, undergone
many changes in the last three hundred years.

During the early boyhood of the poet, his father, 15

John Shakespeare, was a prosperous tradesman. He was a wool dealer and farmer. When Shakespeare was four years old his father became high-bailiff, or mayor of the town.

5 The future dramatist was sent to the village school at about the age of seven. He could already read, having learned his letters at home from a very queer primer. It was called the "horn-book," because it was made of a single printed leaf, set in a frame of
10 wood like our slates, and covered with a thin plate of horn.

The boy remained at school only about six years. His father had failed in many enterprises, and it is probable he needed his son to help him in his work.
15 Just what Shakespeare learned at school we do not know, but his writings show some knowledge of Greek and Latin, for these languages were taught in the schools at that time.

It is certain that Shakespeare's education went on
20 after he left school. That is, he learned something from everything he saw about him and from all that he read. Even the trees in the forest and the streams in the meadows taught him lessons about nature. And this idea he expresses in his own beautiful way
25 in the play "As You Like It," when he makes the banished Duke in the forest of Arden say : —

> " And this our life, exempt from public haunt,
> Finds tongues in trees, books in the running brooks,
> Sermons in stones, and good in everything."

It is quite probable that John Shakespeare unconsciously decided the career of his son, for it was while
he was mayor of Stratford that plays were first presented there, and the players must have obtained his
consent in order to give their performances.   5

We can also learn from his writings what games
Shakespeare was fond of, or, at least, what sports the
boys of his time took delight in.   In Shakespeare's
"Comedy of Errors" he refers to the game of football,
and in the historical play of "Julius Cæsar," there is 10
a fine description of a swimming match between Cæsar
and Cassius.   Cassius tells the story to Brutus of how
Cæsar challenged him to leap into the river Tiber,
armed as they were for battle : —

> "Cæsar said to me, 'Darest thou, Cassius, now   15
>   Leap in with me into this angry flood,
>   And swim to yonder point ? '   Upon the word,
>   Accoutered as I was, I plunged in
>   And bade him follow ; so, indeed, he did.
>   The torrent roar'd and we did buffet it   20
>   With lusty sinews, throwing it aside
>   And stemming it with hearts of controversy."

Cassius then tells how Cæsar's strength gave out and
he cried for help, and how Cassius brought him safe to
land.   25

Other sports of Shakespeare's day were archery,
wrestling, hunting, and falconry, where a bird called a
falcon was let loose into the air to pursue its prey.

When Shakespeare was in his nineteenth year he married Anne Hathaway, and a few years later he set out to seek his fortune in London.

He had played some small parts on the stage at
5 Stratford, and it is not surprising that we soon find him among the players in London, filling such trifling parts as were offered to him, and even, some accounts say, holding horses at the stage door to help support himself and his family.

10 His leisure time was spent in study. "Plutarch's Lives" furnished him with material for his plays of "Julius Cæsar," "Antony and Cleopatra," and parts, at least, of others.

He was a great student of the Bible, so much so
15 that a learned bishop who made a study of his plays found that Shakespeare in all his writings had in five hundred and fifty different places either quoted from the Scriptures or referred to them.

Shakespeare rose to fame rapidly. He was associ-
20 ated in the building of a new theater called the Globe, where his plays were acted before thousands. Then the Blackfriars Theater was built, and these two houses divided the honor of producing his plays.

He gathered up the history of England, the gran-
25 deur of its courts, the beauty of its woods and fields, and the deeds of its people, and told of it all in such masterful dramas that his name leads all other English writers.

The last few years of his life were spent at Stratford-on-Avon, where he had become a large land-owner. He died in the year 1616, at the age of fifty-two.

Nearly every great English writer and poet ever since has referred, in some way or other, to the plays of Shakespeare. The speeches of our statesmen owe 5 much of their strength and beauty to the influence of his writings. It has been said that " Shakespeare is like a great primeval forest, whence timber shall be cut and used as long as winds blow and leaves are green."

THE THREE CASKETS.

[ABRIDGED.]

WILLIAM SHAKESPEARE.

Belmont. A Room in Portia's House. Three Caskets of Gold, Silver, and Lead on Table.

Portia, a beautiful and accomplished heiress, is sought in marriage by a large number of suitors, whose fate is to be determined by the choice they make of one of three caskets — gold, silver, and base lead.

The following are the comments of three of the suitors — the Prince of Morocco, the Prince ♪ Arragon, and Bassanio: —

Enter Portia, with the Prince of Morocco.

PORTIA.

Now make your choice.

MOROCCO.

The first, of gold, which this inscription bears, —
Who chooseth me shall gain what many men desire ;

The second, silver, which this promise carries, —

Who chooseth me shall get as much as he deserves.

This third, dull lead, with warning all as blunt, —

Who chooseth me must give and hazard all he hath. —

How shall I know if I do choose the right?

PORTIA.

The one of them contains my picture, Prince:
If you choose that, then I am yours withal.

MOROCCO.

Some god direct my judgment! Let me see;
I will survey th' inscriptions back again.
What says this leaden casket?

Who chooseth me must give and hazard all he hath.

Must give, — for what? for lead? hazard for lead?
This casket threatens: men, that hazard all
Do it in hope of fair advantages.
A golden mind stoops not to shows of dross;
I 'll then nor give nor hazard aught for lead.
What says the silver, with her virgin hue?

Who chooseth me shall get as much as he deserves.

As much as he deserves! — Pause there, Morocco,
And weigh thy value with an even hand:
If thou be'st rated by thy estimation,
Thou dost deserve enough; and yet enough
May not extend so far as to the lady:

And yet to be afeard of my deserving,
Were but a weak disabling of myself.
As much as I deserve! Why, that's the lady:
I do in birth deserve her, and in fortunes,
In graces, and in qualities of breeding;
But, more than these, in love I do deserve.
What if I stray'd no further, but chose here?
Let's see once more this saying graved in gold:

> *Who chooseth me shall gain what many men desire.*

Why, that's the lady; all the world desires her:
. . . . Deliver me the key;
Here do I choose, and thrive I as I may!

PORTIA.

There, take it, Prince, and if my form lie there,
Then I am yours. [*He unlocks the golden casket.*

MOROCCO.

What have we here?
A carrion Death, within whose empty eye
There is a written scroll! I'll read the writing.

> [Reads] *All that glisters is not gold, —*
> *Often have you heard that told:*
> *Many a man his life hath sold,*
> *But my outside to behold:*
> *Gilded tombs do worms infold.*
> *Had you been as wise as bold,*
> *Young in limbs, in judgment old,*
> *Your answer had not been inscroll'd:*
> *Fare you well; your suit is cold.*

Cold, indeed ; and labor lost ;
Then, farewell, heat, and welcome, frost !—
Portia, adieu ! I have too grieved a heart
To take a tedious leave : thus losers part.

[Exit with train.

Enter Prince of Arragon.

PORTIA.

Behold, there stand the caskets, noble Prince ;
If you choose that wherein I am contain'd,
Straight shall our nuptial rites be solemnized :
But if you fail, without more speech, my lord,
You must be gone from hence immediately.

ARRAGON.

I am enjoin'd by oath to observe three things :
First, never to unfold to any one
Which casket 't was I chose ; next, if I fail
Of the right casket, never in my life
To woo a maid in way of marriage ; lastly,
If I do fail in fortune of my choice,
Immediately to leave you, and be gone.

PORTIA.

To these injunctions everyone doth swear
That comes to hazard for my worthless self.

ARRAGON.

And so have I address'd me.   Fortune now
To my heart's hope !— Gold, silver, and base lead.
Who chooseth me must give and hazard all he hath.

You shall look fairer, ere I give, or hazard.
What says the golden chest? ha! let me see:

Who chooseth me shall gain what many men desire.

What many men desire!—That *many* may be meant
By the fool multitude, that choose by show,
Not learning more than the fond eye doth teach;
Which pries not to the interior, but, like the martlet,
Builds in the weather on the outward wall,
Even in the force and road of casualty.
I will not choose what many men desire,
Because I will not jump with common spirits,
And rank me with the barbarous multitude.
Why, then to thee, thou silver treasure-house;
Tell me once more what title thou dost bear:

Who chooseth me shall get as much as he deserves.

And well said too: for who shall go about
To cozen fortune, and be honorable
Without the stamp of merit? Let none presume
To wear an undeserved dignity.
O, that estates, degrees, and offices
Were not derived corruptly! and that clear honor
Were purchased by the merit of the wearer!
How many then should cover, that stand bare!
How many be commanded, that command!
How much low peasantry would then be glean'd
From the true seed of honor! and how much honor
Pick'd from the chaff and ruin of the times,
To be new-varnish'd! Well, but to my choice:

Who chooseth me shall get as much as he deserves.

I will assume desert. — Give me a key,
And instantly unlock my fortunes here.

> [*He opens the silver casket.*

PORTIA.

Too long a pause for that which you find there.

ARRAGON.

What's here? the portrait of a blinking idiot,
Presenting me a schedule!   I will read it. —
How much unlike art thou to Portia!
How much unlike my hopes, and my deservings!

Who chooseth me shall have as much as he deserves.

Did I deserve no more than a fool's head?
Is that my prize? are my deserts no better?

PORTIA.

T' offend, and judge, are distinct offices,
And of opposèd natures.

ARRAGON.

What is here?

> *The fire seven times tried this:*
> *Seven times tried that judgment is*
> *That did never choose amiss.*
> *Some there be, that shadows kiss;*
> *Such have but a shadow's bliss:*
> *There be fools alive, I wis,*
> *Silver'd o'er; and so was this.*

Still more fool I shall appear
By the time I linger here:
With one fool's head I came to woo,
But I go away with two. —
Sweet, adieu! I'll keep my oath,
Patiently to bear my wroth.

[*Exeunt Arragon and Train.*]

Enter Bassanio.

BASSANIO.

So may the outward shows be least themselves:
The world is still deceived with ornament.
In law, what plea so tainted and corrupt,
But, being season'd with a gracious voice,
Obscures the show of evil?

.   .   .   .

There is no vice so simple, but assumes
Some mark of virtue on its outward parts:
How many cowards, whose hearts are all as false
As stayers of sand, wear yet upon their chins
The beards of Hercules and frowning Mars;
Who, inward search'd, have livers white as milk!
And these assume but valor's excrement,
To render them redoubted.   Look on beauty,
And you shall see 't is purchased by the weight;
Which therein works a miracle in nature,
Making them lightest that wear most of it:
So are those crispèd snaky golden locks,

Which make such wanton gambols with the wind,
Upon supposèd fairness, often known
To be the dowry of a second head,
The skull that bred them in the sepulcher.
Thus ornament is but the guilèd shore
To a most dangerous sea; the beauteous scarf
Veiling an Indian feature; in a word,
The seeming truth which cunning times put on
T' entrap the wisest. Therefore, thou gaudy gold,
Hard food for Midas, I will none of thee:
Nor none of thee, thou stale and common drudge
'Tween man and man: but thou, thou meager lead,
Which rather threatenest, than dost promise aught,
Thy plainness moves me more than eloquence;
And here choose I: Joy be the consequence!

> [*Opening the leaden casket.*

—— What find I here?
Fair Portia's counterfeit!
—— Here 's the scroll,
The continent and summary of my fortune: ——

> *You that choose not by the view*
> *Chance as fair, and choose as true:*
> *Since this fortune falls to you,*
> *Be content and seek no new.*
> *If you be well pleased with this,*
> *And hold your fortune for your bliss,*
> *Turn you where your lady is,*
> *And claim her with a loving kiss.*

PORTIA.

You see me, Lord Bassanio, where I stand,
Such as I am : though, for myself alone,
I would not be ambitious in my wish,
To wish myself much better ; yet, for you,
I would be trebled twenty times myself ;
A thousand times more fair, ten thousand times more rich ;
That, only to stand high on your account,
I might in virtues, beauties, livings, friends,
Exceed account : but the full sum of me
Is sum of — something ; which, to term in gross,
Is an unlesson'd girl, unschool'd, unpracticed :
Happy in this, she is not yet so old
But she may learn ; then happier in this,
She is not bred so dull but she can learn ;
Happiest of all, in that her gentle spirit
Commits itself to yours to be directed,
As from her lord, her governor, her king.
Myself and what is mine to you and yours
Is now converted : but now I was the lord
Of this fair mansion, master of my servants,
Queen o'er myself ; and even now, but now,
This house, these servants, and this same myself,
Are yours, my lord ; I give them with this ring ;
Which when you part from, lose, or give away,
Let it presage the ruin of your love,
And be my vantage to exclaim on you.

From " The Merchant of Venice."

QUOTATIONS FROM SHAKESPEARE.

ADVERSITY.

SWEET are the uses of adversity;
Which, like the toad, ugly and venomous,
Wears yet a precious jewel in his head:
And this our life, exempt from public haunt,
Finds tongues in trees, books in the running brooks,
Sermons in stones, and good in everything.

"As You Like It."

REPUTATION.

GOOD name in man and woman, dear my lord,
Is the immediate jewel of their souls:
Who steals my purse steals trash; 't is something,
    nothing;
'T was mine, 't is his, and has been slave to thousands;
But he that filches from me my good name
Robs me of that which not enriches him,
And makes me poor indeed.

"Othello."

FEAR OF DEATH.

COWARDS die many times before their death;
The valiant never taste of death but once.
Of all the wonders that I yet have heard,
It seems to me most strange that men should fear;
Seeing that death, a necessary end,
Will come when it will come.

"Julius Cæsar."

SHAKESPEARE'S POETRY.

FRANCIS JEFFREY.

FRANCIS JEFFREY was born in Edinburgh in 1773 and died in 1850. He attended the schools of his native city and completed his education in the Universities of Glasgow and Oxford, preparing himself for the pursuit of law.

He was also a writer of essays and criticisms and attained 5 high rank as a judge and writer. He was at one time editor of the famous "Edinburgh Review."

SHAKESPEARE alone, when the object requires it, is always keen and worldly and practical; and yet, without changing his hand or stopping his course, 10 scatters around him, as he goes, all sounds and shapes of sweetness, and conjures up landscapes of immortal fragrance and freshness, and peoples them with Spirits of glorious aspect and attractive grace. He is a thousand times more full of fancy and imagery and 15 splendor than those who, in pursuit of such enchantments, have shrunk back from the delineation of character or passion, and declined the discussion of human duties and cares.

More full of wisdom and ridicule and sagacity than 20 all the moralists and satirists that ever existed, he is also more wild, airy, and inventive, and more pathetic and fantastic, than all the poets of all regions and ages of the world. And he has all those elements so happily mixed up in him, and bears his high faculties so tem- 25 perately, that the most severe reader cannot complain

of him for want of strength or of reason, nor the most sensitive for defect of ornament or ingenuity. Everything in him is in unmeasured abundance and unequaled perfection; but everything is so balanced and kept in
5 subordination, as not to jostle or disturb or take the place of another.

The most exquisite poetical conceptions, images, and descriptions are given with such brevity, and introduced with such skill, as merely to adorn, without loading,
10 the sense they accompany. Although his sails are purple and perfumed, and his prow of beaten gold, they waft him on his voyage, not less, but more rapidly and directly than if they had been composed of baser materials. All his excellences, like those of Nature
15 herself, are thrown out together; and, instead of interfering with, support and recommend each other. His flowers are not tied up in garlands, nor his fruits crushed into baskets; but spring living from the soil, in all the dew and freshness of youth; while the grace-
20 ful foliage in which they lurk, and the ample branches, the rough and vigorous stem, and the wide-spreading roots on which they depend, are present along with them, and share, in their places, the equal care of their creator.

HOME.

HENRY W. GRADY.

HENRY W. GRADY was born in Georgia in 1851. While a student at the University of Georgia, he excelled in debate. On graduation, he determined to make journalism his life-work. As the editor of the "Atlanta Constitution," he rapidly grew into prominence as a journalist and an orator. Mr. Grady died 5 in 1889.

A FEW days later I visited a country home. A modest, quiet house sheltered by great trees and set in a circle of field and meadow, gracious with the promise of harvest ; barns and cribs well filled and the old 10 smoke-house odorous with treasure; the fragrance of pink and hollyhock mingling with the aroma of garden and orchard and resonant with the hum of bees and poultry's busy clucking ; inside the house, thrift, comfort, and that cleanliness that is next to godliness — the 15 restful beds, the open fireplace, the books and papers, and the old clock that had held its steadfast pace amid the frolic of weddings, that had welcomed in steady measure the newborn babes of the family, and kept company with the watchers of the sick bed, and had 20 ticked the solemn requiem of the dead ; and the well-worn Bible that, thumbed by fingers long since stilled, and blurred with tears of eyes long since closed, held the simple annals of the family and the heart and conscience of the home. 25

Outside stood the master, strong and wholesome and upright; wearing no man's collar; with no mortgage on his roof and no lien on his ripening harvest; pitching his crops in his own wisdom and selling them in his 5 own time in his chosen market; master of his lands and master of himself. Near by stood his aged father, happy in the heart and home of his son. And as they started to the house, the old man's hands rested on the young man's shoulder, touching it with the knight-10 hood of the fifth commandment and laying there the unspeakable blessing of an honored and grateful father.

As they drew near the door, the old mother appeared, the sunset falling on her face, softening its wrinkles 15 and its tenderness, lighting up her patient eyes, and the rich music of her heart trembling on her lips, as in simple phrase she welcomed her husband and son to their home. Beyond was the good wife, true of touch and tender, happy amid her household cares, 20 clean of heart and conscience, the helpmate and the buckler of her husband. And the children, strong and sturdy, trooping down the lane with the lowing herd, or, weary of simple sport, seeking, as truant birds do, the quiet of the old home nest.

25 And I saw the night descend on that home, falling gently as from the wings of the unseen dove. And the stars swarmed in the bending skies; the trees thrilled with the cricket's cry; the restless bird called from the neighboring wood; and the father, a simple man of

God, gathering the family about him, read from the Bible the old, old story of love and faith and then went down in prayer, the baby hidden amid the folds of its mother's dress, and closed the record of that simple day by calling down the benediction of God on the family and the home!

And as I gazed, the memory of the great Capitol faded from my brain. Forgotten its treasure and its splendor. And I said, " Surely here — here in the homes of the people — is lodged the ark of the covenant of my country. Here is its majesty and its strength; here the beginning of its power and the end of its responsibility." The homes of the people — let us keep them pure and independent, and all will be well with the Republic. Here is the lesson our foes may learn — here is work the humblest and weakest hands may do.

Let us in simple thrift and economy make our homes independent. Let us in frugal industry make them self-sustaining. In sacrifice and denial let us keep them free from debt and obligation. Let us make them homes of refinement in which we shall teach our daughters that modesty and patience and gentleness are the charms of woman. Let us make them temples of liberty, and teach our sons that an honest conscience is every man's first political law; that his sovereignty rests beneath his hat, and that no splendor can rob him and no force justify the surrender of the simplest right of a free and independent citizen. And

above all, let us honor God in our homes — anchor
them close in His love. Build His altars above our
hearthstones, uphold them in the set and simple faith
of our fathers, and crown them with the Bible — that
5 book of books in which all the ways of life are made
straight and the mystery of death is made plain.

Let us keep sacred the Sabbath of God in its purity,
and have no city so great, or village so small, that
every Sunday morning shall not stream forth over
10 towns and meadows the golden benediction of the
bells, as they summon the people to the churches of
their fathers, and ring out in praise of God and the
power of His might. Let us keep the states of this
Union in the current of the sweet old-fashioned, that
15 the sweet rushing waters may lap their sides, and everywhere from their soil grow the tree, the leaf whereof
shall not fade, and the fruit whereof shall not die.

Let us remember that the home is the source of our
national life. Back of the national Capitol and above
20 it stands the home. Back of the President and above
him stands the citizen. What the home is, this and
nothing else will the Capitol be. What the citizen
wills, this and nothing else will the President be.

A PALACE IN A VALLEY.

DR. SAMUEL JOHNSON.

DR. SAMUEL JOHNSON was born at Lichfield, England, in 1709, and died in 1784.

He was educated at Oxford, where he gained honor as a student in spite of his poverty and defective eyesight.

After leaving college Johnson held a position as an usher, 5 and later was employed by some booksellers.

He gradually began a literary life, publishing some poems, and then conducted "The Rambler" and "The Idler," two periodicals.

He wrote the story of "Rasselas" to pay the expenses of 10 his mother's funeral. His greatest work was a Dictionary of the English Language.

Dr. Johnson's character was a strange union of strength and weakness. His manners were uncouth, but his conversation was rich in wit and wisdom. His genius was recognized during the 15 latter years of his life.

YE who listen with credulity to the whispers of fancy and pursue with eagerness the phantoms of hope; who expect that age will perform the promises of youth, and that the deficiencies of the present day will be supplied 20 by the morrow, — attend to the history of Rasselas, Prince of Abyssinia.

Rasselas was the fourth son of the mighty emperor in whose dominions the Father of Waters begins his course; whose bounty pours down the streams of plenty 25 and scatters over half the world the harvests of Egypt.

According to the custom which has descended from age to age among the monarchs of the torrid zone,

Rasselas was confined in a private palace, with the other sons and daughters of Abyssinian royalty, till the order of succession should call him to the throne.

The place which the wisdom or policy of antiquity 5 had destined for the residence of the Abyssinian princes was a spacious valley in the kingdom of Amhara, surrounded on every side by mountains, of which the summits overhang the middle part. The only passage by which it could be entered was a cavern that passed 10 under a rock. The outlet of the cavern was concealed by a thick wood, and the mouth which opened into the valley was closed with gates of iron.

From the mountains on every side rivulets descended that filled all the valley with verdure and fertility, and 15 formed a lake in the middle inhabited by fish of every species, and frequented by every fowl whom Nature has taught to dip the wing in water. This lake discharged its superfluities by a stream which entered a dark cleft of the mountain on the northern side, and 20 fell with dreadful noise from precipice to precipice till it was heard no more.

The sides of the mountains were covered with trees, the banks of the brooks were diversified with flowers; every blast shook spices from the rocks, and every 25 month dropped fruits upon the ground. All animals that bite the grass, or browse the shrub, whether wild or tame, wandered in this extensive circuit, secured from beasts of prey by the mountains which confined them. On one part were flocks and herds feeding in the pastures; on another, all beasts of chase frisking in the lawns. All the diversities of the world were brought together, the blessings of nature were collected, and its evils extracted and excluded.

The valley, wide and fruitful, supplied its inhabitants ₅ with the necessaries of life, and all delights and super-fluities were added at the annual visit which the emperor paid his children, when the iron gate was opened to the sound of music; and during eight days every one that resided in the valley was required to propose whatever ₁₀ might contribute to make seclusion pleasant, to fill up the vacancies of attention, and lessen the tediousness of time. Every desire was immediately granted. All the artificers of pleasure were called to gladden the festivity; the musicians exerted the power of harmony, ₁₅ and the dancers showed their activity before the princes, in hope that they should pass their lives in this blissful captivity, to which those only were admitted whose performance was thought able to add novelty to luxury. Such was the appearance of security and delight which ₂₀ this retirement afforded, that they to whom it was new always desired that it might be perpetual; and as those on whom the iron gate had once closed were never suffered to return, the effect of long experience could not be known. Thus every year produced new schemes ₂₅ of delight and new competitors for imprisonment.

The palace stood on an eminence raised about thirty paces above the surface of the lake. It was divided into many squares or courts, built with greater or less magnificence, according to the rank of those for whom they were designed. The roofs were turned into arches of massy stone, joined by a cement that grew harder by time, and the building stood from century to century 5 deriding the rains and equinoctial hurricanes, without need of reparation.

This house, which was so large as to be fully known to none but some ancient officers who successively inherited the secrets of the place, was built as if suspicion 10 herself had dictated the plan. To every room there was an open and secret passage; every square had a communication with the rest, either from the upper stories by private galleries, or by subterranean passages from the lower apartments. Many of the columns had 15 unsuspected cavities, in which a long race of monarchs had deposited their treasures. They then closed up the opening with marble, which was never to be removed but in the utmost exigencies of the kingdom; and recorded their accumulations in a book which was 20 itself concealed in a tower not entered but by the emperor, attended by the prince who stood next in succession.

Here the sons and daughters of Abyssinia lived only to know the soft vicissitudes of pleasure and repose, 25 attended by all that were skilful to delight, and gratified with whatever the senses can enjoy. They wandered in gardens of fragrance and slept in the fortresses of security. Every art was practiced to make them pleased with their own condition. The sages who instructed them told them of nothing but the miseries of public life, and described all beyond the mountains as regions of calamity, where discord was always raging, and where man preyed upon man.

To heighten their opinion of their own felicity, they 5 were daily entertained with songs, the subject of which was the happy valley. Their appetites were excited by frequent enumerations of different enjoyments, and revelry and merriment was the business of every hour from the dawn of morning to the close of even. 10

These methods were generally successful; few of the princes had ever wished to enlarge their bounds, but passed their lives in full conviction that they had all within their reach that art or nature could bestow, and pitied those whom fate had excluded from this seat of 15 tranquillity.

Thus they rose in the morning and lay down at night, pleased with each other and with themselves,— all but Rasselas, who, in the twenty-sixth year of his age, began to withdraw himself from their pastimes 20 and assemblies, and to delight in solitary walks and silent meditation. He often sat before tables covered with luxury, and forgot to taste the dainties that were placed before him; he rose abruptly in the midst of the song and hastily retired beyond the sound of music. 25 His attendants observed the change and endeavored to renew his love of pleasure. He neglected their officiousness, repulsed their invitations, and spent day after day on the banks of rivulets sheltered with trees, where he sometimes listened to the birds in the branches, sometimes observed the fish playing in the stream, and anon cast his eyes upon the pastures and mountains filled with animals.

5 This singularity of his humor made him much observed. One of the sages, in whose conversation he had formerly delighted, followed him secretly, in hope of discovering the cause of his disquiet. Rasselas, who knew not that any one was near him, having for some 10 time fixed his eyes upon the goats that were browsing among the rocks, began to compare their condition with his own.

"What," said he, "makes the difference between man and all the rest of the animal creation? Every 15 beast that strays beside me has the same bodily necessities with myself; he is hungry and crops the grass, he is thirsty and drinks the stream; his thirst and hunger are appeased, he is satisfied and sleeps; he rises again and is hungry; he is again fed and is at 20 rest. I am hungry and thirsty, like him; but when thirst and hunger cease, I am not at rest; I am, like him, pained with want; but am not, like him, satisfied with fullness. The intermediate hours are tedious and gloomy; I long again to be hungry, that I may again 25 quicken my attention. The birds peck the berries or the corn, and fly away to the groves, where they sit in seeming happiness on the branches and waste their lives in tuning one unvaried series of sounds. I likewise can call the lutanist and singer, but the sounds that pleased me yesterday weary me to-day, and will grow more wearisome to-morrow. I can discover within me no power of perception which is not glutted with its proper pleasure, yet I do not feel myself delighted. Man surely has some latent sense for which 5 this place affords no gratification, or he has some desires distinct from sense, which must be satisfied before he can be happy."

After this he lifted up his head, and, seeing the moon rising, walked toward the palace. As he passed through 10 the fields and saw the animals around him, "Ye," said he, "are happy, and need not envy me that walk thus among you, burdened with myself; nor do I, ye gentle beings, envy your felicity, for it is not the felicity of man. I have many distresses from which ye are free; 15 I fear pain when I do not feel it; surely the equity of Providence has balanced peculiar sufferings with peculiar enjoyments."

With observations like these the prince amused himself as he returned, uttering them with a plaintive 20 voice, yet with a look that discovered him to feel some complacence in his own perspicacity, and to receive some solace of the miseries of life from consciousness of the delicacy with which he bewailed them. He mingled cheerfully in the diversions of the evening, 25 and all rejoiced to find that his heart was lightened.

From "Rasselas."

TRUE HEROISM.

LET others write of battles fought,
  Of bloody, ghastly fields,
Where honor greets the man who wins,
  And death the man who yields;
But I will write of him who fights
  And vanquishes his sins,
Who struggles on through weary years
  Against himself, and wins.

He is a hero stanch and brave
  Who fights an unseen foe,
And puts at last beneath his feet
  His passions base and low;
Who stands erect in manhood's might,
  Undaunted, undismayed,—
The bravest man who drew a sword
  In foray or in raid.

It calls for something more than brawn
  Or muscle to o'ercome
An enemy who marcheth not
  With banner, plume, or drum,—
A foe forever lurking nigh,
  With silent, stealthy tread;
Forever near your board by day,
  At night beside your bed.

All honor, then, to that brave heart,
   Though poor or rich he be,
Who struggles with his baser part, —
   Who conquers and is free!
He may not wear a hero's crown,
   Or fill a hero's grave;
But truth will place his name among
   The bravest of the brave.

THE PEN.

EDWARD BULWER LYTTON.

BENEATH the rule of men entirely great
The pen is mightier than the sword. Behold
The arch enchanter's wand! — itself a nothing
But taking sorcery from the master's hand
To paralyze the Cæsars and to strike
The loud earth breathless! Take away the sword —
States can be saved without it.

From " Richelieu."

MOUNT VERNON, THE HOME OF WASHINGTON.

CHARACTER OF WASHINGTON.

GEORGE BANCROFT.

GEORGE BANCROFT was born at Worcester, Mass., in 1800 and died in 1891.

He was graduated from Harvard College when he was seventeen, bearing off the second honors of his class.

5 The following year he sailed for Europe and spent five years studying under the most learned professors in Germany, France, and Italy.

On his return to America he became a tutor at Harvard and was afterwards connected with a classical school at Northampton.

10 He was deeply interested in the affairs of the nation, but refused to enter public life, as he had decided to write a history of the United States.

The first volume of this history appeared in 1834, and the series occupied his time for many years.

Mr. Bancroft held the position of secretary of the navy for about a year under President Polk. It was due to his efforts that the Naval Academy at Annapolis, Md., was established.

He was appointed minister to England in 1846 and remained abroad for three years.   5

He returned to this country and resumed his literary work. In 1867 he was appointed minister to Berlin by President Grant.

The "History of the United States" is without a rival. It is generally accepted as an authority. Mr. Bancroft spared no pains in his researches among old manuscripts, and his style 10 is full of interest.

At eleven years old, left, an orphan, to the care of an excellent but unlettered mother, Washington grew up without learning. Of arithmetic and geometry he acquired just knowledge enough to be able to practice 15 measuring land; but all his instruction at school taught him not so much as the orthography or rules of grammar of his own tongue. His culture was altogether his own work, and he was in the strictest sense a self-made man; yet from his early life he never seemed uneducated. At 20 sixteen he went into the wilderness as surveyor, and for three years continued the pursuit, where the forest trained him, in meditative solitude, to freedom and largeness of mind; and Nature revealed to him her obedience to serene and silent laws.   25

In his intervals from toil, he seemed always to be attracted to the best men, and to be cherished by them. Fairfax, his employer, an Oxford scholar, already aged, became his fast friend. He read little, but with close attention. Whatever he took in hand, he applied him- 30

self to with care ; and his papers, which have been preserved, show how he almost imperceptibly gained the power of writing correctly ; always expressing himself with clearness and directness, often with felicity of
5 language and grace.

Courage was so natural to him that it was hardly spoken of to his praise; no one ever at any moment of his life discovered in him the least shrinking from danger; and he had a hardihood of daring which
10 escaped notice, because it was so enveloped by superior calmness and wisdom.

He was as cheerful as he was spirited ; frank and communicative in the society of friends; fond of the fox-chase and the dance; often sportive in his letters ;
15 and liked a hearty laugh. This joyousness of disposition remained to the last, though the vastness of his responsibilities was soon to take from him the right of displaying the impulsive qualities of his nature, and the weight which he was to bear up was to overlay and
20 repress his gayety and openness.

His hand was liberal; giving quietly and without observation, as though he were ashamed of nothing but being discovered in doing good. He was kindly and compassionate, and of lively sensibility to the sorrows
25 of others; so that, if his country had only needed a victim for its relief, he would have willingly offered himself as a sacrifice. But while he was prodigal of himself, he was considerate for others ; ever parsimonious of the blood of his countrymen.

His faculties were so well balanced and combined that his constitution, free from excess, was tempered evenly with all the elements of activity, and his mind resembled a well-ordered commonwealth; his passions, which had the intensest vigor, owned allegiance to reason; and with all the fiery quickness of his spirit his impetuous and massive will was held in check by consummate judgment. He had in his composition a calm which gave him, in moments of highest excitement, the power of self-control, and enabled him to excel in patience, even when he had most cause for disgust. Washington was offered a command when there was little to bring out the unorganized resources of the continent but his own influence, and authority was connected with the people by the most frail, most attenuated, scarcely discernible threads; yet, vehement as was his nature, impassioned as was his courage, he so restrained his ardor, that he never failed continuously to exert the attracting power of that influence, and never exerted it so sharply as to break its force.

His understanding was lucid, and his judgment accurate; so that his conduct never betrayed hurry or confusion. No detail was too minute for his personal inquiry and continued supervision; and at the same time he comprehended events in their widest aspects and relations. He never seemed above the object that engaged his attention; and he was always equal, without an effort, to the solution of the highest questions, even when there existed no precedents to guide his decision.

In this way he never drew to himself admiration for the possession of any one quality in excess ; never made in council any one suggestion that was sublime but impracticable ; never in action took to himself the
5 praise or the blame of undertakings astonishing in conception, but beyond his means of execution. It was the most wonderful accomplishment of this man that, placed upon the largest theater of events, at the head of the greatest revolution in human affairs, he never
10 failed to observe all that was possible, and at the same time to bound his aspirations by that which was possible.

Profoundly impressed with confidence in God's providence, and exemplary in his respect for the forms
15 of public worship, no philosopher of the eighteenth century was more firm in the support of freedom of religious opinion ; none more tolerant, or more remote from bigotry ; but belief in God and trust in His overruling power formed the essence of his character.
20 Divine wisdom not only illumines the spirit, it inspires the will. Washington was a man of action, and not of theory or words ; his creed appears in his life, not in his professions, which burst from him very rarely, and only at those great moments of crisis in the fortunes of
25 his country, when Earth and Heaven seemed actually to meet, and his emotions became too intense for suppression ; but his whole being was one continued act of faith in the eternal, intelligent, moral order of the Universe. Integrity was so completely the law of

his nature, that a planet would sooner have shot from its sphere, than he have departed from his uprightness, which was so constant that it often seemed to be almost impersonal.

They say of Giotto, that he introduced goodness into the art of painting: Washington carried it with him to the camp and the cabinet, and established a new criterion of human greatness. The purity of his will confirmed his fortitude; and, as he never faltered in his faith in virtue, he stood fast by that which he knew to be just; free from illusions; never dejected by the apprehension of the difficulties and perils that went before him; and drawing the promise of success from the justice of his cause. Hence he was persevering, leaving nothing unfinished; free from all taint of obstinacy in his firmness; seeking and gladly receiving advice, but immovable in his devotedness to right.

Of a "retiring modesty and habitual reserve," his ambition was no more than the consciousness of his power, and was subordinate to his sense of duty; he took the foremost place, for he knew, from inborn magnanimity, that it belonged to him, and he dared not withhold the service required of him; so that, with all his humility, he was by necessity the first, though never for himself or for private ends. He loved fame, the approval of coming generations, the good opinion of his fellow-men of his own time; and he desired to make his conduct coincide with their wishes; but not fear of censure, not the prospect of applause, could tempt him to swerve from rectitude; and the praise which he coveted was the sympathy of that moral sentiment which exists in every human breast, and goes forth only to the welcome of virtue.

5   This also is the praise of Washington, that never in the tide of time has any man lived who had in so great a degree the almost divine faculty to command the confidence of his fellow-men and rule the willing. Wherever he became known, in his family, his neighborhood, 10 his county, his native state, the continent, the camp, civil life, the United States, among the common people, in foreign courts, throughout the civilized world of the human race, and even among the savages, he, beyond all other men, had the confidence of his kind.

NATIONAL HYMN.

SAMUEL FRANCIS SMITH.

SAMUEL FRANCIS SMITH was born in Boston in 1808, and died in 1895.

He attended the Boston Latin School, was graduated at Harvard College, and then studied for the ministry at the Andover Theological Seminary. While in Harvard he was a classmate of 5 Oliver Wendell Holmes. At a reunion of his class, held many years after they had left college, Holmes read a poem which he had written for the occasion, called "The Boys," and spoke of Mr. Smith in these words:

> "He chanted a song for the brave and the free, 10
> Just read on his medal, 'My Country, of thee.'"

He referred to the poem beginning "My country, 't is of thee," the national hymn of America, written by Mr. Smith when he was a young theological student, and first sung at a children's celebration, held on one Fourth of July, in the Park Street 15 Church, Boston.

A collection of his hymns and poems has been published under the title of "Lyric Gems."

> MY country, 't is of thee,
> Sweet land of liberty,
>   Of thee I sing;
> Land where my fathers died,
> Land of the pilgrim's pride,
> From every mountain side
>   Let freedom ring.

My native country, thee —
Land of the noble free —
　　Thy name I love;
I love thy rocks and rills,
Thy woods and templed hills,
My heart with rapture thrills
　　Like that above.

Let music swell the breeze,
And ring from all the trees
　　Sweet freedom's song;
Let mortal tongues awake;
Let all that breathe partake;
Let rocks their silence break —
　　The sound prolong.

Our fathers' God, to thee,
Author of liberty,
　　To thee we sing:
Long may our land be bright
With freedom's holy light;
Protect us by thy might,
　　Great God, our King.

GUIDE TO PRONUNCIATION.

A key to the symbols most of which are used in this Reader to indicate the pronunciation of the more difficult words.

I. VOWELS.

ā as in fāte		â as in câre		ĭ as in ĭdea		ōō as in fōōd	
ȧ " senȧte		ē " mēte		ĭ " ĭt		ŏŏ " fŏŏt	
ă " făt		ĕ " ĕvent		ī " sīr		ū " ūse	
ä " ärm		ĕ " mĕt		ō " ōld		ṳ " ṳnite	
a " all		ẽ " hẽr		ȯ " ȯbey		ŭ " ŭp	
ȧ " ȧsk		ī " īce		ŏ " nŏt		û " fûr	

II. EQUIVALENTS.

a = ŏ as in whạt		ọ = ōō as in wọlf		u = ōō as in pṵll	
ê = â " thêre		ó = ŭ " sòn		ȳ = ī " flȳ	
ī = ē " gīrl		ô = a " hôrse		y̆ = ĭ " baby̆	
ọ = ōō " mọve		u = ōō " rṵle			

III. CONSONANTS.

Only the most difficult consonants in this Reader are marked with diacritical signs. The following table may prove useful to the teacher for reference and for blackboard work.

ç = s as in miçe	th (unmarked) as in thin	
e or c (unmarked) = k as in eall	ph = f " phantom	
eh = k as in sehōōl	s = z " ịs	
ch (unmarked) " child	z (like s sonant) " zone	
ġ lik j " cāġe	qu (unmarked) " quite	
ḡ (h. l) " ḡĕt	x = gz " exact	
n̲ = n͜ " ĭn̲k	x (unmarked) = ks " vex	
t̶h̶ " t̶h̶ĕm		

Certain vowels, as a and e, when obscured and turned toward the neutral form, are italicized. Silent letters are also italicized.

WORD LIST.

—o◦o❀o◦o—

The following is an alphabetical list of the most difficult words used in this Reader.

The less difficult words that have been used in the Primer, First, Second, Third, and Fourth Readers are omitted.

This list may be made the basis of a great variety of exercises in correct pronunciation, distinct enunciation, rapid spelling, language lessons, and review work.

For an explanation of the diacritical marks, see preceding page.

The syllable *tion* is not re-spelled in this list, but wherever it occurs should be pronounced *shŭn*.

ăb dĭ cā′ tion	ăd mĭn ĭs trā′ tion	ăl lĕ gŏr′ ĭc al
ăb hôr*red*′	ăd′ mĭ r*al*	ăl lī′ *an*çe
ăb′ sȯ lūt*e* lỹ	ăd ȯ rā′ tion	ăl līed′
ăb străct′ ĕd	à droit′	ăl low′ *an* çes
à bỹss′	ăd văn′ tȧ ġĕs	a*ll*-pĕr vād′ ĭng
ă*e* çĕl′ ĕr ā tĕd	ăd vĕr′ sĭ tỹ	ăl lūr*ed*′
ăc cŏm′ mȯ dāt*e*	ăd vĕr′ tĭ*se* ment	ăl tĕr′ năt*e* lỹ
ăc count′ *ant*	ăd′ vȯ cāt*e*	ăm băs′ sȧ dor
ăc c*o*u′ tĕr*ed*	ăf flĭc′ tion	(dĕr)
ăc c*o*u′ tĕr ments	âir′ ĭ lỹ	ăm′ blĭng
ăc cū′ mŭ lā tĕd	ăl′ bà trŏss	ăm bŭs cād*e*′
ăd′ jŭ t*ant*s	ăl lē′ ġi*an*çe	ăm′ phĭ thē à tĕr

418

ă năl' ŏ ġĭes
ăn' ehŏ răġe
ăn' ĕc dōtes
ăn' ĭ mā tĕd
ăn nĭ vĕr' să ry̆
ăn noy' ançe
ăn tăġ' ŏ nĭst
ăn tĭç' ĭ pā tĕd
ăn tiq' ui ty̆
  (tĭk' wĭ)
ăn' tre (tĕr)
ăp' ȧ thy̆
ăp' ĕr tŭres
ăp pạll' ĭng
ăp pȧ rā' tŭs
ăp pȧ rĭ' tion
ăp prē ci ā' tion
  (shĭ)
ăp prĕ hĕn' sion
  (shŭn)
ăp prĕ hĕn' sĭve
ăp prĕn' tĭçe shĭp
ăp' prŏ bā tĕd
ăp prō' prĭ ȧte ly̆
ā' prĭ eŏt
aq' ui (ăk' wĭ) lĭne
är eādes'
ärch' ĕr y̆
är' ehĭ tĕct

är ehĭ tĕc' tŭr ạl
ȧ rē' nȧ
är' gŭ ment
är quĕ bŭs iērs'
är' sĕ nạl
är tĭc' ŭ lȧte ly̆
är' tĭ fĭçe
är tĭl' lĕr y̆
är tĭl' lĕr y̆ man
ăsp' ĕns
ăs pīr' ant
ăs pĭ rā' tions
ăs sāil' ạnts
ăs sĕm' bled
ăs sĕm' bly̆
ăs sō' ci (shĭ) ā tĕd
ăs sō çĭ ā' tion
ăs suaged' (swājd')
ȧ stĕrn'
ăs tound' ĭng
ăs trŏl' ŏ ġĕrs
ăs trŏn' ŏ mĕr
ăs trŏ nŏm' ĭc
ȧ sȳ' lŭm
Ăth ĕ naē' ŭm
ăth lĕt' ĭc
ăt tĕn' ŭ ā tĕd
ăt' trĭ būtes
ạu thŏr' ĭ ty̆

ăv' ȧ lănche
ăv' ĕ nᵤe
ȧ vĕrred'
aye (äĭ)

băch' ĕ lor (lĕr)
bāil' ĭff
bạl' drĭc
bär bā' rĭ ạns
bär băr' ĭc
băp tĭș' mạl
băr' rȧ cōon
băr' rĭ ĕr
băt tăl' ion (yŭn)
băt' tĕr ĭes
băt' tle ment
bạu' ble
bēe' tlĭng
bĕ gᵤiled'
bĕ lēa' guĕred
bĕl lĭġ' ĕr ent
bĕn ĕ dĭc' tions
bĕn ĕ făc' trĕss
bĕ nĭg' nant
bĕ queath'
bĕ siē' ġĕrs
bĕv' ĕr ăge
bĭg' ŏt ry̆
bĭl' lŏw y̆

bǐ ŏg′ rȧ phў

bǐs′ ϲuǐt

bǐv′ ouac (wăk)

blĕss′ ĕd nĕss

bois′ tĕr oŭs

bō rĕ ā′ lǐs

bound′ ȧ rǐes

boun′ tĕ oŭs lў

brāe

brȧ vā′ dŏ

brĕth′ rĕn

brǐl′ liant (yant)

buoy′ (bwoi′) ɑn çў

bûrgh′ ĕr

bûr′ nǐshed

bŭs′ kǐn

căf′ tɑn

cȧ lăm′ ǐ tў

căl′ ǐ bĕr

căn nȯn āde′

căp′ tǐ vā tǐng

căp tǐv′ ǐ tў

cȧ rēered′

cär′ năġe

cär′ rǐ ȯn

cas′ (kăzh) ŭ ɑl tў

căt′ ȧ lŏgue

căt′ ȧ phrăcts

căt′ ȧ răct

căt′ ĕ ϲhīş ǐng

cȧ thē′ drɑl

căv ȧ lϲēr′ lў

căv′ ǐ tǐes

çĕl′ ăn dīne

çĕ lĕs′ tial (chɑl)

çĕ mĕnt′ ĕd

çĕn′ sure (shu̧r)

çĕr tǐf′ ǐ cȧte

chăl′ lĕnġed

chăl′ lĕn ġĕr

chăm′ pǐ ȯn ǐng

ϲha′ ŏs

ϲhăr′ ăc tĕr īze

chăr′ ǐ tȧ ble

ϲhăsms

chăs′ tǐşe ment

ϲhĕm′ ǐs trў

cheq′ uer (chĕk′ ĕr)

chǐv′ ɑl roŭs

Chrǐs tian′ ǐ tў
   (chăn′)

ϲhrǐs′ tened

ϲhrȯn′ ǐ clĕrs

ϲhrȯn′ ǐ cles

ϲhўm′ ǐc

çǐr′ ϲuǐt

çǐr cŭm′ fĕr ençe

çǐr cŭm scrībed′

çǐt′ ȧ del

çǐv ǐ lǐ zā′ tion

clăm′ bĕred

clăm′ or (ĕr) oŭs

clēr′ ġў mɑn

cō ǐn çīde′

cŏl′ ŏ nǐsts

cŏl′ tĕr

cŏm′ băt ɑnt

cŏm bǐ nā′ tion

cŏm mȧnd′ ĕrs

cŏm mĕnçe′ ment

cŏm mĕn dā′ tion

cŏm′ mȯn wĕalth

cŏm mū′ nǐ cā tĕd

cŏm mū′ nǐ cȧ tǐve

cŏm mū′ nǐ tў

cŏm mūt′ ĕd

cŏm păn′ ion shǐp
   (yŭn)

cŏm pärt′ ments

cŏm pas′ sion
   (păsh′ ŭn)

cŏm plā′ çençe

cŏm plex′ ion
   (plĕk′ shŭn)

cŏm pĕt′ ǐ tors
   (tĕrs)

cŏm′ plĭ ment
cŏn çēal′ ment
cŏn çĕn′ tĕred
cŏn′ çĕn trā tĕd
cŏn clū′ sion (zhŭn)
cŏn cŭs′ sion
   (kŭsh ŭn)
cŏn dĕmned′
cŏn ġēn′ ial (yal)
cŏn grĕ gā′ tion
cŏn jĕc′ tŭre
cŏn′ sĕ quĕnçe
cŏn spĭr′ ȧ çў
cŏn stĕr nā′ tion
cŏn strŭc′ tion
cŏn′ sŭm māte
cŏn tā′ ġiȯn
cŏn tĕm′ nĕrs
cŏn tĕmnĕd′
cŏn′ tĕm plāte
cŏn tĕm plā′ tion
cŏn tĕnt′ ment
cŏn trĭ bū′ tions
cŏn′ trīte
cŏn vȧ lĕs′ çençe
cŏn voy′
cŏn vŭl′ sion
   (shŭn)
cŏpse

cŏ rŏl′ lȧ
cōrps
couch′ ant
coun′ tĕr fĕĭt
coun′tĕr märch ĭng
coûr′ tĕ oŭs
cȯv′ ĕt ĕd
cow′ ard (ĕrd) ĭçe
crĕ dū′ lĭ tў
crĭ tē′ rĭ ȯn
crō′ cŭs
cru̯is̵′ ĕrs
crŭm′ blĭng
cru̯ sād′ ĕrs
cui rass′ (kwĕ ràs′)
çў lĭn′ drĭc al
çўm′ bals

dăm′ s̵ĕls
dĕ çeit′ fŭl lў
dĕ çĕp′ tion
dĕç ĭ mā′ tion
dĕ çĭ′ phĕr ȧ ble
dĕc là mā′ tion
dĕc ȯ rā′ tions
dĕ crĕp′ ĭt
dĕ fi′ ançe
dĕ fi′ cien çĭes
   (fĭsh′ en)

dĕ fīl′ ĭng
dĕ ġĕn′ ĕr ăte
dĕ lĭb′ ĕr ā tĕd
dĕ lĭn ĕ ā′ tion
dĕ lĭv′ ĕr ançe
dĕ lū′ sion (zhŭn)
dē mȧr cā′ tion
dĕ mēan′ or (ĕr)
dĕm ȯ lĭ′ tion
dĕ mŏr′ al īzed
dĕ nŏm ĭ nā′ tion
dĕ rīd′ ĭng
dĕ scrĭp′ tions
dĕs ȯ lā′ tion
dĕ s̵ĭst′ ĕd
dĕs pŏt′ ĭc
dĕs′ tĭ nĭes
dĕ strŭc′ tion
dĕ tĕr mĭ nā′ tion
dĕ voured′
dĭ′ ȧ lĕct
dĭ ăm′ ĕ tĕr
dĭf fū′ sion (zhŭn)
dĭl′ ĭ ġent
dĭ mĭn′ ŭ tĭve
dĭs ăf fĕc′ tion
dĭs̵ ăs′ troŭs
dis cern′ ĭ ble
   (dĭz zĕrn′)

dĭs' çĭ plĭne	ĕm bǎr' rassed	ĕx' çĕl lĕn çĕs
dĭs côrd' ant	ĕm blĕm ǎt' ĭc al	ĕx çĭṣe'
dĭs coŭr' å ġĭng	ĕm broid' ĕred	ĕx çīte' ment
dĭs ĕm bärked'	ė mĕr' ġen çў	ĕx' crĕ ment
dĭ shĕv' eled	ĕm' ĭ grāte	ĕx ė cū' tion ĕrs
dĭs hŏn' ored (ĕrd)	ĕm' pĕr ors (ĕrs)	ĕx ĕc' ŭ tĭve
dĭs ôr' dĕred	ĕm' ŭ lāte	ĕx ĕm' plå rў
dĭs sĕm' bled	ĕn ǎm' ĕl	ĕx ĕmpt'
dĭs sĕv' ĕred	ĕn chånt' ĕrs	ĕx ĕr' tions
dĭs tĭnct' nĕss	ĕn chånt' ment	ĕx hŏr tā' tion
dĭs tĭnc' tion	ĕn chånt' rĕss	ĕx pĕnd' ĭ tŭre
dĭ vĕr' sion (shŭn)	ĕn còm' passed	ĕx pē' rĭ ençed
dĭ vĭ' sions	ĕn cŭm' bĕr	ĕx pĕrt' nĕss
(vizh' ŭns)	ĕn dow' ment	ĕx ploits'
dĭz' zĭ lў	ĕn dūr' ançe	ĕx plŏ rā' tions
dŏc' ŭ ments	ė nū' mĕr ā tĭng	ĕx plō' sion (zhŭn)
dŏ mĭn' ion (yŭn)	ĕn vĕl' ŏped	ĕx prĕss' ĭve
drä' må tĭst	ĕp' ĭ sōdes	ĕx' quĭ ṣīte
drought	ē quĭ nŏc' tial	ĕx tĭn' guished
dŭn' ġeòn	(shal)	(gwĭsht)
dŭ rā' tion	ė quĭp' ment	ĕx traôr' dĭ nå rў
	eq' ui (ĕk' wĭ) tў	ĕx trăv' å gant
ĕd' ĭ fĭçe	ė rŭp' tion	ĕx trĕm' ĭ tў
ĕd ĭ tō' rĭ als	ĕs tĭ mā' tion	ĕx ŭl tā' tion
ĕd ŭ cā' tion	ė tĕr' nal	ĕx ŭlt' ĕd
ĕf fāçed'	eů rē' kå	
ĕl' ė ġў	ė vǎc' ŭ ā tĕd	fǎb' ŭ loŭs
ĕl ė mĕn' tal	ė vǎn' ĭsh ĭng	fǎc' ŭl tĭes
ĕl' ŏ quençe	ĕx ǎm ĭ nā' tions	faḷ' chiòn

făn tăs′ tĭc

făs′ çĭ nā tĕd

fē′ ɑl tў

fė lĭç′ ĭ tў

fė rō′ cious lў
   (shŭs)

fė rŏç′ ĭ tў

fĕr′ ule (ĭl)

feūds

fĭc′ tion

fĭc tĭ′ tious (shŭs)

fĭ dĕl′ ĭ tў

fĭl′ ȧ ments

fĭl′ chĕs

flēer

flŭc′ tŭ āte

fôre′ fĭn gĕr

fŏr′ eĭgn ĕrs

fôr tĭ fĭ cā′ tions

foun dā′ tion

frăn′ tĭc ɑl lў

frȧ tĕr′ nal

frĕn′ zĭed

frĭ vŏl′ ĭ tў

frŭs′ trȧ tĕd

fŭn dȧ mĕn′ tal

fū s̟ĭl lāde′

fûrze

fŭs′ tian (chɑn)

găl′ lɑnt lў

găl′ ló𝑤s

gär′ nĕred

găr′ rĭ sons

gäunt′ lĕts

gėn′ ŭ ĭne lў

gė ŏm′ ė trў

gės tĭc′ ŭ lā tĭng

geȳ′ sĕr

gĭb′ bĕt

gĭl′ lў flow ĕr

gôr′ geoŭs

grȧ dā′ tions

grăp′ plĭng

grăt ĭ fĭ ɕā′ tion

grăt′ ĭ fȳ ĭng

grēaves

grĕn ȧ dĭēr′

guăr ăn tēes′

guīle′ ful

guĭn′ ėa

gȳ rā′ tions

hăb ĭ tā′ tion

hȧ bĭt′ ŭ al

hăl′ bĕrt

hăl′ yards (yĕrds)

här′ bĭn gėr

här mō′ nĭ oŭs

haṵ′ bĕrk

hĕalth′ ĭ lў

hĕdge′ rō𝑤

hĕif′ ĕr

hĕr′ ɑld rў

hĕrb′ ăge

hĕr′ ŏ ĭne

hĕr′ ŏ ĭsm

hĭck′ ŏ rў

hĭg′ gles

hĭll′ òck

hĭs tŏr′ ĭc al

hón′ eў sŭe kles

hŏs pĭ tăl′ ĭ tў

hŏs′ tĕl rĭes

how ădj′ ĭ

hŭb′ bŭb

hŭr′ rĭ cāne

huṣ s̟ärs′

ī′ çĭ cles

ĭd′ ĭ ŏt

ĭl lū′ mĭ nā tĕd

ĭl lū′ sion (zhŭn)

ĭl lū′ sŏ rў

ĭl lŭs′ trȧ tĕd

ĭm mē′ dĭ ăte lў

ĭm′ ăge rў

ĭm bĭbe′

ĭm mŏr tăl′ ĭ tў

ĭm pēarled′

ĭm pĕnd′ ĭng

ĭm pĕr çĕp′ tĭ blў

ĭm pē′ rĭ ɑl

ĭm pĕr′ tĭ nençe

ĭm pĕt′ ŭ oŭs lў

ĭm plĭç′ ĭt lў

ĭm′ pŏ tent

ĭm prĭş′ oned

ĭm prăc′ tĭ cȧ ble

ĭm prọve′ ment

ĭm prụ′ dent

ĭn ăd vĕrt′ ent

ĭn ăp′ plĭ cȧ ble

ĭn căn tā′ tions

ĭn clĕm′ en çў

ĭn clĭ nā′ tion

ĭn cŏn vēn′ ience

(yens)

ĭn côr′ pŏ rā tĕd

ĭn crĕd′ ĭ ble

ĭn cŭm′ bent

ĭn cûr′ rĭng

ĭn dĕ fīn′ ȧ ble

ĭn dĕn tā′ tion

ĭn′ dĭ gŏ

ĭn dĭ vĭs′ ĭ ble

ĭn′ dŏ lençe

ĭn ĕf′ fȧ ble

ĭn ĕf fĕc′ tŭ ɑl

ĭn ĕx hȧust′ ĭ ble

ĭn ĕv′ ĭ tȧ ble

ĭn′ fan trў

ĭn′ fĭ del

ĭn ġē̇ nū′ ĭ tў

ĭn ġĕn′ ŭ oŭs

ĭn hăb′ ĭt ɑnts

ĭn ĭm′ ĭ tȧ ble

ĭn i′ ti ate

(ĭsh′ ĭ āt)

ĭn jŭnc′ tions

ĭn jū′ rĭ oŭs

ĭn ŏf fĕn′ sĭve

ĭn quĭş′ ĭ tĭve lў

ĭn săn′ ĭ tў

ĭn serōlled′

ĭn sĕp′ ȧ rȧ ble

ĭn sĭg nĭf′ ĭ cant

ĭn sĭg′ nĭ ȧ

ĭn′ sŏ lent

ĭn spĭ rā′ tion

ĭn stɑll′ ments

ĭn stĭnc′ tĭve lў

ĭn strŭct′ or (ĕr)

ĭn′ strụ ment

ĭn tĕg′ rĭ tў

ĭn tĕl lĕc′ tŭ ɑl

ĭn tĕm′ pĕr ăte

ĭn tĕr çēde′

ĭn tĕr chāng′ ĭng

ĭn tĕr fēr′ ĭng

ĭn tĕr mĕd′ dle

ĭn tē′ rĭ or (ĕr)

ĭn tĕr mē′ dĭ ăte

ĭn tĕr prĕ tā′ tion

ĭn tĕr′ prĕt ĕr

ĭn tĕr rŭp′ tion

ĭn tĕr rŏg′ ȧ tŏ rў

ĭn tĭ mā′ tions

ĭn trĕnch′ ments

ĭn trĕp′ ĭd

ĭn trụ′ sĭve

ĭn văl′ ŭ ȧ ble

ĭn vĕnt′ ĭve

ĭn vĭn′ çĭ ble

ĭn vĭ tā′ tions

ĭn vŏl′ ŭn tȧ rў

ĭr rĕg ŭ lăr′ ĭ tў

ĭr rĕl′ ĕ vant

ĭr rĕ prĕss′ ĭ ble

ī sŏ lā′ tion

ĭ tĭn′ ĕr ant

jăve′ lĭns

jŏck′ eўs

jŏc′ ŭnd

jŏl lĭ fĭ cā′ tion

jū′ bĭ lant

jū′ bĭ lēe

jū′ nĭ pĕr

lăb′ ў rĭnth

lā′ dled

lâirs

lăm ĕn tā′ tion

lăn′ yard (yĕrd)

lăt′ ĭ tūde

lĕc′ tŭr ĭng

lĕg′ å çў

lĭ ā′ nås

lĭb′ ĕr al lў

lĭb ĕr ā′ tion

lĭ brā′ rĭ an

liēģe

lieŭ tĕn′ ant

līme′ kĭlns

lĭn′ nĕt

lĭt′ ĕr å tŭre

līthe

lū′ mĭ noŭs

lūt′ å nĭst

lŭx ū′ rĭ ant

lўr′ ĭc

må gi′ cians

  (jĭsh′ ans)

măg nå nĭm′ ĭ tў

măg nĕt′ ĭc

măl′ å dў

măn ĭ fĕs tā′ tion

măn′ ĭ fĕst ĕd

măr′ ĭ tĭme

mā′ son rў

mau sŏ lē′ ŭm

mēa′ gĕr

mė ẹhăn′ ĭc al lў

mė ẹhăn′ ĭcs

mĕd ĭ tā′ tion

mĕm′ ŏ rå ble

mė mō′ rĭ als

mĕn′ å çĭng

mēn′ ial (yal)

mē′ tė ors (ĕrs)

mė trŏp′ ŏ lĭs

mĕt′ tle sȯme

mī′crȯ scȯpe

mĭ li′ tia (lĭsh′ å)

mĭ nūt′ ĕst

mĭ răc′ ŭ loŭs lў

mĭs′ sĭle

mō′ mĕn tå rў

mȯ mĕn′ tŭm

mŏn′ ås tĕr ў

môrt′ gảģe

môr tĭ fĭ cā′ tion

moun′ taĭn oŭs

mŭl′ tĭ plў

mŭs′ ẹŭ lar (lĕr)

mū tĭ lā′ tion

myr′(mĕr′)mĭdŏns

mўs tē′ rĭ oŭs

mўs′ tĭc al

năt′ ŭ ral ĭst

năv′ ĭ gā tor (tĕr)

nĕc′ tar (tĕr) ĭnes

nĕg′ lĭ ģençe

nĕv ĕr the lĕss′

nĭche

nīght′ ĭn gāle

noi′ sȯme

noŭr′ ĭsh ment

nū′ mĕr oŭs

nŭp′ tial (shal)

nûrs′ ĕr ў măn

ȯ bē′ dĭ ençe

ŏb lĭt′ ĕr ā tĕd

ŏb ṣẹrv′ an çẹs

ŏb ṣẹrv′ å tȯ rў

ŏb′ stĭ nå çў

ŏc cŭ pā′ tion

ŏc′ ŭ lar (lĕr)

ȯ′ dor (dĕr) oŭs

ŏf fi′ cious nĕss
  (fĭsh′ ŭs)
ŏm′ ĭ noŭs
ŏm nĭp′ ŏ tençe
ō′ pĭ ŭm
ŏr′ an ger (ĕnj ẽr) y̆
ôr′ ꞓhĭs
ō rĭ ĕn′ tal
ôr′ nȧ ment
ôr thŏg′ rȧ phy̆
ō vẽr whĕlmed′

păl ĭ sādes′
pa͟l′ try̆
păr′ ȧ gráph
păr′ ăl lĕls
păr′ ȧ pĕt
pärched
pärch′ ment
pär′ don ȧ ble
pȧ rĭsh′ i͝on ẽrs
pär′ lĭa ment
pär sĭ mō′ nĭ oŭs
pär′ son ȧg̣e
pär ti (shĭ) ăl′ ĭ ty̆
pär′ tĭ cle
pär tĭc ŭ lär′ ĭ tĭes
pas′ sion ȧte
  (păsh′ ŭn)

pā′ trĭ ärꞓh
pā′ trĭ ŏt ĭsm
pa͟wn′ brō kẽr
pĕa͟ṣ′ ant ry̆
pĕn ĭn′ sŭ lȧr
pĕn′ nĭ lĕss
pĕn′ nòn çĕlle
pẽr çĕp′ tion
pẽr chànçe′
pẽr′ fĕct nĕss
pẽr fôrm′ an çĕs
pē rĭ ŏd′ ĭc als
pẽr′ mȧ nent ly̆
pẽr pĕt′ ŭ al
pẽr pĕt′ ŭ āte
pẽr sĕ vēr′ ançe
pẽr′ sòn ȧg̣ ĕs
pẽr spĭ ꞓȧç′ ĭ ty̆
pẽr suad′(swād′)ĕd
pẽr tûrbed′
pĕs tĭ lĕn′ tial
  (shȧl)
phĭ lŏs′ ŏ phẽrs
phĭl ŏ sŏph′ ĭc al
phŏ tŏg′ rȧ phẽrs
phy̆s′ ĭc al ly̆
pĭck′ ȧ nĭn nĭes
pĭc tŭr esque′(ĕsk′)
pĭn′ ions (y̆ŭnṣ)

pĭn′ nȧ ꞓles
plȧ cärd′
plȧin′ tĭve
plăn′ tȧins
plăn tā′ tions
pōach′ ẽr
poiṣed
pŏ lĭt′ ĭ cal
pŏl lūt′ ĕd
pŏp′ ŭ lȧçe
pŏp ŭ lā′ tion
pŏn′ iard (yẽrd)
pŏr′ rĭn ġẽr
pŏṣ ses′ sions
  (zĕsh′ ŭnṣ)
pŏs tẽr′ ĭ ty̆
pō′ ten tȧtes
pŏt′ tẽr
praē′ tŏr
prāi′ rĭe
prĕç′ ĕ dent
prĕ çĭp′ ĭ tā tĕd
prĕ çĭp′ ĭ toŭs
prĕ lĭm′ ĭ nȧ ry̆
prē′ lūde
prē mȧ tūre′
prĕ pär′ ȧ tŏ ry̆
prĕṣ ẽr vā′ tion
prĕ ṣẽrves′

pri̇ mē′ val

prĭm′ ĭ tĭve

prĭṣm

pri̇ vā′ tion

prŏc lȧ mā′ tion

prŏd′ ĭ gal

prȯ fe̦s′ sion

  (fĕsh′ ŭn)

prȯ fū′ sion (zhŭn)

prō′ grăm me

prȯ jĕct′ ĭles

prŏm e̅ nädes′

pro̅ pōr′ tioned

pro̅ prī′ e̅ tor (tĕr)

pro̅ ṣā′ ĭc

prŏs pĕr′ ĭ tẙ

prŏs′ pĕr o̯ŭs

prŏs trā′ tion

pro̅ vō′ cȧ tĭve

prow′ ĕss

prȳ′ ĭng

psa̦l′ tĕr

pū ĭs′ sa̦nçe

pū′ nẙ

pŭp′ pĕts

pûr sū′ a̦nçe

qua̦d′ ru̯ pĕds

qua̦r′ tĕr mȧs tĕr

răm′ mĕr

rēa′ ṣon ȧ blẙ

rĕ çĕss′ ĕs

rĕç′ ĭ pĕ

rĕç ĭ tā′ tion

rĕck′ lĕss lẙ

rĕc′ o̯m pĕnse

rĕc′ tĭ tūde

rĕ doubt′ ĕd

rĕ dound′ ĭng

rē ëch′ (ĕk′) ŏed

rĕ frăc′ to̯ rẙ

rĕ gā′ lĭ ȧ

rĕg ŭ lā′ tion

rĕ lī′ a̦nt

rĕ lĭn′ quĭsh

rĕ mĕm′ bra̦nçe

rĕ mŏn′ stra̦nçe

rĕ môrse′ lĕss

rĕp ȧ rā′ tion

rĕp rĕ ṣe̦nt′ ȧ tĭve

rĕp rĕ ṣe̦nt′ ment

rĕp′ rĭ măñd

rĕp′ tĭle

rĕp ŭ tā′ tion

rē′ quĭ ĕm

rĕ ṣe̦nt′ ment

rĕ ṣĭst′ a̦nçe

rĕ̦ṣ′ o̯ na̦nt

rĕ splĕn′ de̦nt

rĕ ūn′ ion (yŭn)

rĕv′ ĕl rẙ

rĕv′ ĕr end

rĕv′ ĕr ent lẙ

rĕv′ ĕr ẙ

rĕv o̯ lū′ tion ȧ rẙ

rhi̇ nŏç′ e̅ rŏs

rhȳmes

rĭb′ a̦nd

rĭd′ ĭ cūle

right′ eous nĕss

(rī′ chŭs)

rŏ măñçe′

rōod

rō′ ṣe̯ ăte

route

săc′ rĭ fice (fĭz)

săd′ dened

sȧ găç′ ĭ tẙ

săl′ tire (tĕr)

săl vā′ tion

săp′ lĭngs

săt′ ĕl lītes

săt′ ĭr ĭsts

sĕaf′ fo̯lds

sĕath′ lĕss

sehĕd′ ŭle

schŏl' ar (ĕr) shĭp	sŏ lĭd' ĭ tў	sŭmp' tŭ oŭs nĕss
scrīve' nĕr	sŏ lĭl' ŏ quў	sū pĕr cär' gŏ
scȳthe	sŏn' nĕts	sū pĕr flū' ĭ tĭes
sēa' fâr ĭng	sôr' çĕr ў	sŭ pē rĭ ŏr' ĭ tў
sĕ clū' sion (zhŭn)	sọu	sū pĕr năt' ŭ ral
sĕc' rĕ tå rў	sŏv' ĕr eĭgn tў	sū pĕr stī' tion
sĕ lĕc' tion	spē' cies (shēz)	sū pĕr vi' sion
sĕn å tō' rĭ al	spĕc tā' tors (tĕrs)	(vĭzh' ŭn)
sĕn sĭ bĭl' ĭ tў	sphĕr' ĭc al	sŭp' ple nĕss
sĕn' tĭ ment	spĭr ĭt ŭ ăl' ĭ tў	sûr' çēase
sĕn tĭ mĕn' tal	spŏn tā' nĕ oŭs lў	sûr vey' or (vā' ĕr)
sĕp' ŭl ehĕr	squạd' rȯn	sûr vīv' or (ĕr)
sĕ pŭl' ehral	stāte' lĭ ĕst	sŭs pi' cion
sĕ quĕs' tĕred	stātes-gĕn' ĕr al	(pĭsh' ŭn)
shăe' kles	stĕr' ĭle	sўe' ŏ phant
shå grēen'	stŏ lĭd' ĭ tў	sўl' lå ble
shăl' lóp	străt' å ġĕm	sўm' bŏl īze
shärp' shōot ĕrs	strĕn' ŭ oŭs	sў rĭn' gå
shrŭb' bĕr ў	stŭ pĕn' doŭs	sўs tĕm ăt' ĭc
sīeve	sŭb ôr' dĭ nåte	
sĭg' nĭ fīed	sŭb ôr dĭ nā' tion	tăe' tĭes
sĭm plĭç' ĭ tў	sŭb tĕr rā' nĕ an	tăff' răil
sĭ mŭl tā' nĕ oŭs	sŭb' tlĕr	tăn' ġĭ ble
sĭn gŭ lăr' ĭ tĭes	sŭe ces' sion	tăn' tå līzed
sī' zar (zĕr)	(sĕsh' ŭn)	tăp' ĕs trĭed
smŭg' glĕrs	sŭe çĕs' sĭve lў	taut
sō' joŭrn ĕrs	sŭf' fĕr ĕrs	taw' drў
sŏl' åçe	sŭm' må rў	tē' dĭ oŭs nĕss
sŏl' ĕm nīze	sŭm' mȯned	tĕl' ĕ scōpe

tĕ mĕr′ ĭ tў

tĕr′ mĭ nāte

tĕr′ rȧç ĕs

tĕs′ tȧ ment

thē ŏ lŏǵ′ ĭc ɑl

thē′ ŏ rĭes

thŭn′ dĕr oŭs

thwȧrt′ ĕd

tĭt′ u̇ lar (lĕr)

tŏe′ sĭn

tŏl′ ĕr ȧ ble

tour′ (tōōr′) nĕў

trȧ dĭ′ tion ȧ rў

trăn scĕn dĕn′ tɑl

trăns fĭg′ u̇res

trĕach′ ĕr oŭs lў

trĕm′ u̇ loŭs nĕss

trĭ ăn′ gu̇ lar lў (lĕr)

trī′ còl ored (ĕrd)

trĭ ŭm′ phɑl

trŏp′ ĭc ɑl

trŭst′ wor thў (wûr)

trўst′ ĭng

twăng′ ĭng

ŭn āid′ ĕd

u̇ năn′ ĭ moŭs

ŭn ăs sūm′ ĭng

ŭn băr rĭ ᴇāde′

ŭn çēas′ ĭng lў

ŭn coiled′

ŭn còm′ fort ȧ ble (fĕrt)

ŭn cŏn′ scious lў (shŭs)

ŭn cŏn trōl′ lȧ ble

ŭn däunt′ ĕd

ŭn dĕ çēived′

ŭn dĕ fĕnd′ ĕd

ŭn dĕ fīled′

ŭn dīght′

ŭn dŭ lā′ tions

ŭn fā′ vor ȧ ble (vĕr)

ŭn flĕdǵed′

ŭn flĭnch′ ĭng lў

ŭn fôr′ tŭ nȧte

ŭn frĕ quĕnt′ ĕd

ŭn gòv′ ĕrn ȧ ble

ŭn ĭn tĕr rŭpt′ ĕd

u̇ nique′ (nēk′)

ū nĭ vĕr′ sĭ tў

ŭn măn′ nĕr lў

ŭn mĭs tāk′ ȧ ble

ŭn ŏb ṣĕrved′

ŭn ôr′ gɑn īzed

ŭn rĕ lĕnt′ ĭng

ŭn ŭt′ tĕr ȧ ble

ŭn vā′ rĭed

ŭn wĭeld′ ў

ŭp brāid′ ĭng

ŭp hēav′ ɑls

ū su′ (zhṳ′) rĭ oŭs

vā′ ᴇan çĭes

văg′ ȧ bŏnd

vā′ grant

văl′ iant (yɑnt) lў

văl′ or (ĕr) oŭs

văn′ quĭsh ĕs

vȧ rī′ ĕ tĭes

väunt′ ĭng lў

vĕǵ ĕ tā′ tion

vē′ hĕ ment

vĕ lŏç′ ĭ tў

vĕnǵe′ ançe

vĕn′ òm oŭs

vĕr′ dŭr oŭs

vĕr′ ĭ fīed

vĕt′ ĕr ɑns

vĕx ā′ tion

vĭ brā′ tion

vĭ çĭn′ ĭ tў

vĭ çĭs′ sĭ tūdes

vĭǵ′ ĭ lɑnçe

vĭg′ or (ĕr) oŭs

vĭnt′ åge

vīr′ ġĭn al

vĭ tăl′ ĭ tў̆

vŏl cā′ nȯ

wĕdged

whey (hwā)

whorls (hwûrls)

work′ man shĭp

(wûrk′)

wound′(wōōnd′)ĕd

wrĕtch′ ĕd nĕss

PROPER NAMES.

Additional Signs Used in the Following List.

ẹ as in dẹ (Fr.).　　　　　ö (= ĕr) as in Götz (Ger.).

ï (= ē) as in pïque (Fr.).　　ü as in Düs′ sel dorf.

K (= ch) as in Rĭch′ tĕr (Ger.).　　Ŵ (= V) as in Ŵĭl′ hĕlm (Ger.).
(K)

N as in Pepin′ (Fr.).
(N)

Ā′ brå hăm

Ăb ў̆s sĭn′ ĭ å

Aē′ sŏp

Ăg′ as siz (sē)

Ā′ jăx

Al′ cott

Ål̆′ låh

Ăm′ brēe

Ăn′drẹas Füt′tĕral

Ăn′ tŏ nў̆

Å paĕç′ ĭ dēṣ

Å pŏl′ lȯ

Är′ bå çēs

Är mā′ då

Ăr′ rå gŏn

Ăs′ cham

Au gus ti′ na
(Ow gōōs tē′ nä)

Au rō′ rå Lēigh

Ä vi′gnon(vïn′yŏn)

Âyr

Å zōreṣ′

Ăz′ tĕc

Băb′ ў̆ lon

Băl ĕs tiẹr′

Bär′ nẹ vĕlt

Băs sä′ nĭ ȯ

Bås tille′ (tēl′)

Bĕl shăz′ zar

Bĕr när din′ de St.
Pierre
(däN′ dẹ säN
Pĭ är′)

Bĭṣ′ märck

Bȯ hē′ mĭ å

Bŏs′ cå wĕn

Bue′ na Vis′ ta
(Bwä′ nä Vēs′ tä)

Bul′ wĕr Lў̆t′ ton

Bûr′ gŭn dў̆

Büsch′ ĭng

Caen (kŏN)

Çaē′ ṣar

Cå lē′ nŭs

Căm′ ĕ lŏt

Cär lўle′

Cä′ sä Gui′ di
(Gwē′ dē)

Cas′ si us (Kăsh′ ŭs)

Cäs tĭl′ la (yä)

Cä vi te′ (tä′)

Chăl dē′ ans　[pĕc

Chä pul′ (pōōl′) tå‑

Chär nĕy′

Chĕlms′ ford (fûrd)
Cher′ (Shĕr′) boûrg
Chris′ tŏ phĕr
Çin′ trä
Clăn ru̦′ ădh
Clĕ ŏ pā′ trä
Cōle′ rĭdge
Cor′ me ray (Kôrm′rē)
Cor reg i′ dor
(Côr rĕ hē′dō)
Count dẹ Bü rĕn′

Dăl nĕss′
Dà măs′ cŭs
Dï ŏ dä′ ti
Dï ŏg′ ĕ nĕṣ
Dō min′ gō
Don An to′ ni o de
Ul lo′a (Dŏn Än tō′nĭ ō dĕ Ool yō′à)
Don Juan de Aus′-
trĭ à (Dŏn who ahn′dĕ Ows′-
Dŏn Quĭx′ ŏte (Eng.)
Dŭ ĕs′ sà
Düs′ sel dŏrf

Ĕb ĕn ē′ zĕr
Ė ġўp′ tian (shan)
Ĕn tĕp′ fu̦hl

Faust (Foust)
Fe′ (Fā′) lĭx Gräs
Fï dē′ lē

Găl′ ăx ў
Găl ĭ lē′ ŏ
Gā′ zà
Gà zĕlle′
Gĕs′ lĕr
Ġĭŏt′ tō
Glau′ cŭs
Glĕn′ cōe
Glĕn erē răn
Gŏ lï′ ath
Gŏt′ fried (frēt)
Göt′ tĭng en
Götz von Ber′ lich-
ing en (fŏn Bĕr′ liK Ing ĕn)
Gnĕsch′ ĕn

Hāgue
Hä′ vre
Hē′ brew (bru̦)
Hĕl′ sĕg gĕn [rō
Hernän′dō Pï zär′-
(är)
Hŏ rā′ ti us (shŭs)
Ĭs′ lä dĕ Cu̦′ bä

Jà māi′ cà Plāin
Jo′hännWŏlf′gäng
(Yō) von Göe′thẹ
(fŏn)
Knōwleṣ
Lăb′ rà dôr
Lä Cä pē tāine′

Lä hōre′
Lăn′ çĕ lŏt
Leïp′ sïe
Les Mi se rables′
(Lä Mē sä räbl′)
Leў′ den
Lï ġē′ ĭ à
Lŏr rāine′
Lou vain′ (văN′)
Lŭck′ now
Lū dŏ vï′ eŏ
Lu̦ ne′ (nā′) tä
Lux em bourg′
(Loox sŏN boor′)

Mà cau′ laў
Măg′ dà lĕn
Mà nĭl′ à
Ma roōn′ [tẹ năe′
Mar′quis dẹ LăN-
Märsei llais′(săyă′)
Mä zĕp′ pà
Mī′ eha el Ăn′-
ge (jà) lō
Mī′ das [văn′ tēṣ
Mi guĕl′ dĕ Çer-
Mĭl′ an
Min dä nä′ ō
Mŏ hăm′ mĕd
Mŏn′ mouth
Mŏnt′ eălm

Mont chev reu′ il
   MöN che̜ vre̜′ y̆

Mŏnt′ mo rĕn çĭ

Mŏn tō′ jo (hō)

Mō rŏe′ eō

Mŏs′ kōe-ström

Năz′ à rēne

Nĕb ŭ ehad nĕz′ zar

Nêer′ wĭn dĕn

Nĭn′ ĕ veh

Nôr′ folk

Nŏr wē′ ğĭ an

Nō′ tre Däme

Ò ly̆m′ pĭ à

Ò thĕl′ lŏ

Păl′ ĕs tīne

Päl′ mäs

Pà ri′ sian (rĭzh′ an)

Pär năs′ su̜s

Perrenot′ (Pĕrnō′)

Pĕt′ rĕl

Piēd mŏn tēse′

Phĭ lĭ bĕrt′ de̜ Brü-
   xelles (sĕl′)

Phĭl ĭs′ tĭ à

Pic ci o′ la (Pĭt chŏ′ là)

Plā′ tō

Pŏm pe′ ii (pā′ yē)

Pōr′ ti (shĭ) à

Pôr tĭl′ lo (yō)

Pōr′ tu̜ gue̜se

Pŏt′ ĭ phàr

Prĭeur′ de̜ lä Märne

Prŏ mē′ thĕ u̜s

Prŏ ven (vŏN) çäl′

Rā ē′ nä €rĭs tē′ nä

Ra̜′ leĭgh

Răs′ sĕ las

Rĕğ′ ĭ nald Hē′ ber

Re̜ ne′ (nā′)

Rĕp′ plĭ ĕr

Rĕyn′ olds̜

Rich′ e lieu
   (Rĕsh′ e̜ lōō)

Rich′ (RĭK′) tĕr

Rŏss′ bach (bäK)

Sain (săN) tïne′

Sa̜lĭs′ bur (ber) y̆

Săm′ son Ăg on ĭs′
             tēs̜

Săn′ €hō Păn′ zà

Săr′ à çĕn

Săr à gŏs′ sà

Sär′ tor Rĕ sär′ tu̜s

Săxe-W̆eī′ mar

Sē′ poy

Shà lŏtt′

Sŏe′ rà tēs̜

Sphinx (Sfĭnks)

Stōke Pō′ ğes

Su̜′ bĭg

Tā′ nĭs

Telesile′ (Tālāzĭl′)

Tĕll märeh′

Thē′ ŏ dōre

Thō′ reau (rō)

Trō′ jan

Tŭs′ ea ny̆

Ty̆re

Ty̆r′ ol

Ū′ krāine

Ve (Vā) läs′ eō

Vĕn dē′ an

Vĕ sū′ vĭ u̜s

Vīs′ count de̜ Fŏn′-
       te nāy

W̆ĕr′ thĕr

Wĕst mĭn′ stĕr

W̆ĕtz′ lär

W̆ĭl′hĕlm Meĭs′ tĕr

Wĭn dĕr mēre

Words′ worth
   (Wûrdz′ wûrth)

Wy̆e